Incorporating Images

Incorporating Images

FILM AND THE RIVAL ARTS

Brigitte Peucker

PRINCETON UNIVERSITY PRESS

PRINCETON, NEW JERSEY

Copyright © 1995 by Princeton University Press
Published by Princeton University Press, 41 William Street,
Princeton, New Jersey 08540
In the United Kingdom: Princeton University Press,
Chichester, West Sussex
All Rights Reserved

Library of Congress Cataloging-in-Publication Data
Peucker, Brigitte
Incorporating images : film and the
rival arts / Brigitte Peucker.
p.   cm.
Includes index.
ISBN 0-691-04098-2 (cl) — ISBN 0-691-00281-9 (pa)
1. Motion pictures and the arts.
2. Motion pictures—Aesthetics.
I. Title.
PN1995.25.P48   1994
791.43′01—dc20   94-18110

This book has been composed in Sabon

Princeton University Press books are
printed on acid-free paper and meet the guidelines
for permanence and durability of the Committee
on Production Guidelines for Book Longevity
of the Council on Library Resources

Printed in the United States of America

1   2   3   4   5   6   7   8   9   10

1   2   3   4   5   6   7   8   9   10
(Pbk.)

FOR SPENCER

———————————————————————————

Contents

CONTENTS

Illustrations

Acknowledgments

THIS STUDY has benefited from advice and support of many kinds. Of these, conversations with students undoubtedly have been most important to its shaping; although there are many whose questions have provoked my thought, I wish to single out David Black—a longtime friend—Alisa Aydin, Andrew Anker, Kevin Affonso, and Derek Dreher. In addition, the encouragement of colleagues and former colleagues has been enormously valuable: Peter Demetz first suggested that I pursue my interest in film and, over the years, Donald Crafton, Miriam Hansen, David Rodowick, Jennifer Wicke, Antonia Lant, Tim Corrigan, and Eric Rentschler provided various forms of support and counsel. For their continuing friendship—intellectual and personal—I owe a debt of gratitude to Richard and Cynthia Brodhead, Geoffrey Hartman, Thomas and Martha Hyde, Jocelyne Kolb, Konrad Kenkel, David Marshall, Candace Waid, and especially Maria DiBattista and Paul H. Fry, who read the manuscript and gave me the benefit of their astute and sensitive comments. For his computer wizardry, technical assistance, and generosity I wish to thank Anthony J. Niesz of the Yale Language Laboratory. Over the years, my friends at Yale's Audio-Visual Center and the Yale Film Study Center have offered a great deal of assistance, and Mary Geesken of MOMA was very helpful in providing stills. I also wish to thank my editor, Mary Murrell, for her calm and professional advice.

Various parts of this study were presented to audiences from whose comments I profited enormously. The section on Rohmer's *Marquise of O.* was first presented at the Whitney Humanities Center at Yale in the fall of 1985, and again at Cornell University the following spring. Other excerpts from this manuscript were also read at the Whitney Humanities Center, at Ohio State University, and at a conference of the International Association for Philosophy and Literature. Yale University provided assistance in the form of faculty leave, and a grant from the A. Whitney Griswold Foundation helped subsidize my work.

Most importantly, perhaps, I wish to thank Paul H. Fry and Spencer Fry for their invaluable presence and conversation.

Incorporating Images

Introduction

BODIES AND BOUNDARIES

THIS BOOK examines the problematic space that film occupies between the established arts of painting and literature. An agonistic dynamic governs the relation of film to these sister arts, as cinema struggles for self-legitimation through the appropriation, revision, and subversion of literary and painterly tropes. In a series of paradigmatic readings, I will elucidate the issues generated by the incorporation of these discourses in the cinematic text; their conjunction, I claim, is articulated most persistently through the figure of the human body.

There are varied and interrelated reasons for the prominence of the body at the site of this articulation. Following Vivian Sobchak's semiotic phenomenology, we know that the perceiving mind that makes film experience possible is an embodied mind and that this experience "entails the visible, audible, kinetic aspects of sensible experience to make sense visibly, audibly, and haptically."[1] Even the most important claims concerning the generic heterogeneity of film have been developed in the face of a persistent tradition of organic theories of art modeled upon the human body, theories that are difficult to lay to rest. Moreover, the reality/illusion opposition that all of the arts plays upon is problematized especially by the medium of film; the repeated subject of discussion from Arnheim to Baudrillard, this opposition plays itself out in the thematization of nature-culture thresholds typically expressed through the body, especially in questions concerning sexuality and death.[2] This book, then, positions the body within a matrix defined by questions regarding the nature of film as a medium, questions involving movement and the image, film's composite generic status, and its manipulation of illusion and the real.

The first chapter focuses on the textual and spectatorial consequences of the introduction of movement into visual representation that film occasions. Endowing the image with a semblance of three-dimensional materiality by the very fact of its movement, film's images of moving bodies are not life itself, but "life-like," a simulacrum whose phantasmatic status evokes the uncanny.[3] As Comolli puts it, cinema is conscious of itself as a "machine for simulation" that achieves only a "mechanical and deathly reproduction of the living."[4] Fragmented by close-ups, bodies in film stand in for the fragmented texts in which they appear, texts necessarily pieced together shot by shot and sequence by sequence. Linked to the uncanniness of the phantasmatic bodies it contains, film's self-understanding as a fissured text brings with it an underlying fear of castration and of death. It is for this reason, among others, that preferences for organic works of art in the traditional criticism of literature and the visual arts are to some extent internalized by film as part of its struggle to attain the status of high culture. Over and against this tendency, film and its proponents tend to champion its technological, mechanically reproducible aspect, compared to which organic models have become obsolete, and in the process reconfirm and affirm the very fragmentation that they fear.

Chapter two explores another aspect of the manner in which film models itself upon the body, analyzing the relation of the literary and pictorial frequently figured by film as sexual relations gone awry. As W.J.T. Mitchell has pointed out, aesthetic disputes involving generic boundary crossings are often represented as social and familial.[5] In cinema, what is at issue is the fear that film, as a hybrid form comprised of image and narrative, is nothing less than a "monstrous birth"; this unease, generated by a perceived lack of formal unity and expressed in the Horatian trope of the monster, is a long-familiar topic in aesthetics. The problem of film's heterogeneity as a medium will necessarily be confined here to analyzing the manner in which a variety of texts gender and sexualize the encounter of image and narrative as they vampirize the more traditional arts. The union—or collision—of these two textual systems is represented repeatedly in cinema by suggestions of adultery, incest, miscegenation, and bisexuality. The films discussed here are not confined to one culture or period, but are taken from a range of—primarily canonical—texts.

In the third chapter, yet another relation of body to text forms the backdrop for an inquiry into the presence of literature and painting in film. Concentrating on the way in which some texts can figure a permeable boundary between the real and representation, this chapter establishes a context for such manifestations in film with a discussion of trompe l'oeil effects of diverse kinds and of hybrid genres such as tableau vivant. Playing on the gap between signifier and signified, the movement between representation and the real suggests the troping of a preoccupation familiar from realist aesthetics. I contend that fear of death provides the motivation for the (figured) entry—or flight—into the text, just as the opposite gesture of making representation "come to life" likewise has its origins in this fear. Read broadly, trompe l'oeil effects and tableau vivant in film take up once more the discussion of cinematic movement, and the relation of the real to film provokes questions concerning the three-dimensionality of the cinematic image, in which cinema sees another form of triumph over painting. In the films under discussion, literature and painting continue to be figured as gendered, and sexuality is expressed as necrophilia or in pornography, and functions as a metaphor for the "incorporation" of textuality. The deliberate production of affective spectatorial responses such as vertigo and nausea—means of creating bridges between body and text—ultimately points to an elision of a Kantian aesthetics of disinterestedness with an affective aesthetics tied to the body that is in keeping with the (imagined) "materiality" of film.

In arguing these points, I frequently refer to the writings of Diderot and Kleist. Of Diderot it can truly be said that his imagination is in various ways concerned with the "proto-cinematic," at least as regards his interest in the sister arts and in generic boundary crossings. It is, after all, Diderot who claimed that Chardin, Greuze, and other painters had told him that his literary images could be transferred onto a canvas almost without change: "This seems to be the result of my habit of arranging my own figures in my head as though they were on a canvas; perhaps of my actually transferring them to one, since I am always gazing at a large wall as I write . . . so that I have gradually come to see everything in terms of attitudes, passions, expressions, movements, perspectives, and arrangements suitable for use in works of painting."[6] This speculation, written, of course, by a critic of painting and a theater man, in itself substantiates the implication of an essay by Roland Barthes to the effect that film theory has its origins in the eighteenth century.[7] I have occasionally turned to Kleist in order to be able to meditate upon the manner in which the body is understood both to underscore a crisis of signification *and* to inform a textual system. The confrontation that Kleist's writings stage between Kantian and empiricist aesthetics, as well as his sustained interest in the visual arts, make his writings not only natural candidates for cinematic adaptation, but productive of insights concerning cinematic textuality as well.[8]

In retrospect, I have become aware of the extent to which Balzac's *Sarrasine* thematizes and figures some of the questions to which Barthes alludes, but which are not the focus of *S/Z*. Formulating these questions once again in the mirror of Balzac's story may serve to clarify and contextualize them, though I do not wish to set up direct correspondences between these issues in *Sarrasine* and in film. In Balzac's story one body constitutes the model for sculpture, painting, and narration; transposed repeatedly from one medium into another, it may be said to embody the meeting point of all of the arts.[9] This body is defined by its uncanniness: notably, it appears at once alive and dead, and is a fragmented—castrated—body.[10] Conversely, when from the perspective of the narrator this body appears briefly to be entwined with the figure of a young woman, the narrator perceives in the hybrid creature "death and life . . . in a fantastic arabesque, half hideous chimera, divinely feminine from the waist up."[11] In thus alluding to the Horatian trope of generic transgression (comely woman above, grotesque fish below), Balzac strengthens the connection of this body, now figured as androgyne, with the instability of generic boundaries. Both as castrato and as androgyne, this is a body under the sign of death, a body that repeatedly "dies" into representation. As Barthes points out, its problematic status with regard to representation raises a number of issues integral to the realist's project, such as the relation of original to copy and the shift between the three- and the two-dimensional implied in the transposition of sculpture to painting. For the sculptor Sarrasine who attempts to model this body, "the perfect statue would have been an envelope containing a real woman."[12] Interestingly, Barthes originally intended to use a Kleist novella, *The Marquise of O.*, as the tutor text for *S/Z*.[13]

My own approach to painting and literature may benefit from some amplification here. Rarely do I discuss specific paintings in detail; rather, my concern is with how film figures static visual representation in its texts, how it engages it, how it seeks to outdo it and how, in the process, it defines its own modalities.[14] Whether it involves the representation of the moving, three-dimensional figure emerging from the canvas, as in *The Cabinet of Dr. Caligari*, whether it appears in film's definition of its spaces (as in Fritz Lang or Fassbinder), whether it serves to delimit the relation of the body to representation and to death (as in Hitchcock or Greenaway), or whether it is used in defining the ontology of film's images, painting is often made to carry a heavy burden in cinema. My aim in this essay is to suggest a number of relationships between painting and the spaces and images of cinema with regard to their manner of situating the human body. In the case of the literary—perhaps a more accurate term in the context of this study than "literature"—I do not dwell upon issues of adaptation or specific genres, but am concerned with similarly abstract issues: with problems of narration and the temporality of cinema, with narrative progress and closure, and with the recurrent theme of writing. Intermittent references to theater naturally occur at the conjunction of literary and painterly contexts.

Although German films—ranging from *The Student of Prague* (1913) to *Wings of Desire* (1987)—are more often drawn upon than those of any other national cinema, I frequently refer to the work of Hitchcock and to films by Griffith, Dreyer, Rohmer, Greenaway, and others to broaden my claims.[15] The films discussed have been chosen primarily, though not exclusively, from among so-called art films, but I want to suggest that it is not only films that are acutely self-conscious about their invocation of the sister arts that manifest traces of a coming-to-terms with other modes of (high cultural) textuality. Film's heterogeneity, producing the dialectical tension between "writing" and images that, from the standpoint of Adorno and Horkheimer, silent film in particular reinforces, does not, in fact, end with silent cinema's demise, but is inherent to the medium itself.[16] While this tension is often featured quite obviously in experimental films, it is not wholly suppressed in the mainstream. Although the classical style is designed to cover the heterogeneity of film as a textual system, this project is often not entirely successful, and a film's "fictive homogeneity" is insufficient to mask the "antithetical" materials of the cinematic medium.[17] If film's encounter with the literary and painterly is not usually a sustained one in the typical Hollywood product, the traces of this encounter are often inscribed there nevertheless. They are obviously present in all of Hitchcock, including his Hollywood films, just as they are present, for example, in films by Douglas Sirk and William Wyler, and, more recently, in those of Robert Altman and Steven Spielberg. Indeed, insofar as this problematic is expressed in the opposition between reality and illusion, it is, as Teresa de Lauretis has suggested, persistently thematized in the many recent movies in which boundary crossings are featured.[18] Ultimately, my reading of the issues that derive from the discursive interplay of the literary and painterly with and within cinema entails the claim that they are closely involved with problems of aesthetics, that they are phenomenological, and that they have a bearing on issues that extend beyond the terrain of historical and cultural specificity and touch upon film's ontological status.

7

Movement, Fragmentation, and the Uncanny

> The body in films is also moments, intensities, outside a
> single constant unity of the body as a whole, the
> property of a some *one*; films are full of fragments, bits
> of bodies, gestures, desirable traces, fetish points . . .
> —*Stephen Heath* [1]

EARLY SPECULATIONS concerning the nature of film hovered uneasily around the subject of movement, around issues of life and lifelessness, body and soul, the fantastic and the uncanny effect. "The essence of cinema," Georg Lukács wrote in 1913, "is movement itself," and he was already reflecting a widespread belief. [2] Earlier, a Grand Café program advertising films by the Lumière brothers describes in detail what these films record, namely, "all the movements which have succeeded one another over a given period of time in front of the camera and the subsequent reproduction of these movements by the projection of their images, life size, on a screen." [3] Wildly affirmative of cinema, in which he saw the basis of all new directions in the arts, the Expressionist poet Yvan Goll proclaimed in 1920 that cinematic movement would have the catalytic effect of ozone or radium upon all media and genres, which for the moment were "dead and mute." [4] With Viking Eggeling and perhaps Hans Arp in mind, Goll speculated that the future would soon bring *Kino-malerei* or "movie-painting" into existence. A year earlier, another German writer, Carl Hauptmann, theorizing about Rodin against the historical backdrop of the *Laocoön* controversy, made the claim that sculpture's manifest desire to suggest movement—indeed, the desire of all of the visual arts to transcend the moment—could now be realized in cinema. [5]

But the introduction of movement into the realm of visual representation was thought to have negative consequences also. Cinematic bodies—the human figures subjected to motion in films—were generally perceived as attenuated, as "merely" the sum of their actions and movements, and were often contrasted negatively with so-called theatrical bodies. Eleonora Duse's is a frequently cited example of the stage actor's body, the theatrical body capable of projecting "full presence" or "soul," or—as even Lukács put it—a body in which being and acting were indissolubly one.[6] As observed in theatrical performances, the actor's body was thought to be redolent of fate, mystery, and tragedy, whereas, according to Lukács, bodies in films should not even be considered human, but rather as constituting life of a wholly new and fantastic kind.[7] Thus, cinematic representations of the human body were adjudged to be unmetaphysical and soulless, to constitute one-dimensional creatures whose life is one of pure surface—to be somehow monstrous, unnatural, precisely because visual representations, whose stillness the limits of technology had made to seem natural, were now capable of being subjected to movement. Still, Lukács's reading differs from some insofar as he felt that the cinematic representation of human beings ought not to be perceived as inadequate, as founded upon a lack, but rather simply as a consequence of the *principium stilisationis* of cinema. According to Lukács, neither fate nor causality determines cinematic life; since, he believes, movement alone constitutes or defines the cinema, he is able to argue that while the human figures represented on the screen may have lost their souls, they have precisely for this reason regained their bodies.

During this period of silent cinema, it comes as no surprise that the body language of pantomime and gesture occupied a central position in the discussion concerning the place of film with regard to the established arts. For some, the presence of the body on stage, contrasted with its actual absence from the cinematic frame, ensures the primacy of even theatrical pantomime over film, not to mention the primacy of drama, with its access to the spoken word.[8] Others, like Carl Hauptmann, claim that the human soul is best expressed in body language, seeing in the foregrounding of gesture (*Gebärde*) a primal, privileged domain of signification available to film.[9] Usually, however, it is suggested that the silent cinema's muteness—and even the facial expression of cinematic figures, whether exaggerated or blank and, in either case, mask-like—contributes to the uncanniness and "soullessness" of its figures. It is this effect, as Walter Benjamin reminds us, that Charlie Chaplin uses to such advantage; his "mask of uninvolvement" makes Chaplin into a "marionette in a fair sideshow."[10] Contributing to this marionette-like effect are Chaplin's body movements, his "exercises in fragmentation," as Miriam Hansen puts it; utterly self-conscious about the effects of the cinematic apparatus on the representation of his body, Chaplin is the film actor par excellence who, by "chopping up expressive body movement into a sequence of minute mechanical impulses . . . renders the law of the apparatus visible as the law of human movement."[11] But Chaplin's recuperative strategy of exposing the fragmentation imposed upon the body by cinema was a personal solution to a perceived threat, not a strategy that could find universal application.

UNNATURAL CONJUNCTIONS: THE HETEROGENEOUS TEXT

In 1916, Paul Wegener's lecture, "The Artistic Possibilities of the Cinema," with its emphasis on the "kinetic lyricism" of the cinema and on the play of pure motion for its own sake, established him as a forerunner among the artists and filmmakers—including Hans Richter—who would develop the abstract film in Germany.[12] Wegener's interest is in what he calls the "fantastic domain" of "optical lyricism," a term perhaps not as far from Gilles Deleuze's concept of the "movement-image" as the nearly seventy years that separate their two texts might suggest; for Deleuze, too, the lure of filmmaking lies in the possibility of reproducing pure movement "extracted from bodies or moving things," movement as a function of a series of equidistant instants reproduced in a sequence of shots.[13] Not surprisingly, it was the tantalizing implication of movement suggested by series photography—comic photographs of a man fencing with himself and playing cards alone—that originally drew Wegener to the cinematic medium in 1913, and that, at one and the same time, suggested to him the suitability of the cinema for transmitting the fantastic tales of E.T.A. Hoffmann.[14]

The significance of series photography to the development of cinema is well documented. In the United States, Eadweard Muybridge published photo sequences to illustrate his studies of animal locomotion, and was already using an invention of his own, the zoopraxiscope, to project short sequences during his lectures in 1880. Thus living bodies, especially human figures, came to be linked with movement—indeed, were vehicles for portraying movement—in series photography from its very inception.[15] It is probable that the images of the fencer that Wegener saw were very much like those produced by Muybridge, and that they demonstrated the graceful postures assumed by the human body while fencing, postures that the camera could record in sequence. What Wegener saw additionally, however, is the absence of an opponent in these photographs, prompting him to make the connection between this uncanny absence in the photographic frame and the potential of film to express uncanny effects. We shall return to the nature of these effects later.

While I shall be concerned here with the conjunction of Wegener's interest in cinematic motion and his representation of the body by means of what Deleuze calls the "fixed primitive image,"[16] it is nevertheless clear that Wegener's interest in itself is of a more abstract order. There is one particular aspect of the fascination with the play of shapes dissolving into one another, with motion subjected to temporal rhythms such as that found in the films of Richter, that fixes Wegener's attention, and that is the possibility of conjoining the natural with the artificial: "I can imagine," he writes, "a kind of cinema which would use nothing but moving surfaces, against which there would impinge events that would still participate in the natural world but transcend the lines and volumes of the natural."[17] The images produced by the conjunction of the organic and the inorganic—of the natural or "living" and the artificial or "dead"—could, by means of the camera and of montage, become moving images emphasized as such. For Wegener, it is pure motion, divorced from the actual status of the object as inherently animate or inanimate that is of interest—the kind of motion, in other words, that cinema is innately capable of rendering.[18] Further examples that Wegener puts forward—as when he suggests that "microscopic particles of fermenting chemical substances could be filmed together with small plants of various sizes"[19]—strongly confirm the impression that the ontological status of such composite images, liberated from the binary link of being to life and non-being to death, is at least in part the object of his fascination. It is, furthermore, precisely the potential for such a juxtaposition of natural and artifical in Hanns Heinz Ewers's script for *The Student of Prague* that Wegener claims to have found so compelling: "*The Student of Prague*, with its strange mixture of the natural and artificial . . . interested me enormously."[20]

The pairing and the permutations of the natural and artificial take on a particular resonance for this film on several levels, including, of course, the thematic one (to be pursued later) that is suggested by the various "supernatural" elements of the plot. Intriguingly, it finds expression in the manner in which the film is an assemblage of varying spaces, spaces that, while not atypical of films of this period, do not often coexist jarringly in later narrative cinema. Kracauer's distinction, in *Theory of Film*, between the "two tendencies" of cinema—the "Lumière tendency," with its documentary interest in the natural, recording the details of the physical world, and the "Méliès tendency," with its formative interest in the artificial, in theatrical vision—is illustrated aptly by several different sequences of *The Student of Prague*, pointing to the way in which the cinema, in its desire for a uniquely cinematic space, appropriates the spaces and modes of as many of the arts as it can press into service, with the consequence of presenting itself repeatedly as a mixed mode, a heterogeneous text.[21]

Not surprisingly, given such emphases, *The Student of Prague* is utterly self-conscious about its position vis-à-vis the more established arts; for example, the opening images, which constitute a setpiece made up of nineteenth century mourning pictures, including a weeping willow with a tombstone. On this tombstone is inscribed the text of Alfred de Musset's "La nuit de Décembre," a poem that establishes themes of mimetic artifice, of the double, and of death. To say nothing of its recognizable allusion to the visual arts, the literary space that this short sequence announces—the poem as epitaph, the space of writing at the moment at which it most obviously marks an absence, a text "signed" by the poet, as one might find it in an anthology—appears again at the end of the film, as though to enclose the cinematic narrative in literary brackets, to frame the moving images of its narrative with the static spaces at once of writing and of death. (In some prints this opening sequence survives only as the text of the poem itself, which is then less clearly distinguishable from the film's title cards, but nevertheless still serves to stress the status of the literary as writing.) Since its function in the narrative is to foreshadow his tragic end, the student Baldwin is able to enter this preliminary scene, and the melancholy movements of his body and that of the willow itself, staged and stagy, suggest that the scene as a whole is more than a mere illustration of the poem. It is meant pointedly to predict that the film will animate writing, will bring it to life.

Immediately following this sequence, a theatrical prologue points to the stage as a space in which all movement must be generated either by the bodies of the actors or by overtly mechanical means—by such mechanisms, for example, as the swing used for the deus ex machina, mechanisms that had become sophisticated in the nineteenth century but that would suddenly seem archaic in the cinema. In this connection a further speculation of Wegener's seems pertinent: he hoped that film would make it possible to use "marionettes or small three-dimensional models which could be animated image by image, in slow or rapid motion depending on the speed of the montage," thus giving rise "to fantastic images which would provoke absolutely novel associations of ideas in the spectator."[22] In this passage, Wegener restates his fascination with the frisson produced by film's capacity to animate the inanimate. Though this effect was experienced more intensely during an earlier period in the development of cinema, it is still produced today; as one critic has recently noted, "the experience of film involves a mysterious equivocation between terror and the sense of a utopia in which divisions between life and death are effaced."[23]

One might well see in the marionettes mentioned by Wegener equivalents of the automata that recur in Hoffmann's stories, uncanny figures connected with crises of perception and desire. Wegener's formulations imply not only that film offers technical possibilities for the animation of puppets, but also that the apparatus of cinema naturalizes the movements of the marionettes because, once they become images in a film, their movements—"animated image by image"—seem no more mechanically produced than the movements of human actors. From this perspective, Wegener's remark gestures towards Kleist's "On the Marionette Theater," an essay to which we shall return.

For today's spectator, the rapid juxtapositon of *The Student of Prague*'s two opening sequences—the literary-painterly space with the theatrical space—occasions a feeling of Brechtian distancing no doubt already experienced while reading the two cards following the film's title, the first announcing "A Romantic Drama in 6 Acts," the second that the film was shot on location "in Castle Belvedere in Prague, Palace Fürstenberg, Lobkovitz and other historic places." Once again, the claim of romance, with its Méliès-like insistence on artifice and the film's self-proclaimed generic identity as drama are relativized by the counterclaim of photographed reality reminiscent of Lumière, a reality that, moreover, is overtly situated within history. The narrative itself, which opens with a short series of genre scenes of student life, is thus placed within a series of brackets that raise conflicting expectations and make contesting claims about the status of the text and its generic identity.[24]

As Thomas Elsaesser points out, Wegener, Wiene, Murnau, Lang, and many others involved in this phase of German filmmaking deliberately addressed themselves to the task of elevating cinema to the status of an art form, and he astutely observes that it is within the confines of the German art cinema that the forms of the fantastic flourish.[25] In a later essay, Elsaesser again addresses the historically specific predominance of aesthetic self-consciousness in German silent cinema, noting that its typical foregrounding of the act of narration resulted in "a profusion of nested narratives, framed tales, flashbacks, *en abîme* constructions and interlacing of narrative voices."[26] One explanation for this phenomenon lies precisely in the self-conscious attempt to develop a new art form as noted by Elsaesser in his earlier text. We can see its consequences in the barely formulated theoretical issues that lie buried in essays and films such as Wegener's—issues expressed, for example, in formulations suggesting transgressive boundary crossings between the natural and artificial. Such passages suggest that film, at the moment of flaunting its capacity to introduce movement into the visual arts on the one hand and to give visual expression to narrative on the other, is at pains to contain an uneasiness about its hybrid nature, an uneasiness that nevertheless leaves its mark upon these texts.

For the contemporary spectator—and perhaps also for the spectator of 1913—there is one scene in *The Student of Prague* that stands out most vividly for the juxtaposition of its spaces and for the intricacy with which it poses the problem of the interrelation of the arts.[27] Identified by a title as the "Preparation for the Hunt," the space of this sequence resembles a stage set whose back wall is covered from floor to ceiling by tapestry-like paintings. For a few instants only the eye is allowed to linger upon the two figures in riding attire that occupy the foreground, whereupon a third figure enters through the door. At this moment the space of the scene is radically disrupted. What had been a typical tableau scene, appropriate to its theatrical space, is relegated to being "merely that," for when the door in the center of this wall opens, it reveals another space—an actual birch wood, not a set. Since the door opens into nature without the mediation of an architectural space, the spectator has the impression of a theater set imposed directly upon a natural scene; there is a distinct awareness of the conjunction of ontologically disparate spaces. Startling as it is, this effect is heightened when all three characters leave through the door, which remains open to reveal the receding figures as they wend their way among the trees. Tellingly, the shot is held another few seconds, thus emphasizing the juxtaposition of natural scene and tapestry-like mural whose subject is the hunt.[28]

There follows an abrupt cut to figures on horseback moving from background to foreground in a movement that seems magically continuous with that of these same figures from the foreground to the background in the previous frame. Here, in fact, there occurs a moment in which movement seems almost to exist independently of the figures that produce it. As these figures approach, it becomes clear that they are mounted huntsmen surrounded by a pack of hounds, who leave the castle grounds through a wrought-iron gate in the foreground. Ever more animated, the bodies of horses and hounds in constant motion, these figures emerge as though freed from the constraints of a frame. A montage of shots follows that not only presents a natural landscape full of the play of light and shadow, with trees reflected in bodies of water in the manner that Danish directors had already learned to project on screen, but serves also to impart the intoxication so obviously felt with what Deleuze calls the "emancipation of the image."[29] Since this sequence serves little diegetic purpose, its montage of shots seems relatively long: the static camera is placed in various positions and the horsemen and dogs pass in front of it, their bodies passing in and out of the cinematic frame with increasing speed. Repeatedly, these figures evoke offscreen space, the space outside the cinematic frame on which André Bazin bases his distinction between cinema and painting.[30]

Obviously what is at issue here is the release of the body from the tableau space of theater with its relatively fixed perspective and, more particularly, from the space of the tapestry-like wall mural that entraps and contains it. The film brings the mural of the hunt to life, as it were, and the dramatic organization of this sequence of shots, with its ever faster motion, builds to a triumphant crescendo, leaving no doubt that this moment is constructed in order to proclaim cinema as an advance over earlier, more culturally established art forms.[31] Wegener's radical departure from the circumscribed theatrical space of the castle interior celebrates film's ability, in the words of Kracauer, to "record the visible world," and even to transcend it in the play of "pure movement" that Wegener admired.

"Its Strange Mixture of the Natural and Artificial": The Presence of Kleist

It seems appropriate at this point to turn to Kleist's "Marionette Theater," which to a remarkable extent forms a subtext not only for Wegener's lecture on "kinetic lyricism," with its search for a pure motion that transcends the limitations imposed upon the human body by its physical capacities and by consciousness, but also simply for various images within the film itself.[32] Kleist's dialogue includes several narratives, the first of which, told by a dancer, makes the somewhat outrageous claim that marionettes (*Gliederpuppen*) have more grace (*Anmut*) and greater fluidity of motion than human dancers. The second narrative, the only one told by the "I" of this exchange, tells the story of a young man who, happening to glance into the mirror one day while bending over to dry himself, tells his companion that he sees a resemblance between himself and the famous Spinario sculpture of a young man extracting a splinter from his foot. Although his companion has also just made the same observation, the companion does not admit this and, on the contrary, tells the young man rather brusquely that he is seeing things—literally, that he is seeing ghosts.[33] From this moment on, the young man is wholly changed: he begins to spend his time contemplating his reflection in the mirror, becoming self-conscious in the process and losing his natural grace. The reading of body movements is also of crucial importance in the third narrative, in which a bear must discern thrusts from feints while fencing.

Each of these narratives leaves its traces either in *The Student of Prague* or in Wegener's essay. The language of mechanics that Kleist's speaker uses to describe the movements of the marionettes—language concerning the curves that their motions are said to describe, the rhythms of these motions, and the "machinist" who controls them—renders them both abstract and technological, much like the cinematic motions described by Wegener. The film combines images from the other two narratives, placing the student Baldwin, Prague's most skillful fencer, before a mirror and allowing him to thrust and parry with his mirror image, an image that will become his ghostly double. Ironically, the dismissive remark that he must be seeing ghosts also dismisses uncanniness at the very moment of suggesting it. Further, the Kleist text contains a passage that Cynthia Chase has called "an appendage" to these narratives, a remark by the dancer to the effect that the newly available artificial limbs enable human dancers to execute their steps more gracefully than they could with their natural limbs.[34] Not only does the dancer suggest the substitution of marionette for human, as noted above, but he also sanctions that monstrous conjunction of artificial (dead) and natural (living) parts that forms one of the central concerns of *The Student of Prague*, in which Wegener locates an important aspect of cinematic experimentation.

In the narratives and "appendage" of the "Marionette Theater," the discourse of the body clearly occupies a more central position than most have recognized.[35] Paul de Man has commented upon the humorously ironic connection of the Spinario figure removing a thorn from his foot to the *Laocoön* group that has been the object of so much attention from those who seek, like G. E. Lessing, to delineate the boundaries between the arts: both sculptures portray their subjects in pain.[36] Laocoön's body in pain, repeatedly idealized by commentators, elicited sublimated desire in Winckelmann.[37] Kleist's text, typically, also links the visual work of art with sexuality: the narrator of the story has, after all, been observing the young man in a public bath and has prefaced his anecdote with words to the effect that the young man had lost his innocence by means of a mere observation.[38] It is not only a fall into self-consciousness that is at issue here, as this suggestive word-play on losing one's virginity makes clear.

But the latent eroticism of the Kleist essay is not my topic here: more pertinent is the manner in which the young man of the second narrative, an erstwhile beholder of the sculpture and now a beholder of his own image in the mirror, is no longer in control of that image just when he most desperately seeks to "embody" the work of art, with the result that he is not only alienated from his image, but from his own body as well. The nature of the young man's narcissism requires some elaboration:[39] though he is not wholly subsumed by a mirrored self at which he gazes and which confirms his gaze, gazing back in a mutually sustaining erotic relation, he is alienated from a beloved image. What Kleist's young man sees, as he loses one grace after another, is the degree to which he is unlike Spinario's figure, his desired mirror image.[40] The young man's situation appears to resemble a grotesquely skewed version of the Lacanian mirror stage, in which the haunting presence of the sculpture in the memory is substituted for the confirming gaze of the mother, and this presence causes the self to appear ever less idealized. Here, then, is an analogue for the fragmented Imaginary of early cinema: searching for an identity while gazing into the mirror, it sees the presence of the arts that have engendered it, but cannot yet visualize an idealized version of itself in the mirror's surface.

"BITS OF BODIES": THE FRAGMENTED TEXT

Like the young man of Kleist's anecdote, Baldwin, the central character of Wegener's film, has lost control of his mirror image. In Baldwin's case this image returns to pursue and haunt him as his Double. There have been various readings of the return of and to the Double during the fin de siècle, usually having to do with the effects of industrialization and mass production.[41] Quite clearly, however, the function that the Double takes on in *The Student of Prague* has at least as much to do with the anxiety created by the production of the moving image itself as with the technology of this production, and must be seen within the experimental—and potentially problematic—context of movement both attached to and divorced from the human body. Walter Benjamin's observation that the strangeness experienced by an actor before the camera "is basically the same kind as the estrangement felt before one's own image in the mirror" is interesting in this regard; Benjamin goes on to note that this image has become "separable, transportable."[42] In *The Student of Prague*, the image-producer (Baldwin, Wegener) sells his image, which then chases and pursues him, flaunting its mobility all the while, until the end of the film, when its destruction also occasions the end of the narrative and of the film. Obviously, the double takes its place within a group of fantastic figures familiar to us from other German films of this period. As Elsaesser has pointed out: "One of the most typical figures of the fantastic in the German cinema is that of the sorcerer's apprentice, i.e., the creation and use of magic forces which outstrip their creator and over which he loses control."[43] While Elsaesser convincingly reads the Double as a part of the self that emancipates itself and turns against its creator, his argument that this phenomenon is occasioned by the alienation of the producer from his product in capitalism—undoubtedly inspired by Benjamin—is incomplete.[44] As Benjamin's remarks also suggest, the anxiety expressed in the narrative of Wegener's film would seem to have much in common with that of primitive peoples who fear that the camera will steal their image and hence possess them.[45]

The narrative calls to mind other fears as well, such as the feeling of uncanniness described by Jentsch and somewhat disparagingly quoted by Freud in his essay on the uncanny concerning "doubts whether an apparently animate being is really alive; or conversely, whether a lifeless object might not be in fact animate."[46] As we recall, it is precisely this boundary between animate and inanimate that is the focus of Wegener's interest: "uncanniness" would seem to describe the effect cinematic motion produced in him. Although Freud goes on to cite Jentsch's claim that "the impressions made by wax-work figures, artificial dolls and automatons" in particular elicit this kind of reponse,[47] he is eager to substitute the castration complex as the origin of the Uncanny for the tamer speculations concerning an "intellectual uncertainty" evoked by such figures put forward by Jentsch. And yet, even as Freud asserts the superiority of his theories to those of Jentsch, the theme of motion remains present in Freud's thinking too—as, for instance, in the contention that "dismembered limbs, a severed head, a hand cut off at the wrist, feet which dance by themselves—all these have something peculiarly uncanny about them, especially when, as in the last instance, they prove able to move of themselves in addition."[48] Freud's images of mutilation, fragmentation, and movement have a role to play in regard to the perception of the cinematic

18

image: the body is too much the terrain threatened by the "cutting" of film to be left conveniently out of the picture.

Clearly, the theme of the Double as it is figured in *The Student of Prague* expresses cinema's fascination with the ontology of the image, and it poses questions concerning the nature of cinematic representation, especially with regard to the manner in which narrative and visual coherence in films are anchored in the human body. It is true that Wegener was fascinated with the detachment of movement from the body, with the possibility of leaving the domain of narrative cinema, bound as it is to the human figure, for that of "kinetic lyricism."[49] In Wegener's essay, as in Kleist's text, it is implied that increased formalization will produce increased aesthetic pleasure,[50] and that the cinema machine, the product of modern technology, can successfully realize the dancer's interpretation of the marionette theater as a place where movement is unencumbered by Kleist's "inertia of matter."[51] But, should it not already be apparent, it should be noted that *The Student of Prague* is by no means the abstract film that Wegener envisions, but rather one in which the—doubled—body is prominent.

Early instances of animating visual representation often involved photographic studies of the human body in motion: the human model, after all, was the most easily controlled object for such experimentation. In series photography, each photograph tends to represent the whole body, centered within the frame, and early narrative cinema displayed the whole human figure within its frames as well. The close-up of a body part had to be "invented," of course, and the story of the occasion on which Griffith chose for the first time *not* to include the whole body of an actor within the frame records the shock that was felt at this act of "mutilation": "You'll cut off his feet," was the enraged cry of Billy Bitzer, the cameraman; apparently the Hollywood moguls put it another way: "We pay for the whole actor, Mr. Griffith. We want to see him."[52] Unlike theater, which generally puts the actor's whole body on display on the stage, cinematic space is created as bodies move into, across, and out of the frame and are "fragmented" in the process by close-ups, pans, and tracking shots. It is in the interest of the camera to dismember the human body as it creates the film, perversely playing on the spectator's desire for the whole actor during the process. We might also call to mind a French film described in an essay of 1913, a film in which a wooden horse assembles itself out of many pieces and then proceeds to gallop away in what is surely a commentary on the nature of the image.[53] Seen in this context,

Wegener's gesture of splitting—or fragmenting—the actor and thereby effectively doubling him should be read simultaneously as a figuring of cinema's tendency to fragment the body and as an effort to shore it up by duplicating its wholeness.

Film is at its most uncanny, one early German theorist claimed, where "connecting limbs" (*Zwischenglieder*)—frames or sequences necessary to the continuity of motion and of action—are omitted.[54] In such statements film itself is figured as a body whose organic wholeness is tampered with, an object that has lost a limb (*Glied*). If cinematic narrative is, in fact, a "mechanism entailing mutilation," as it in some sense must be, it should be noted that mutilation, cutting, or découpage function only as one set of terms in a dialectic, over and against suturing and montage, to create cinematic narrative and cinematic space.[55] On the subject of parts and wholes, it is useful to consider Barthes's discussion of Diderot's tableau:

> Diderot is for us the theorist of this dialectic of desire; in the article on "Composition," he writes: "A well-composed picture [*tableau*] is a whole contained under a single point of view, in which the parts work together to one end and form by their mutual correspondence a unity as real as that of the members of the body of an animal; so that a piece of painting made up of a large number of figures thrown at random on to the canvas, with neither proportion, intelligence, or unity, no more deserves to be called a *true composition* than scattered studies of legs, nose and eyes on the same cartoon deserve to be called a *portrait* or a *human figure*." Thus is the body expressly introduced into the idea of the tableau, but it is the whole body that is so introduced—the organs, grouped together and as though held in cohesion by the magnetic power of the segmentation, function in the name of a transcendence, that of the *figure*, which receives the full fetishistic load and becomes the sublime substitute of meaning.[56]

The student of Prague's body is split (the mirror image or reflection is severed from the body that produces it) and doubled (the mirror image acquires a life of its own); the film contains, therefore, a figure of its own hybrid status as text, its discomfiting suspicion that its own body is not all of a piece. Early cinema suspects that the arts of which it is comprised set it at odds with itself; it suspects that it is composed of scattered limbs that do not quite come together as a figure. In the earliest of Fritz Lang's Dr. Mabuse films, a minor character is tagged as decadent and weird because he is a Cubist—because, it is said, he admires paintings in which "legs, nose, and eyes" do not come together in the customary way. In this same film, Hugo Balling—an obvious allusion to Hugo Ball, the Dadaist—is one of the evil personae of Dr. Mabuse himself. Clearly, these references both are and are not admiring, for film both wants to deny its acts of dismemberment and is envious of an avant-garde that it quotes in order to place itself on the cutting edge.

Man and the Cinema Machine: Magician, Psychoanalyst, Scientist: The Case of Dr. Caligari

The early filmmaker's perplexed play upon the wholeness and fragmentation of the human body, its appearance and disappearance within the cinematic frame, its metamorphosis from "real" body to "mere" image and back again is nowhere in greater evidence than in the films of Georges Méliès.[57] In *The Famous Box Trick* (1898), the image is literally split and doubled as a magician—the role in which Méliès so frequently cast himself—cuts a boy in two with his wand, magically creating two boys. Méliès presents himself repeatedly as a conjuror or illusionist, often in conjunction with machinery of various kinds, thus drawing attention to a need to situate himself within the spheres of technology and imagination that together define cinema. What Linda Williams has astutely called the "drama of dismemberment and reintegration" that Méliès so often performs upon bodies—both male and female—in his films, need not only be read as an attempt to come to terms with the problem of sexual difference and the threat of castration, but should also be seen—perhaps more simply—as yet another of the ways in which the filmmaker narrativizes the operations that the cinematic apparatus performs upon the image of the human body, fragmenting and making it whole again from frame to frame.[58] As Williams has noted, Méliès obsessively positions his own body within the machine that he manipulates, exploring ever anew the place of the body as such in cinema.

In German cinema the prototype of the figure that conjoins magician with filmmaker is that of Dr. Caligari; indeed, Robert Wiene's *The Cabinet of Dr. Caligari* (1919) complicates the figure of the filmmaker-magician additionally: it offers the spectator superimposed allegories of both filmmaking and psychoanalysis, supported by the multiple identity of Caligari as carnival entertainer, hypnotist, student of the "unconscious," and head of an insane asylum.[59] The cabinet in which Caligari's "creature" and sideshow exhibit, Cesare, is kept recalls both the cinematic apparatus that contains, controls, and projects the cinematic body (represented by Cesare) and the unconscious over whose frightening forces Caligari has control (embodied in Cesare, alternatively called "the sleeper"). At the moment, for example, when Jane, the female lead, approaches the cabinet, peering inside the upright box, there is a cut to Caligari pointing his phallic cane threateningly at her; Jane, having looked inside, runs away shielding her eyes. On the one hand, this scene suggests that Caligari has revealed to Jane the libidinal drives situated in the unconscious (as well as the sexual power of the analyst), while, on the other hand, it encapsulates two aspects of directorial anxiety, suggesting both the uncontrollable power attached to the image itself and the invasive power associated with the camera.[60] Jane lingers at the site, both repulsed and attracted by what she has seen: her ambivalence towards Cesare, image and id, refigures Wiene's anxiety about the power of his medium as an anxiety of authority reminiscent of Wegener's and typical for the early filmmaker: the image, once created, assumes an autonomy over which no one can claim control.

In *Caligari*, this anxiety concerning the moving image must be viewed against the backdrop of a painterly set that represents the ultimate in constructed spaces. It has become a commonplace of German film history to claim that *Caligari* was intentionally made to incorporate "high art" values. It was hoped that its Expressionist decor would make the film more marketable, and certainly *Caligari*'s enormous popular success in Paris would suggest that its producer and director had made the correct decision.[61] Designed by the studio painters Warm, Röhrig, and Reimann, *Caligari*'s sets of painted canvas constitute a mise-en-scène over which it was possible to exercise complete control (most notable, perhaps, are the rays of light painted onto the walls and floors).[62] Obliquely slanted doors and windows are for the most part also painted onto the set, and furniture, especially built to conform to the distortions of the decor, is kept to a minimum. The stylization of the set, as is well known, extends to the lighting, the costumes, and even to the gestures of the actors. In fact, this highly subjective world, which the framing narrative eventually situates as the vision of a madman, is, from the point of view of filmmaking, utterly contrived and composed. More so than *The Student of Prague*, *Caligari* represents the earliest stages of the moving figure's release from the painted canvas, for its primitivism is decidedly not determined by the limitations of film technology or film form.

As the narrative proper of film begins, it is carefully marked as a narration: Francis's story begins with a series of title cards alternating with the tableaux that illustrate it, and this pattern is punctuated by frontal shots of Francis in the act of narration. The first three tableaux are contained by iris-in and iris-out shots: these opening frames present virtually at one and the same time the "graphic signals" of cinematic grammar and what is quite obviously a painted set. The first of these tableaux depicts the mountain village of Holstenwall on the slope of a fragmented, many-planed mountain designed in simplified imitation of Cézanne or Feininger: this is simply a painting, absolutely static and flat. The second shot of Holstenwall, however, a close-up of the fair, though motionless, is not wholly confined to the two-dimensional space of painting, as we see a portion of flat stage in the foreground. Finally, the third shot of the narrated story introduces movement into the scene in the form of the human figure, that of Caligari, who emerges near the bottom of the frame, walking up a stairway defined by lines that, in the second shot, had appeared to be part of the painted backdrop. As Caligari walks toward the camera, he looms ever larger until the shot ends with an iris-in on a close-up of his face. These shots are distinguished, then, by the ever greater complexity of their spaces, the second shot revealed only in retrospect to have greater depth than the spectator was first able to discern; what initially appeared to have been a trompe-l'oeil effect (the stairway) is revealed as an actual prop. While, however, at the end of this progression the human figure creates a theatrical space as it moves across the stage, the spectator never-theless remains aware of the manner in which this space is generated from and bounded by painting.[63] Keeping in mind the many iris shots that enclose the tableaux and separate them from one another, we can read in their superimposed movement their control and dominance over the image—they form expanding and contracting frames around the tab-leaux, first revealing and then withdrawing them from our view. In yet another act of appropriation, cinema imposes its capacity for movement upon the stasis of painting.

The narrative continues in a series of frames in which the human figure is contained in this half-painterly, half-theatrical space, recalling from a somewhat different perspective what Michael Fried has called the "rapprochement between the aims of painting and drama" in eighteenth-century France.[64] Characters repeatedly recede into and emerge from the painted backdrop: at several junctures what appeared to be a painted door is opened to reveal another space, much as the door of the palace in *The Student of Prague* is opened to reveal "natural," cinematic space. One such instance occurs when Jane enters Caligari's tent and is shown the upright cabinet containing Cesare that before it is opened simply ap-pears to be lines painted on the canvas wall—a compelling reminder of the way in which film can gesture toward depth, towards three-dimensionality, as well as of the way the cinematic image is released from pictorial space. (The play upon flatness and depth represented by the "hidden door" is found frequently in early films: Fritz Lang, for instance, makes similar use of a wallpaper-covered door in *Metropolis*.) Designed by artists, anxious about its status among the sister arts, *Caligari* seeks to establish its origins in painting, theater, *and* narrative: witness the sustained emphasis on the act of storytelling.[65] Insofar as *Caligari* "contains" an "agitation"[66]—and it very clearly does—an important aspect of this agitation appears to involve both cinema's place vis-à-vis high culture and, concomitantly, the consequences of its difference from other modes of representation. One such difference, as we have been saying, consists in its ability to introduce movement into visual art.

As critics have pointed out, *Caligari* is divided into a series of static tableau, so that, although a rather complex plot is developed in the film, it still progresses by means of a series of staged compositions that retain their connection to painting.[67] (The garden scene of the frame story, in distinction to the narrative proper, manifests an approach to setting, movement, and space that is noticeably more cinematic.) The static quality of the succession of silent moving pictures that this film presents to the spectator's view approaches the mode Lyotard calls "acinéma," situated "at the two poles of cinema taken as a writing of movements: thus, extreme immobilization and extreme mobilization."[68] With regard to immobilization, it will be useful here to turn to Michael Fried's reading of Diderot and to consider the concept of the sister arts in the eighteenth century, the period during which it most notably flourished.[69]

As Fried points out, in his early writings on theater Diderot advocates a new kind of dramaturgy that rejects *côups de théatre*, unexpected twists and turns of the plot, and orients itself instead toward a certain kind of painting in order to find inspiration for tableaux—for "visually satisfying, essentially silent, seemingly accidental groupings of figures."[70] Similar to the way in which Diderot felt that the spectator in the theater should be "thought of as before a canvas, on which a series of such tableaux follow one another as if by magic," the tableaux in *Caligari* are somewhat loosely connected, not to say disjointed.[71] While the ideological significance that the tableau carries for Diderot has perhaps little directly to do with the tableau approach to film narrative in *Caligari*, nevertheless the more formal aspects of Diderot's notion shed light on the relation of early cinema to painting.[72] Furthermore, these frontally shot tableaux have something else in common with the kind of painting preferred by Diderot, paintings that completely exclude the beholder from the site of representation: they, too, exteriorize the spectator and exclude her or him from their action, unlike films made in the dominant mode of narrative cinema, which seek to conflate the camera eye with that of the spectator. Janet Bergstrom calls attention to the fact that it is characteristic for Weimar cinema to allow "for modes of viewing more commonly associated with the fine arts, specifically with looking at paintings."[73]

In Diderot, as read by Fried, the exclusion of beholder from the canvas is related to the idea of pictorial unity, an idea with which Diderot was much preoccupied. Diderot's model is an organic one; as mentioned earlier, the unity of a composition has its analogue for Diderot in the unity of the figure or body: "Each function performed by the body has an effect not only upon one of its parts, but upon the whole body. There is a 'general conspiracy of movements,' an interdependence of all the parts, which the artist must know and feel in order to represent them."[74] This kind of unity is missing in the tableaux of *Caligari*; the discrepancy between the moving human figure that generates theatrical space and the pictorial space that hems it in figures once more the problem of generic heterogeneity. Mediating between these two kinds of space, however, is the figure of Cesare, which I have already associated with the cinematic image.

As we know, the somnambulist is Caligari's creature and Caligari "brings him to life," as it were, but the precise nature of his influence over Cesare's actions is allowed to remain ambiguous; it is never completely clear whether or not Caligari orders him to murder or simply releases him to do as he will. (In actuality, somnambulistic episodes are thought to be hysterical symptoms, symbolic representations of unconscious wishes that cannot be fully inhibited.) After Caligari opens the painted canvas "door" up for the first time to reveal to the crowd the cabinet containing Cesare, Caligari points his baton-like cane at him and the somnambulist slowly enters the state between waking and sleeping characteristic of his condition: at first he is motionless for several moments, then his eyes open very slowly and he raises his eyebrows, next his arms move out in front of him like a doll's, and then, placing one foot carefully before the other, he begins to walk, marionette fashion. This gradual and deliberate transition from complete stasis to movement emphasizes his emergence from the painted canvas. Cesare's leotards and his heavy, mask-like makeup set him apart from the other characters who populate the film, and further emphasize the angularity of the movements that allow him to merge repeatedly with the oblique lines of the set. His eyes, though open, hold an unseeing, "lifeless" stare, much like those on the sideshow poster that

Fig. 1. Cesare's emergence from Caligari's cabinet evokes the emergence of the moving figure from the painted canvas.

has his painted image, Munch-like, upon it. Here, too, in the juxtaposition of poster and moving creature, there is a play upon stillness and motion, high art (the quotation of Munch) and the simulated, "unnatural" motion to which the human body is subjected in cinema. Cesare, in other words, literally lives up to the often quoted pronouncement ascribed to Hermann Warm, one of the film's designers: "Films must be drawings brought to life."[75]

In part, Cesare's uncanniness arises from the fact that he is neither awake nor asleep, neither dead nor alive, and the ambiguity concerning his status is figured in the circus wagon scene, where Caligari's cabinet—now no longer vertical and like a built-in closet, but rather on the floor, horizontal and coffin-shaped—is discovered to contain not Cesare himself, but rather a doll or effigy made in his likeness and seemingly distinguishable from the real Cesare only in its incapacity to perform any motion at all. This is an image of another kind—a mere replica of the body, akin to sculpture—and Caligari makes use of it in order to delude Francis and the police into believing that the sleeper is safely in his cabinet and not at large in the village. In contrast with the doll that has been substituted for his body and that appropriately transforms the cabinet into a coffin, Cesare seems frighteningly alive. In one sense, Cesare as "monster" stands in, then, for the phantasmatic cinematic body, the body that critics and audiences of the period took to be soulless, one-dimensional, and lacking in presence, a frightening instance of nonorganic life. Yet we must ask ourselves what further significance this figure has for the film, and, in order to locate it, we must return to Diderot's tableau.

In the drama as Diderot envisions it, the tableau represents a fixed moment that halts narrative progression, interjecting stasis into movement, as it were, and deferring for that moment all subsequent movement or narrative development. During this short period of suspended time, the action is fixed or frozen at a point of heightened meaning, a point at which the gestures of the bodies within the tableau are especially capable of expressing the enduring significance of their relations to one another. It seems hardly surprising that Barthes has likened this frozen instant to the "pregnant moment" of Lessing's *Laocoön*, as there is a sculptural quality in the fixity of the tableau scene that, though it is confined to the present moment, nevertheless implies both a past and a future, much as Lessing would have sculpture do.[76] By its very nature, then, the tableau in relation to the drama is fetishistic, in the sense that it suspends time, deferring the narrative process, while the body, which functions as a sign guaranteeing unity *within* the tableau as well as being an analogue *to* the tableau, stands in a fetishistic relation to the tableau itself.

Furthermore, the Diderotian tableau bears a strong resemblance to the tableau vivant, which has a role to play in the relation of the fetish to masochism: characters assume tableau vivant postures in Sacher-Masoch, whose novels, as Deleuze notes in his study of masochism, "display the most intense preoccupation with arrested movement; his scenes are frozen, as though photographed, stereotyped or painted."[77] In Sacher-Masoch's novels the narrative flow is interrupted by the stasis of sculpture: these moments have the function of deferring or suspending literary movement, of halting the progress of the narrative in order to defer knowledge about its course. In psychoanalytic terms, what is ultimately being deferred is the knowledge, derived originally from viewing the body of the mother, that castration is possible. *Caligari*'s tableaux are significant because in some sense they slow down the very automated forms of movement that were associated with the uncanny effect. Since the tableau expresses a hesitation concerning narrative development, the choice of this form suggests that the stasis of painting is being pitted against the sequential flow of literary narrative, in a manner similar to what Jean-Louis Comolli, in writing about theatrical elements in *La Cécilia*, has termed a "superimposition, disphasing, dislocation of two representations, one over the other, one against the other."[78]

The perception of fragmentation or dismemberment is a virtual sine qua non of the cinematic body for the spectator of films even during the Weimar period; this fear of fragmentation is an anxiety that the makers of films were at great pains to counteract. I have thus far deferred the issue of castration in order to draw attention to the textual surface of the films and essays under discussion, since it is here that questions of origination and the struggle for territory play themselves out. Now, however, this issue can no longer be deferred. As Elsaesser has claimed, Cesare in his sheath-like clothing is obviously a kind of "phallus-fetish," yet we should keep in mind that, in characterizing him in this manner, we are already implying that he figures at one and the same time as a sign of sexual power—the phallus—and as the defense against dismemberment, against its loss—the fetish.[79]

On both the image and the narrative plane, Cesare is a phallus without a body, ironically the very sign of castration. Cesare's phallic power is evoked by the film both in the scene in which Jane looks at him in the vertical cabinet and in the later scene in which Cesare—now even more clearly a cinematic image, as he is visible only as a shadow projected upon the wall behind her bed—armed with the dagger that doubles him, prepares to thrust it into Jane's body. And yet, as Petro has pointed out, there is at the same time a curious identification between Jane and Cesare, obvious for the first time, perhaps, in the crosscutting between Cesare, whom Francis takes to be sleeping in the open, horizontal coffin, and Jane asleep in her bed.[80] The ambiguity concerning phallic power and its lack is figured again when, precisely at the moment when Cesare is about to stab Jane, he drops the dagger—refuses to kill or violate her—and picks her up instead.[81] Characterized as he is by doubleness and ambiguity, Cesare is made to signify the heterogeneity of the moving image in yet another sense, expressive of the Oedipal relation of the moving image as "son"—now powerful, now powerless—to its literary and painterly "fathers."

As a troubling presence within the cinematic text, a presence that figures the instability of film in its fluctuating identifications—not to say agonistic struggles—with the literary and the pictorial, *and* as an emblem of the fragmented text and the anxiety about the lack of cohesion in the tableau, Cesare, in this allegory of self-conception must be removed from the text. Having furthered the narrative as the murderous agent of Caligari, he must then be neutralized, suddenly collapsing in a ravine in order to facilitate the transformation of Caligari from sideshow entertainer and hypnotist who aims for control over the visual field into the head of an insane asylum, the reigning power over the very place whose function is to exercise interpretive control over the texts of mind and body. In this regard, the final scene of the film (part of the framing story) is significant, since both allegories are once again merged here. The asylum over which

Caligari presides is rendered as a Foucauldian theater of madness in which the inmates, each contained within a separate delusional scenario, are displayed to the spectatorial view.[82] Evoking and transforming the carnival of the film's beginning, this scene is composed of figures who relate to one another only as aspects of a show. Tellingly, it is in this scene that we can locate once again the recurrent anxiety concerning the heterogeneity of the cinematic medium, in particular concerning the coherence of independent images and the problem of connecting these fragments into a cohesive whole by means of the cinema machine itself. Viewed from the perspective of *Caligari* especially, it is no accident that this reconstitutive process has an analogue in the interpretive procedures of psychoanalysis.

The unifying figure of the film, of course, is that of Caligari himself, who has the ability, in his psychoanalytic guise, to read these figures as cases, to interpret them and "put them in their place." Thus he is finally able to say of Francis "I recognize his mania," by this means reversing the perspective of the narrative: it is important to keep in mind that between the figure of Caligari as the magician and that of Caligari as the authorized interpreter of the film's images—the supposedly authoritative analyst of the film's concluding frames—there intervene the scenes in which he is presented (in Francis's account) as the mad doctor, who, having become obsessed with a figure in a text that he is reading, no longer has control over the text of himself. Virtually until the final frames, the terms of the Oedipal scenarios of which this film is constituted are constantly shifting. Even the final "resolution" introduces ambiguity into the frame as the film concludes with an iris-in on Caligari who announces, having just removed his glasses, that he will "cure" Francis, the narrator of the tale. Focusing on Caligari's face, this shot manages to make Caligari appear less uncanny and more benign. Readers of E.T.A. Hoffmann, however, and readers of Freud, too, may find this conclusion more unsettling than reassuring, for in the fall of 1919, several months before *Caligari* was released by Decla, Freud had published his essay on "The Uncanny," which includes his extensive analysis of Hoffmann's *The Sandman* and its many tricks with optical lenses.[83]

In a thinly veiled act of one-upmanship, Freud's essay seeks to replace Jentsch's reading of the uncanny effect as residing in "intellectual uncertainty" (concerning whether something is living or dead, real or imaginary) with his own conviction that it centers on the issue of castration, emblematized by the loss of a limb, for example, or by a threat to the eyes. By means of this interpretive act, Freud seeks to establish the centrality of the Oedipal complex in yet another dimension of psychic life. As is well known, Freud locates the threat of castration in Hoffmann's tale in the figure of Coppola-Coppelius, a seller of lenses and optical devices.[84] It is arguably within this constellation of allusion that the semantic field surrounding *Glied*—limb or link, as in one early critic's complaint concerning the fragmentary omission of "connecting limbs"[85] in film—and marionette (*Gliederpuppe*) is brought into relief by the hitherto missing term, *männliches Glied* or penis, which suggests as well another meaning of *Glied*—one generation of a family. Although I cannot claim irrefutably that an actual allusion to Freud's essay is being made in the final frames of *Caligari*, it nevertheless seems highly probable that in this film that merges filmmaker with psychoanalyst and that attempts to counteract figuratively the filmmaker's fear of fragmentation by firmly linking the cinematic process with its double or mirror image—the analyst's recuperative act of narrative integration—something of the sort is at work. At the risk of repeating a cliché, it seems expedient to point to the manner in which the image of glasses, lenses, and other optical devices understandably recurs in cinema—in the films of Lang and Hitchcock, for example—burdened as it is not only with anxiety about its position with regard to literature and painting, but also about altering and distorting the visual field through the camera eye.

In any case, it seems appropriate here to cite Samuel Weber's reformulation of the Freudian uncanny, which elaborates upon this effect, by finding in it "a certain indecidability which affects and infects representations, motifs, themes and situations," but which is not confined to this indecidability, but includes a second movement, a

> desire to penetrate, discover, and ultimately to conserve the integrity of perception: perceiver and perceived, the wholeness of the body, the power of vision—all this implies a *denial* of that almost-nothing which can hardly be seen, a denial that in turn involves a certain structure of narration, in which this denial repeats and articulates itself.[86]

According to Weber, then, an assertion of the power of vision is at the same time an act of denial of that "almost-nothing," the uncanny, which Freud links to castration, and thus an assertion of that "wholeness of the body" upon which the wholeness or unity of Diderot's tableau is posited. This ambiguity or doubleness concerning the power of vision is obviously manifest in *Caligari*, where the relations among fragment, fetish, and whole are so continuously and variously played out. The cinematic text, whose own body is perceived as heterogeneous or fragmented and whose figures are perceived as uncanny, asserts the power of its vision in order to claim unity for itself on a higher plane. By the same token, the power of vision in Weber's analysis is linked to the power to discover, suggesting yet another area of overlap between Weimar cinema and psychoanalysis. In this same essay on the uncanny, Freud himself concedes that he "should not be surprised that psycho-analysis, which is concerned with laying bare these hidden forces [fear of castration, the Oedipal struggle], has itself become uncanny to many people for that very reason."[87] We have seen Dr. Caligari set aside the power of his spectacles, but are we sure that we can trust the power of the spectacle, irising in, that showed him doing it?

FRITZ LANG, THE APPARATUS, AND THE FISSURED TEXT

In Germany especially it comes as no surprise that psychoanalysis and cinema developed side by side; as early as 1913 Rank's study of the Double had originated in Wegener's *Student of Prague*, and, in this same year, Lou Andreas-Salomé compared cinematographic technique to the mechanism by means of which mental images are produced.[88] Indeed, as Jean-Louis Baudry points out, Freud originally imagined the psychical apparatus as an optical device, not as a magic writing pad.[89] Obviously, it is not only the fact that during the Expressionist period the cinema provided an additional medium for the presentation of the dramas with "psychological" subject matter that were flourishing on the stage that forged a link between psychoanalysis and cinema. Nor was this connection promoted only by the repeated suggestions made during this period that the camera provided a means to study human behavior more closely. Not even the analogy—made by Lukács, among others—between the narrative logic of film and the logic of dream offers a wholly adequate explanation for the persistence with which the figures of analyst and filmmaker merge.[90] Raymond Bellour may offer the most compelling explanation when he points out that the invention of hypnosis and photography alike were signs of a strong image-making tendency that became radicalized at the end of the nineteenth century by cinema, "the mechanical invention that made possible for the first time the imaginary reproduction of movement and life," and by a psychoanalytic theory that attempted to explain the subject by means of a set of representations.[91] Another, perhaps more trivial, reason for the blurring of boundaries between cinema and psychoanalysis undoubtedly lies in the similarity of the cultural positions that they held in

Germany during this period:[92] both found themselves in some sense on the avant-garde fringe, and both were perceived as puzzling hybrids, as remarkable convergences of the imagination and science, which latter category in the case of cinema took the form of technology.[93] It is this uncertainty concerning the site of psychoanalysis and cinema between the rational and irrational, between imagination and science, that is so often expressed in Weimar cinema, though it is not absent from experiments with protocinematic and cinematic forms in other countries: in the United States, Alexander Burke described his "picture plays" as "the art of tableau vivant plus the science of photography,"[94] while in France Méliès says of his Montreuil studio that "it is the coming together of a gigantic photographic workshop and a theatrical stage."[95]

The futuristic machinery, fantastic vehicles, and various optical devices of Méliès films—all of which call the cinema machine itself vividly to mind—find their most obvious German counterparts in the films of Fritz Lang. Rotwang, the mad creator and scientist of *Metropolis* (1926), is a figuration of the filmmaker whose uneasy identity as magician and scientist—the Weimar filmmaker often cannot decide which—places him within the Méliès tradition. This dual identity is emblematized by the Romantic cottage that Rotwang inhabits deep within the futuristic city itself: gabled, without a single right angle, complete with magic doors and inscribed with pentagrams, it contains within it both a vast, modern laboratory (which could never be spatially accommodated by the cottage) and a winding, Expressionist stairway to the catacombs, the subterranean equivalent of the unconscious. Here as elsewhere, in a variety of different guises, we see the question repeatedly and apprehensively posed during this period: how do imagination and technology coexist in cinema?

On the model of Méliès, who had constructed robots before he became a filmmaker, Rotwang creates a mechanical woman, the "false Maria," and, in the process of doing so, loses his hand.[96] The artificial hand he wears, covered with a black glove, is an ominous reminder that in the literature of Romanticism man's hubristic attempt to create life is punished by violence to the mind or body; Rotwang is aligned with the many of Hoffmann's "false artists" who have this aim, while representing additionally the filmmaker who animates the lifeless image by technological means.[97] With his gloved artificial hand, Rotwang is an emblem of the fragmented and heterogeneous nature of the cinematic text; his robotic woman has an inner, mechanical core and an outer layer of human flesh, skin, and hair ("scientifically transferred" to it from the body of the "real Maria" in Rotwang's laboratory) and is therefore also heterogeneous, a product of mixed media emblematizing fears concerning the nature of the life that film confers.

The cinema machine in its technological and "magical" aspects, as well as the inherent heterogeneity of cinema, are pervasive concerns in Lang's work. In *The Testament of Dr. Mabuse* (1933), for instance, the cinema machine is an especially ominous latent presence in an example of doubling that is suggestive for this inquiry. In this film Dr. Baum, the mad psychoanalyst (inspired by Dr. Caligari), virtually "becomes" his patient, Dr. Mabuse (once also a great analyst), by virtue of his obsessive interest in this insane criminal mastermind: Baum is presented as a dedicated scientist and professor for whom Mabuse is a fascinating case study of the first order. It is both Mabuse's "superhuman logic" and his use of hypnosis that Baum originally finds so compelling. Gradually, as Baum attempts to explain the intricacies of Mabuse's psyche to himself and to his students, he comes to internalize the psychological situation of the object of his scrutiny: this doubling is figured with crude literalism in a scene in which Mabuse's "spirit" leaves his body and enters Baum's. Here, too, as in the literature of German Romanticism, the boundary between the supernatural—an explanation from without—and madness—an explanation from within—is deliberately blurred by the film, but what is perhaps more important is the manner in which the irrational is represented as insusceptible to control by the scientist, who at the moment of transfer becomes an artist of destruction. Central to this issue is the printing press that produces the counterfeit money by means of which Mabuse-Baum hopes to destroy the economy and assume power. While the havoc created by this machine is, of course, a reference to the inflationary times during which the film was made, the press functions additionally as a duplicating machine, a machine whose ability to reproduce the image mechanically has been appropriated illegitimately and thus, by analogy, produces false and dangerous currency for aesthetic as well as economic consumption. The fact that a printing press is normally the means by which the written word is disseminated merely adds to the sense in which this allegory of the filmmaker, while negative, nevertheless links filmmaker with writer and hence suggests the complicity of writing with filmmaking.

Having taken over Mabuse's crime organization when Mabuse becomes his patient, Baum gives Mabuse's men their orders in the basement of a deserted factory, in a room blocked off at one end by a theater curtain behind which they may not look on pain of death. Here Baum's voice alone—disembodied, technologically transmitted by a gramophone—

dominates the scene. Behind the curtain the outlines of a figure are visible, but when the curtain is finally pulled and the scene is demystified, this figure, representing film's phantasmatic body, is revealed as merely a flat wooden cutout, a facsimile, lit from behind. If Mabuse in the earlier film is the *Spieler*, player or actor as well as gambler, in this second film he is the *Puppenspieler*, "the great showman of marionettes," as Lang himself called him, yet also the *Puppe*, the marionette or doll.[98]

While this Mabuse doll with Baum's recorded voice orders and organizes ever more appalling crimes, the real Mabuse can only express himself in writing, furiously producing the scenarios for these crimes in his cell. He has become a vehicle for automatic writing: as Baum tells his students during his lecture on his patient's pathology, when Mabuse was brought to the asylum, he was mute and expressed himself only in scribbles. Gradually, however, single words become discernible among the scribbles. These words are then joined together in sentences, until finally detailed scenarios are recorded on the sheets of paper that Mabuse fills continuously. While in the earlier Mabuse film (*Dr. Mabuse the Gambler*, 1922) Mabuse's power resided in his penetrating gaze, which was even, as one critic has claimed, "the controlling principle of the narrative," here his power finds expression in the written text.[99] Like Freud, who rejects an optical model for the psychical apparatus in favor of the figure of the writing pad, in this second Mabuse film Lang substitutes a kind of psychic, automatic writing for the power of the gaze. As we shall see, it is this kind of writing that emblematizes the pre-text of Lang's films.

Lang's "scene of filmmaking," the room with the curtain, finally works to expose the apparatus as the technological construct that it is— comprised of a loudspeaker, lights, and a curtain that acts as a screen— and to suggest both the lifelessness of cinematic bodies and their uncanny power. Here cinema falls apart into its various components: light, image, sound, and the soulless facsimile of a body: Lang lays bare the cinematic codes. It has often been noted that Lang uses offscreen sound in a menacing way,[100] but the radical separation of voice (Baum's) from the body from which it supposedly emanates (Mabuse's and, since it is recorded, Baum's as well), suggest that there is something more at stake here than the flaunting of technical expertise. Lang is pointing to the paradox recently described by Mary Ann Doane according to which sound, though theoretically enabling film to represent a "more organically unified" body, actually serves, when separated from the image of the human body that supposedly produces it, to expose cinema's material heterogeneity.[101] In *The Testament of Dr. Mabuse*, the inharmoniousness of the codes of cinematic representation is even more apparent than elsewhere in Lang's work: here language itself is separated into recorded voice and writing, the image is as heavily fetishized as ever, and narratives and plots are doubled and played off against one another.[102]

Lang's text rhetorically threatens to disassemble into its component parts, and it figures this threat repeatedly in variations on the theme of fragmentation: in the opera performance which Lohmann, the detective, never succeeds in seeing in toto, in the name (Mabuse) that is incompletely etched upon a window and, most importantly, in Mabuse's writings, whose pages are both pieced together (by Dr. Kramm, for whom they constitute a clue to a mystery), and torn into fragments by the mad Dr. Baum in the final scene. Lang makes use of sound bridges to link the scenes of this film to one another and images—including images of writing—are made to perform the same function. It could be argued, however, that this further isolation of the constituents of cinema in these bridging moments not only serves the function of attaching the scenes to one another, of forging a unity from the sum of its parts, but conversely that such a use of sound, image, photograph, and written text further underscores the very fragmentation that it masks. After Mabuse has died, his corpse is revealed to the spectator's eye only twice and only partially: once the camera focuses on his feet, to which a name tag has been affixed, and once the head alone is revealed, as the sheet that covers the body is pulled back for inspection. The discontinuous and fragmented body of the film, it is suggested, finds its analogue in Mabuse's corpse, which, though dead and only partially visible, nevertheless figures an organic unity that the film would like to claim for its own in the very moment of flaunting its heterogeneity and fragmentation.

The Testament of Dr. Mabuse presents the tyrannical psychoanalyst-filmmaker (Mabuse/Baum) as a creator of destructive texts (it is notable that the Mabuse doll and the exposed apparatus find their recent counterparts in Syberberg's *Our Hitler*), which also function as representatives of cinematic narrative. Mabuse's writings, emerging directly from the unconscious, are linked to the hieroglyphs, cryptic signs, and suggestive letters that are everywhere in Lang's films: primitive drawings decorate maps and encoded systems of signs guard hidden worlds of secrecy and intrigue, be they workers' uprisings, as in *Metropolis*, or spy networks, as in *Hangmen Also Die* (1942). But these primitive marks do not on the surface appear to arouse the spirit of interart rivalry in Lang's work; indeed, they are often forms of pictorial writing and hence suggestive of image-linked cinematic writing, like the signifying elements of cinema that Vachel Lindsay and Abel Gance called hieroglyphs.[103] Retaining the significance that they were first accorded by Expressionism, these signs represent the "dark regions of the soul": a broken pre-text evoking primary process, they are too undeniably prior to be shunted aside, and instead they appear as the preliminary jottings around which the finished film narrative is structured. But precisely in this claim that writing is semiotic, not linguistic—also a mere offshoot of the semiotics of which cinema itself consists—we can see a challenge to the primacy of verbal writing after all.

The power of language—the power of the word—is overwhelming in *Dr. Mabuse*, and much of that power resides in Mabuse's name, a well-guarded secret in the film's narrative; in the earlier Mabuse film he is called "the great Unknown." When, at various moments within the film Mabuse is referred to as "the man behind the curtain," "the man in the dark," and "the man behind the scenes," he is constructed both as a powerful enigma and as a creature of the cinema. One character, Hofmeister, goes mad when he is not allowed to speak Mabuse's name, and is only released from his madness when Mabuse's name is restored to his memory. In its written form, "Mabuse" is also a name to conjure with. It is, arguably, one of the hieroglyphs of cinematic language, one of the pre-texts upon which Lang's film is based: when it is discovered that Hofmeister has left fragments of the letters that spell "Mabuse" etched upon a window with his ring, the process of deciphering these bits of letters involves a solution on a glass plate that is, as Fisher notes, reminiscent of the photographic process and additionally recalls Freud's magic writing pad.[104] Since the solution to the mystery—the name of Mabuse—involves the identification of these traces as mirror writing (a solution achieved with a solution), the connection with cinema is all the more manifest. Insofar as Lohmann, the detective who is pitted against Mabuse/Baum, is a reader and interpreter of texts, he occupies a position akin to that of the analyst. This parallelism is confirmed rather than weakened at the moment when it is denied, and Lohmann speaks the concluding words of the film as the asylum attendant shuts the door upon Baum, words to the effect that this is no longer a job for the police.

As is so often the case in Lang, *The Testament of Dr. Mabuse* works to identify art with death (witness the title). Indeed, the so-called testament itself is generically complex, a heterogeneous text: its "scenarios" are illustrated with Expressionist figures and some of its writing—in the Expressionist lettering familiar from *Caligari*—seems primarily decorative in its function even as it contributes to the aim of Mabuse's testament, that of devising crimes of radical destruction and death.[105] On the level of the image track, another of the more obvious examples of the linkage of art and death involves a montage of shots that focuses on the works of art decorating Baum's study, primarily the primitive masks favored by Expressionism. It only remains to crosscut these masks with a row of human skulls to have made the point. Lang does this not only to establish the visual similarity between the death's-head and the masks, but also to suggest the manner in which visual representation seeks to ward off death by the process of conjuring it up.

Figured most obviously and centrally in *Destiny* (*Der müde Tod*, 1921), where Death is the dominant figure, Lang's preoccupation with the relation of death to representation is crucial to an understanding of his films: it is what Lang himself called his "Viennese tone." *Destiny* contains three narratives located in three different places and times, contained within a framing narrative concerning a woman's desire to retrieve her lover from Death.[106] Even though she is given three opportunities to retrieve him, Death places her each time within a predetermined, closed narrative that effectively thwarts female desire. Characterized by repetition, each story sets up a triangle with distinctly Oedipal overtones in which a figure in power blocks the union of the lovers, and the young man of each would-be couple dies. This narrative logic proves inexorable, suggesting the entrapment of all plots within an ur-plot that blocks and overpowers the erotic and propels the overall course of narrative towards the ultimate closure of death, a configuration that conforms precisely to Julia Kristeva's assertion that all narrative is based on "the third-person Father" who is Death itself.[107]

In *Destiny*'s frame narrative, Death is repeatedly posed in front of a seemingly endless wall—or screen—that encloses his domain and whose flat surface is inscribed with hieroglyphs. He is the guardian of a text located somewhere between visual representation and writing—the kind of text that in Lang stands in for the filmic pre-text—and he will not relinquish its code. Moving but little, with an expression that changes rarely, Death as a character figures stasis and, in the first of the three narratives, Death's name, El Mot, plays on "the word," confirming the relation specifically of language to death. It remains for the magician, a character in the third narrative who subjects written texts—Chinese pictograms, another form of hieroglyph—to motion, to stand in for the filmmaker. In this Mélièsian scenario, set in an exoticized Imperial China, the magician animates the written text, turning the emperor's scroll into a snake that dances to his magic wand.[108] Ultimately, however, the film-

Fig. 2. Lang's hieroglyphic texts, in this instance inscribed on Death's "screen," suggest the indebtedness of cinematic representation to both writing and the pictorial image.

maker-magician has no power to reverse the course of the Oedipal narrative—he can only delay its relentless movement towards closure by means of a series of visual tricks (including animation and spectacular displays of various sorts) that he has at his disposal. It should be noted, then, that death determines at least two relations in this film: it actually advances narrative, insofar as it produces the movement towards narrative closure, as well as being manifest in the absence that defines representation per se. Further, if every film is a series of little murders that take place as each frame in the sequence is replaced by another, if "film narrative leaves behind a trail of corpses," as Timothy Corrigan has put it, then filmic movement is implicated in the orientation towards death.[109]

In the context of such a reading, Raymond Bellour's observation concerning a configuration of shots that he sees as typical of Lang's style takes on a new dimension. Noting Lang's characteristic use of a static long shot of three parts, "two actions separated by a moment of stasis,"[110] Bellour reads this pattern as follows: "Adopting this method of disrupting the standard development of a plot, Lang impairs the narrative and, seemingly at least, distorts time in favor of pure scrutiny, thereby conferring a sense of strangeness on the action that is thus stretched out."[111] In terms of the present analysis, then, Lang's manner of proceeding subjects the narrative process to a series of imagistic interruptions, retarding its progress towards closure by interpolating static images that evoke a way of looking associated with the motionless visual arts. Although the progress of narrative towards its completion is deferred in this manner, the usually motionless image featured in the frames that intervene is itself oriented towards death by virtue of its static nature. In this alternation between narrative and image, Lang's style of editing acknowledges the way film takes up a position between them and connects them both with death.

Destiny seems at times to be a cinematic representation of "Beyond the Pleasure Principle" (which Freud published in 1920), assembled from and positioned among several different arts or sign systems. Indeed, one of the signs that Death inscribes in the sand, one that *can* be decoded, suggests this: it is the alpha/omega that in the Christian tradition signifies "In my beginning is my end," but in Freudian terms could be said to trace the simultaneous movement towards origins and death. In *Destiny*, Death is not only the guarantor of narrative closure, but more generally the producer of culture per se: the opening frames of the film, for example, reveal a tombstone inscribed with writing that makes this connection graphically. Although, as *Destiny* suggests, Lang's films as texts are discontinuous and fragmentary rather than organic and fully alive, they figure this predicament as shared in a variety of ways by the other arts as well.

If writing in Lang brings death (often in his films letters lure their recipients into fatal traps), and if narrative is presided over by a ruthless, unrelenting father, allusions to painting are made in a somewhat different spirit. In *Destiny*, one particular allusion is intricately connected with Lang's mise-en-scène and with his attitude toward the relation of cinema to painting. This allusion is to Caspar David Friedrich's "Two Men Contemplating the Moon," with its spectator figures, the so-called *Rückenfiguren* with their backs turned and heads averted from the beholder.[112] In the painting two male spectators form part of a foreground composed of rocks and trees whose gnarled roots and branches are at once threatening and protective. The moon in the distant background, while at the center of a circle described by the determining lines of the painting's decorative foreground, is seemingly connected with the foreground only as the object of the gaze. (This separation of the foreground and background without the mediation of a midground is characteristic of Friedrich's style.)[113] As in other Friedrich paintings, what is truly uncanny resides not so much in the conventional representations of death (for instance, the ghostly, haunted-looking space in which the men are enclosed), but in the quality of the light emanating from the background. The decorative surface of the foreground, the grille-like pattern of branches and roots against the light, takes on the quality of a defense against that light: the painter appears intentionally to have imposed this pattern between himself (and the beholder) and the moon, a figure for the potentially death-bringing sublime.[114]

In Lang's film, the setting of "Two Men Contemplating the Moon" has become the locale of a minor, typically Romantic scene in which an apothecary, dressed like Friedrich's two men in an 1820s' cloak, pulls up a mandrake root by moonlight. Lang's cinematic allusion to the painting is not merely an attempt at historical accuracy; although the mise-en-scène of the framing story suggests Germany in the 1820s, the story is supposedly of no time and no place, claiming for itself the universality of a folk tale, encoded in such scenes by the motionlessness of painting. As Warm and Röhrig, the designers of *Caligari*, also designed *Destiny*, it comes as no surprise that when released in France, the film was praised as a work in the spirit of Dürer and Grünewald, or that Friedrich's painting would be quoted precisely in the scene involving the apothecary whose costume so strongly resembles Dr. Caligari's.[115] But more is at stake here, both in terms of Lang's subject and his mise-en-scène. Friedrich's decorative surface—the branches and roots in relief against a moonlit sky—is retained in the scene involving the apothecary. What is significant, considering the Lang text as a whole, is this relation of surface to threatening, diffuse background in Friedrich and its resemblance to a similar recurring structural element in Lang's mise-en-scène. This relation suggests a complicity between the aims of Lang films and some Friedrich paintings that, as Joseph Koerner points out, often construct their foregrounds as "screens."[116]

This structural element involves the perforated or fissured surface found everywhere in Lang and particularly prominent in *Destiny*. Whether it is a patterned curtain, a wrought-iron gate, or a series of pillars behind which danger lurks, the visual surface at its most ornamental—where it is most obviously a lure for the eye—is particularly suspect and most vulnerable. This surface is less likely than any other to be able to contain the agent of death; indeed, it seems to be its special function to reveal this agent. In later Lang films, where cinematic space has become more sophisticated, this fissured structure takes on a more architectural, less decorative dimension—witness the floors through which, in both *Metropolis* (1926) and *The Testament of Dr. Mabuse*, water first leaks and then bursts. What is at stake in these images is the filmic text itself that, like some of Friedrich's paintings in their staged ambivalence toward the sublime, represents itself as erecting a visual barrier against death. But, as Bellour suggests of the static shot between the two "narrative" shots— that it can only delay, and not sustain the force of narrative development—the decorative surface cannot long resist the pressure of death-bringing narrative movement. Although it understands Friedrich's work to be death burdened, it would seem that the Lang film is envious of the equilibrium that Friedrich's paintings are capable of achieving, and, more importantly, that it envies painting because its composition is not subject to destruction by narrative pressure in the way that the composition of filmic images inevitably is.

Fig. 3. The perforated surfaces in Lang's films have the fragmented human body as their analogue.

Finally, the perforated surfaces, in their various manifestations, as well as the fragmented, fissured text that is the film, have as their ultimate analogue the human body. This is apparent in the scene in *Metropolis* in which water first oozes out of a gash in the floor, looking unbearably like blood emerging from a wound.[117] It seems hardly necessary to look at the wound in *Siegfried* (1922) for confirmation. Perceiving itself as fragmented or fissured, film represents itself repeatedly as a wounded, mutilated, or castrated body, a body that simultaneously aspires to and denies the possibility of organic wholeness.

MAGICIAN AND SURGEON

It has perhaps seemed wilfull to have kept Benjamin's "Work of Art in the Age of Mechanical Reproduction" (1935–36) out of the discussion for so long. Like the earlier theorists and critics of film cited at the beginning of this chapter, in this essay Benjamin, too, is anxious to distinguish between the "presence" of the stage actor and what he takes to be its impossibility for the film actor. For Benjamin, presence is connected to the aura. Citing Pirandello, he suggests that it is dependent on the corporeality of the actor, the actual presence of his body on the stage.[118] Like earlier theorists and filmmakers, Benjamin seems at first troubled by the problem of fragmentation in film, particularly regarding the nature of the film actor's performance: "The stage actor identifies himself with the character of his role. The film actor is very often denied this opportunity. His creation is by no means all of a piece; it is composed of many separate performances" (859). The splitting of the film actor's work into a series of episodes, only to be reconstituted by montage, is only one aspect of the problem as Benjamin sees it: he also points out the role of the camera, which "need not respect the performance as an integral whole" (858). Again relying on Pirandello, Benjamin suggests that the strangeness that an actor feels before the camera must be "basically the same kind as the estrangement felt before one's mirror image" (860), a point relevant to reading *Student of Prague*. Rhetorically, Benjamin still appears at this point in his essay to privilege the auratic, organic stage performance over that of the film actor, and his formulations—with the partial exception of his concept of the aura—are very much rooted in the discourse concerning this topic in the twenties.[119]

Benjamin's distinctions curiously continue to revolve around the topic of the body and, of course, around the question of fragmentation. This is most intriguingly the case in the dichotomy he establishes between the painter and the cinematographer, a dichotomy based on the difference in their respective relations to reality, here imaged as relations to the human body. "The magician heals a sick person by the laying on of hands," Benjamin writes, whereas

> the surgeon cuts into the patient's body. . . . Magician and surgeon compare to painter and cameraman. The painter maintains in his work a natural distance from reality, the cameraman penetrates deeply into its web. There is a tremendous difference between the pictures they obtain. That of

the painter is a total one, that of the cameraman consists of multiple fragments which are assembled under a new law. (862–63)

Benjamin's strategy here is recuperative and political: he clearly rejects
the aura about which he has written with such ambivalence, rejects "auratic" art of which painting is the example, and probably bases his choice
of "magician" as a metaphor for the painter on his idea of the cult value
of auratic art and its origin in ritual. "Magician," then, (the German
word is "*Magier*") is also used in the sense of "shaman," for, as Benjamin
claims, the magician is "still hidden in the medical practitioner" (862).
Portrayed as a high priest of art, the painter in Benjamin's reading indulges in magical practices and illusions that are distanced from and can
have no real effect upon reality, portrayed here as a sick body. On the
other hand, the cameraman, by cutting deeply, not just touching—by regarding reality with an incisively critical lens, as it were—can redeem the
fragmentation inherent in the cinematic medium by thus intensifying it
and paradoxically creating "an aspect of reality which is free of all equip-
ment" (863), a reality "cured" and in some sense redeemed again.

This juxtaposition of magician and surgeon (the opposition is not as
radical as it appears to be at first glance, since they are still united—negatively—in the medical practitioner for Benjamin) refigures the problem
posed in *The Cabinet of Dr. Caligari* and in *Destiny* as well. In the latter
film, the figure of the apothecary, who digs magical roots by moonlight
and has a crow as a familiar, whose shop is stocked with pharmaceutical
vials and a skeleton, expresses the ambiguity concerning the boundaries
of magic and science that we have seen embodied in Dr. Caligari, in
whose cloak the apothecary is clothed.[120] In this scene, *Destiny* places the
figure of the filmmaker (the apothecary) into a mise-en-scène derived
from painting, an art Lang films envy, and portrays him in the act of
pulling the magical and dangerous mandrake root—the root that has a
human shape and grants its possessor sexual potency, yet whose
"scream" of pain may induce madness—out of its surface. In this Oedipal
scenario, Lang's film portrays the filmmaker as attempting to disem-
power the art of the painter—to "castrate" painting, as it were, by appro-
priating its magic for itself. As we have seen, this act of appropriation
remains a rhetorical gesture for *Destiny*, since the film repeatedly suggests
that the visual surface, the resource that Lang films borrow from painting, cannot finally withstand the pressure of narrative movement to
which it must be subjected.

The Cabinet of Dr. Caligari in particular represents one aspect of film's crisis of self-understanding, its place between magic and science, and thus figures film's uncanny relation to psychoanalysis as well. All of the films under discussion here to a greater or lesser extent pose the problem of heterogeneity and fragmentation as an Oedipal problem. In an act of redemptive reversal, Benjamin's gesture of putting the surgical knife into the hands of the cinematographer reverses the power structure of painting—of auratic art in general—and cinema, and in some sense grants the "power of castration" to film, with which Benjamin clearly wishes to identify himself against the tradition.[121]

"KNIFE PHOBIA"

Both as a postscript to Benjamin and a transition to Hitchcock, I would like to turn for a moment to G. W. Pabst's *Secrets of a Soul* (1926). Appropriately categorized by film historians as a film of the "New Objectivity" (*Neue Sachlichkeit*), *Secrets of a Soul*, one of whose opening shots includes a still of Freud, wants to portray the "wishes and desires of the unconscious" in a "case study . . . taken from life." For its dream images, Pabst sought the advice of Hans Sachs and Karl Abraham, two associates of Freud; also in the interests of science and realism, the Russian actor Pawel Pawlow who played the analyst in this film was forced to undergo a crash course in Freud's writings.[122] Long an admirer of Freud, Pabst obviously intended in *Secrets of a Soul* to claim psychoanalysis for science, as the analytical method capable of explaining and curing "mysterious disorders," as one of the title cards puts it. Pabst's interest in the writings of Marx and the films of Eisenstein was very much alive during this period, and the desire to demystify psychoanalysis probably also has its origins there. The so-called objectivity of Pabst's style in this film, however, is limited to a poetic realism not yet influenced by an Eisensteinian dialectical montage. Nevertheless, the obvious aesthetic pleasure evinced in the images of the film, both in those dream images interpreted by the analyst Dr. Orth (whose name has its etymological origins in "straight" or "correct") and in those that the spectator alone can read, is successfully masked when these images are presented as clues for "correct" interpretation. One set of images is of particular interest: these are those that interrupt and illustrate the analysand's narrative to Dr. Orth. Presented against a white background—upon a screen—they establish the connection between dream images and cinematic images, between the technique of psychoanalysis and that of film—a connection which Benjamin would also make in the "artwork" essay.[123] By this means, Pabst acknowledges the residue of the unconscious in cinema while he subjects this residue to the regularizing effects of correct reading. Since the neurosis to which the main character in *Secrets of a Soul* is prey is what the film calls "knife phobia," it is tempting to read in this film, product of the "New Objectivity" though it may be, yet another instance of the fragmentation anxiety of cinema that Benjamin attempts to turn to its own advantage. Indeed, within the Western tradition film's self-consciousness concerning fragmentation is by no means historically or culturally specific.

"Doing It with Scissors": Dismemberment in Hitchcock

In 1974, having concluded his address before the Film Society of Lincoln Center with a quotation from Thomas de Quincey's essay, "Murder as One of the Fine Arts," Alfred Hitchcock added a brief footnote to his speech: "As you can see, the best way to do it is with scissors."[124] Hitchcock refers, in this typically macabre moment, not only to the infamous murder weapon in *Dial M for Murder* (1953), but to the art of film editing or cutting per se. Knowingly or unknowingly, he refers also to a pervasive concern in the body of his films with fragmentation, castration, and dismemberment. It is as though, for Hitchcock, filmmaking *were* an art of murder, of killing off the living body on and as the strip of celluloid that would render it cinematic. Fortunately, Hitchcock was able to thematize this preoccupation with fragmentation, for the popularity of the murder-mystery genre that gave it structure sanctioned its repeated playing out.[125]

It is perhaps not surprising that psychoanalytically inflected readings of Hitchcock films have always seemed particularly appropriate, as the texts themselves bear the marks of authorial neurosis. But we should also look to the traces left in Hitchcock films by pressures inherent to the medium itself. Indeed, in Hitchcock's work we find what appears to be a rather remarkable, mutually reinforcing correspondence between the preoccupations of the authorial psyche and the imaginings of cinema itself, a powerful doubling held in check by the strong formalist impulse and narrative logic that characterizes the films. If film, as an art of murder, relies on cutting, it must also rely on formal practices to shore it up and make it whole.

Hitchcock's films absorbed the themes and preoccupations of an earlier cinema: *The Lady Vanishes* (1938), for instance, is built around automobile and train chases that refer to "Griffith-era melodramatics" and stand in for narrative movement.[126] And, given Hitchcock's early film experience in Germany, the allusion this film makes to Dr. Caligari is not entirely unpredictable: Caligari is split into the figures of Dr. Hartz, posing as both brain surgeon and psychoanalyst, and Signor Doppo, an Italian magician who operates a "vanishing lady" apparatus.[127] Together, this team of villains humorously figures Caligari as filmmaker, an association reinforced by the reference in Hitchcock's title to the Méliès 1896 substitution-trick film, *The Vanishing Lady*, in which a woman repeatedly disappears by means of the cinema machine.[128] New to this figuration of Caligari as filmmaker is the role of surgeon, and it is a telling addition for Hitchcock: the surgeon's intent, too, is to work upon the female body. Since the threat posed by Dr. Hartz as surgeon is never fully realized in this film, the theme of the fragmented body is displaced into a minor episode near the film's beginning during which the body of a young woman (called Iris, as though in oblique allusion to Buñuel) is gratuitously, as Petro puts it, "fragment[ed] . . . in erotic display."[129] Here the camera itself is seen in its capacity as "knife," fragmentating the body by presenting it in a multiplicity of images—in pieces. The shower scene in *Psycho* (1960) manifests this technique in its most developed form.

Fragmentation as a thematic preoccupation in Hitchcock films surfaces quite obviously in *Rear Window* (1954), where it is suggested that a female body is cut up and buried under the shrubbery, with some of its parts dumped into the East River. This theme is only partly disguised by the humor in which it is almost always cloaked. As Tania Modleski points out, even the women that James Stewart's character, Jeffries, jokingly nicknames "Miss Lonelyhearts" and "Miss Torso" have a role to play in this film's fantasy of dismemberment.[130] Lisa, the heroine, turns herself into a fragmented spectacle during a moment of self-display in which she enumerates her body parts to Jeffries one by one, finally subsuming them all under her name: Lisa Carol Freemont. But, as if to displace this preoccupation from Jeffries, Stella, the Thelma Ritter character, is given the most amusing, shocking, and in some ways the most significant lines concerning the things that are done to the human body. Chiding Jeffries about his voyeurism, Stella suggests that "they used to put your eyes out with a red-hot poker" for similar crimes, thus alerting the audience to an act of castration that may already have symbolically taken place, as Jeffries is confined to a wheelchair with a broken leg and generally seems uninterested in the leading lady. It is Stella, further, who suggests that Mrs. Thorwaldsen's body lies scattered about the city, with one leg in the East River, as though in ironic allusion to the dismembered Orpheus, torn to pieces by the maenads because he had scorned their sexual advances. Stella's remarks invoke the erotic within the context of a threatening female sexuality like that of the maenads, here displaced into the male aggression of Mr. Thorwaldsen, who has indeed murdered his wife, thus presenting yet another variation on the theme of Jeffries's "rejection" of Lisa's advances. Further, with her reference to "putting the eyes out," Stella unwittingly brings the Oedipus complex into play and harnesses the erotic to the scopic drive, not surprising in a film as rife with cinematic allusions as *Rear Window*;[131] as Raymond Bellour has argued convincingly, scopophilia in Hitchcock inevitably ends in violence.[132]

If Jeffries is a stand-in for the filmmaker as well as the spectator here, and this has been suggested, then he is a director of early silent tableau films, projected on the screen-like windows he watches with such concentration.[133] Jeffries provides another instance of the director as surgeon, a director whose fantasy of dismemberment is enacted: though Miss Lonelyhearts and Miss Torso remain literally intact, Mrs. Thorwaldsen does fall victim to a man with a knife. Yet the stark rectangular shapes of the apartment-building windows, the screens across which figures move and narratives are played out, also recall painters' canvases, and the artifice of Hitchcock's mise-en-scène—the painted, theatrical quality of the set—underscores their painterly dimension. Figured repeatedly in Hitchcock's films, the privileged space of painting in his oeuvre remains enigmatic, repeatedly marking both the place of the feminine and the place of death.[134]

Hitchcock's capacity for figurative abstraction, like Lang's, pervades even the smallest details of his films. In another instance of *Rear Window*'s black humor, Stella's fascinated musings about cutting up bodies take place just as Jeffries is cutting up his breakfast. What is noteworthy about this conjunction—if only in retrospect, in the context of other films—is the visual and verbal link it effects between the dismembered female corpse and food, creating the distinct suggestion of cannibalism that *Frenzy* (1972) will be at pains to reinforce repeatedly. Tellingly, in *Rear Window* we find a still life of fruit and flowers over the fireplace in Jeffries's apartment, occupying the place where a portrait so often hangs in Hitchcock films. This painting, in front of which a detective pauses as though it contained a clue, features the natural as food (fruit) and, by extension, stands in for the body of the woman as mother.[135] In *Frenzy*, the spectator becomes increasingly aware that Kent, the "garden of England," is also the place where the bodies of women are dumped by the greengrocer–sex murderer who has a particular fondness for his mum. The strong attachment to the mother that characterizes so many of Hitchcock's male figures is also the source of a sadistic aggression turned against the female.

Modleski's convincing explanation for the fantasy of the "body-in-pieces" that *Rear Window* works through relies on the Lacanian mirror stage for its articulation: for the child, bodily unity and perfection are modeled by the body of the mother. On the other hand, the male child's fantasy of dismemberment is disavowed by projecting it onto the body of the woman, who then, "in an interpretation which reverses the state of affairs the male child most fears, eventually comes to be perceived as castrated, mutilated, 'imperfect.'"[136] An earlier film by Hitchcock, *The Thirty-Nine Steps* (1935) contains a "mirror portrait" that is interesting from this point of view. Here, in what seems a bitterly ironic inversion of the bourgeois domestic scene—or, perhaps, its ultimate exposure—the camera lingers on a mirror over a fireplace in a deserted apartment, a mirror that reflects the image of a desperate woman facing it, a woman involved in espionage, whose life is threatened, and about whom the worst is suspected. This woman is soon to die, punished for the ambiguity that surrounds her, although after her death the film rehabilitates her as a patriot. But as an image in the mirror, desirable but under the sign of death, she functions not only as a negative and threatening image of the mother, but also as an image of a feminine self for the man who looks at her.

If, then, to return momentarily to *Rear Window*, Jeffries's voyeuristic eroticism is to be superseded by a "mature" sexuality that involves a rapprochement with Lisa—and the film suggests that it is—then the spectator can expect that Jeffries's still life must be replaced by "Mona Lisa," by the representation of the woman whom Jeffries will not want to call "*my* Lisa" until the end of the film. And, indeed, "Mona Lisa" is the title of a song being composed by a neighbor of Jeffries, a song that is completed with the film's completion and functions as the equivalent of a musical portrait, the "low culture" version of the quintessential masterpiece. It is fortunate for Lisa that she is not "fixed" by painting, given its implication for Hitchcock, though the reference to the Mona Lisa, characterized in the popular imagination by her elusive smile, suggests that no woman can be.

The first Hitchcock film in which the cinematic representation of painting is central is *Blackmail* (1929), the story of the near-seduction of a young woman who is lured into the apartment of an artist to "see his etchings."[137] Stabbing and killing the artist in defense of her virtue, the woman brandishes the knife as the artist himself has brandished the paintbrush with which he, at first with her assistance, has sketched out a female nude. Having twice appropriated the phallus—once in the form of brush, then in the form of knife—the guilty woman becomes the prey of a blackmailer who, ironically, meets his end in a chase sequence through the British Museum, the first of several museum settings in Hitchcock. This chase is recurrently intercut with a static image of the woman, centered in the frame, now "a portrait at last," as if aligning her with the immobility of painting put her in her proper place.[138] The blackmailer on the other hand is connected with the movement characteristic of narrative and the cinematic image, although, in an ironic reversal typical of Hitchcock, it is the blackmailer who dies, while the woman emerges from her ordeal unscathed. As though, however, to attest to the dual function of visual representation to preserve life and to kill it off by fixing it in an image, the blackmailer meets his end by falling through the glass cupola into the Egyptian collection, representing a culture for which the art of visual representation and the art of preservation go hand in hand. The mother's "mummy" in *Psycho* similarly serves, as we shall see, to kill off and to preserve.

Before turning to *Psycho*, however, a brief excursion into the second version of *The Man Who Knew Too Much* (1956) is in order, for here, too, the figure of the surgeon-doctor has a role to play. Displacement again informs the textual system: the topic of the fragmented body is introduced into the film in a joke by the very American James Stewart character, Dr. McKenna, who recites a catalog of the body parts that have financed the vacation upon which he and his family have embarked: one patient's appendix, another's gall bladder, the triplets produced in the womb of yet another. It is perhaps not surprising that someone who thinks about body parts in terms of profit should have the experience that Dr. McKenna has in this film. During the search for the kidnappers of his son, Dr. McKenna mistakenly enters a taxidermist's establishment with the look of an artist's studio and the atmosphere of a mortuary. There follows a somewhat gratuitous episode, peripheral to the diegesis, during which McKenna wanders among fierce-looking stuffed animals and animal parts on display—a fitting punishment, perhaps, for one so inured to

Fig. 4. The theme of the fragmented body takes a comic turn in *The Man Who Knew Too Much*.

dismemberment as to think of gall bladders and appendixes primarily as separable from their owners. In *The Man Who Knew Too Much*, the theme of the fragmented body is countered by that of the preservation of body parts and corpses, the taxidermist's stuffed and mounted trophies. But it is also supplemented in this sequence by the action of a camera that stalks and "shoots" these animals, much as though it were the gun that had made them displays. If the camera is hunter and gun, it nevertheless, like the taxidermist, creates an image to preserve the body that it has killed off.[139] But, also like the stuffed animals in this regard, that image, though lifelike, is dead, incapable of motion except by mechanical means. This theme, too, will be the subject of *Psycho*.

Taxidermy is Norman Bates's hobby; he likes "stuffing things," as the spectator of *Psycho* is only too well aware. Beaks open, wings arrested in flight, the stuffed birds that decorate what he calls the parlor of his motel are threatening, their beady, dead eyes signifying, yet also lacking the deadly power of the gaze that connects them with Norman. Interestingly, the birds are displayed in a room that also contains paintings, behind one of which is the hole in the wall through which Norman observes Marion. Pointing to the integral connection for Hitchcock of the camera, sexual penetration, and murder via the scopic drive, Bellour's convincing psychoanalytic reading of this film constructs the significance of the chain "phallus-bird-fetish-mother-eye-knife-camera."[140] Against the backdrop of this psychoanalytic scenario, then, it may seem somewhat trivial to focus on the way in which these connections speak to cinema's self-positioning vis-à-vis "real life," on the one hand, and other modes of representation, on the other. And yet, this scene constitutes an important dimension of Hitchcock's meditations on the nature of cinematic representation.

Among the stuffed birds suspended from the walls of the room are birds of prey—such as the large owl with wings outspread—that frame the figure of Norman in conversation with Marion. Lit from the front, they cast film-noir shadows on the wall and ceiling behind them. Other birds on perches, placed near arrangements of dried or artificial flowers— constituting, that is, a still life of sorts—decorate the bureau. The lighting of these birds, too, contributes to the manner in which they stand out in relief, stressing their three-dimensionality. Indeed, at one point during his conversation with Marion, Norman reaches out to rest his hand upon one of the birds, emphasizing its status as an object. In pronounced distinction to, yet thematically rhyming with, these bird figures are several paintings that hang on the wall. Behind Marion hangs an oval painting depicting a group of angels of which the one in the center is rising heavenward with outspread wings; behind Norman hang two paintings of classical subjects containing female nudes, one of which, significantly, is a rendering of "Susannah and the Elders," whose subject foreshadows Norman's act of voyeurism. The two-dimensionality of the painterly representations is accentuated by the three-dimensionality of the birds with their large shadows. One of the paintings behind Norman, in which the white skin of the naked female body is prominent while everything else is cloaked in shadow, stresses the corporeality of its subject. Against the birds, however, the painting seems curiously flat, a mere decorative surface.

After Marion has excused herself and leaves the parlor, Norman does something that in some ways is more surprising than the murder he will soon commit: he lifts "Susannah and the Elders" from the wall, revealing a jagged, eye-shaped hole with a point of light at its center, a hole that resembles an eye with its pupil. Hitchcock then cuts to Marion undressing on the other side of the wall, then to a close-up of Norman's eye aligned with the eye-shaped peephole, retrospectively revealing the shot of Marion to have been from his point of view. Like the wallpapered doors in Weimar cinema that suddenly open to reveal another, unexpected space, this moment addresses the idea of the "space behind the painting," suggesting, as the stuffed birds do, that cinema has access to three-dimensional representation. Cinema goes beyond painting in its ability to simulate reality, this scene claims: the space behind the painting is not only three-dimensional, but contains movement.

Modeled upon the eye, the peephole has jagged edges that suggest a torn canvas as well as the organ of sight. Not only does the peephole have an organic model, but it has a cinematic one as well: its shape echoes the holes through which Fritz Lang characters repeatedly do their invasive spying. Especially in the shot in which the eye and the peephole are merged, this moment evokes the conjunction of camera and eye, and positions the cinema as a pornographic peepshow. By implication, then, it suggests that cinema also involves the body in a more problematic way than painting, precisely because it is able to simulate corporeality more readily than painting can. In the ensuing shower scene, in which the slashing knife so obviously functions as an extension of the invasive eye/camera/phallus, the price for that corporeality is paid. Marion's naked body, echoing yet exceeding the painted female nudes, falls victim to the camera/knife in a scene that provides the spectator with a "veritable visual dictionary of possibilities of framing and fragmentation."[141]

Other "stray" images in *Psycho* underline its preoccupation with defining the cinematic body: when Lila enters the mother's bedroom, she is startled by her own mirror image, and her eyes stray to a bronze sculpture of Dürer's praying hands, body parts as clichéd representative of high culture. But it is the preserved corpse of the mother that most obviously takes up the issue of the nature of the cinematic body: the mummy, as body rather than image, exceeds both the flatness of painting and the photograph's capacity to "embalm time."[142] When we finally see this mummy in conjunction with the swinging light bulb in the cellar, it appears to be animated by the "play of light and shadows which also designates cinema itself"; this lighting effect suggests, that is, the capacity for movement that characterizes the cinematic image, giving "life" to the empty eye sockets of the skull.[143] When Norman impersonates—*is*—his mother and thereby psychically keeps her alive, Hitchcock's narrative is simply fleshing this moment out.

A final meditation on fragmentation, the body, and filmmaking in Hitchcock takes us briefly to *Spellbound* (1945) and to *North by Northwest* (1959), where references to the body of the woman as sculpture have something to say about the generation of cinematic images. Famous for its dream sequence based on drawings by Salvador Dali, *Spellbound* actually contains only a radically attenuated form of the sequence originally planned; its best-known image is undoubtedly that of a woman using scissors to cut drapes covered with huges eyes, an image inspired by Buñuel and Dali's *Un Chien Andalou* (1929). Combining images of castration with images of theater, this figuration is a variant on the idea of the filmmaker as surgeon. Within the narrative of *Spellbound*, it is displaced onto Gregory Peck's character who, ostensibly a psychoanalyst, must also perform surgery, and it is displaced as well into the intermittent suspicion that he is a knife murderer. Like Pabst's *Secrets of a Soul*, *Spellbound* purports to be a serious film about psychoanalysis; Pabst's "knife phobia," the fear of castration, is played upon within the diegesis of Hitchcock's film, too, but is ultimately presented as a red herring.

The choice of painting for the dream sequence is a telling one, suggesting the constructed nature of dream images. Dali's dream sequence is also, of course, a painting set to motion rather than a cinematic sequence. Announcing its flatness in a style typical of this painter, its suggestions of three-dimensionality are pure artifice. Interestingly, the dream sequence had originally featured the Ingrid Bergman character becoming a statue in the mind of the psychoanalyst; in a reversal of Galatea coming to life, the woman was to have been subsumed by sculpture, dying into art.[144] When, in *North by Northwest*, Eva Marie Saint is called a "little piece of sculpture" for which the villain "must have paid plenty" at an art auction, the implication of this remark is rather different. At the end of the film, however, when a statue with which Eve's character has become identified is dropped, breaks into pieces, and reveals hidden microfilm—pointing also, as Stanley Cavell supposes, to "the present film,"—something more is at stake.[145] If, in one sense, the statue in *North by Northwest* could be said to give birth to the film, to generate it, then the fate of this statue demonstrates that the female figure must be shattered—fragmented—in order to produce it.

Hitchcock's films, so narrative oriented, so intent on the twists and turns of the plot, mask a continuous preoccupation with the stasis of painting, suggestive of and displaced by the death around which every Hitchcock plot inevitably turns. In most of these instances from Hitchcock's films, it has been the body of the woman that is fragmented or dismembered, that is conflated with the "dead" space of the pictorial, and is most intimately bound up with the uncanny and paradoxical capacity of cinema both to fragment the body and to animate it. I am deferring some of the most important illustrations of these claims for a later chapter, while the next chapter will take up the issue of the fragmented body from another point of view. Suffice it to say in conclusion that in 1927 Hitchcock chose to send a Christmas card to his friends depicting the famous caricature of himself in profile: the card was a jigsaw puzzle, meant to be taken to pieces and then reassembled.[146]

Monstrous Births: The Hybrid Text

> If a painter should decide to join the neck of a horse to
> a human head, and to lay many colored feathers taken
> from here or there so that what is a comely woman
> above ended as a dark, grotesque fish below,
> could you, my friends, if you were allowed
> to see it, keep from laughing?
> —*Horace*[1]

As a latecomer, film alludes to, absorbs, and undermines the discourses of the other arts in order to carve out a position for itself among them. Place precariously between the sister arts of literature and painting especially, film harbors a twofold insecurity that changes its guise—the symptoms of its presence—from film to film, filmmaker to filmmaker. When one or another of these arts is emphasized, this is sometimes a strategy to shift the spectator's attention away from whichever art it is that most immediately threatens to encroach on the territory of the film, for it is too jealous of its boundaries to take the encroachments of the neighboring arts lightly. But it is precisely the source of film's insecurity—the sense of being perceived as a heterogeneous form, a hybrid medium that emerges amid the ruins of traditionally sanctioned cultural forms—that in fact enables the assortment of powerful displacements and repressions at its disposal. Film may set the arts of which it is comprised at odds with each other, as though it were itself unconcerned in the conflict: where it most feels the immanence of the literary, it forms an alliance with the pictorial that either transforms the literary or calls its integrity and adequacy as an artistic medium into question; and where it is most likely to be humbled by the older and more dignified forms of still representation, just then it flaunts its diegetic flexibility, its accommodation of temporality, by using allusion or direct quotation willingly to foreground its indebtedness to literature.

Although Western film as a whole is preoccupied with its place in the tradition—for contemporary film has by no means given up the concern with its status vis-à-vis the other arts—it is perhaps more obviously true of film at its beginnings, when its practitioners first began to develop its language and mode of narration. The films of D. W. Griffith offer an early case in point. Griffith is rightly acclaimed for the ingenuity with which he translated the conventions of novelistic and dramatic narratives into authentically cinematic narratives by means of camerawork and editing. But in films such as *Birth of a Nation*, Griffith also made use of so-called "historical facsimiles," recreations of historical moments such as the signing of treaties that he based visually on historical paintings, although he cited historical writings as his source. No doubt occasioned by Griffith's concern for historical accuracy, these tableaux are especially interesting for the way in which they suspend the cinematic moment between the literary and the painterly. In order to record momentous occasions, Griffith interrupts his narrative, resisting its overwhelming of privileged moments by the momentum of sequence and thus challenging the adequacy of narrative as such, while at the same time sheltering his enterprise under the sponsorship of an art that is equal in dignity to the traditional forms of storytelling. Thus his retreat from one neighboring art, historical painting in the tradition of Benjamin West and Gilbert Stuart, takes the form of homage to another, the golden age of American history writing. In gesturing toward the writing of history as the embodiment of high culture, furthermore, Griffith at the same time leads the attention away not only from historical painting but from an even more pervasive source of his conventions, the Victorian novel. Yet if this last is indeed a covert motive of his facsimiles, it is intriguingly undermined by the fact that amateur theatricals such as those in Thackeray's *Vanity Fair* characteristically based their tableaux on paintings. Thus the displacement of Griffith's indebtedness returns along its own path to its source in the narrative line, perhaps resituating painting as the most powerful prior model after all.

It is a commonplace of film history that during Griffith's years as an actor in the theatrical melodrama, he absorbed its conventions and techniques with their curiously pictorial predisposition: the narrative of the theatrical melodrama tends to be episodic, oriented around a series of tableaux that were often based upon paintings and had the function of prolonging visually evocative moments by freezing them into "living pictures." From these conventions, it can be argued, Griffith later developed analogues for the new cinematic medium—fades, dissolves, subjective (or "vision") shots, and parallel plotting. Within six years—between directing his first one-reeler in 1908 and *Birth of a Nation* in 1914—Griffith is said to have effected a nearly complete transposition of nineteenth-century theatrical modes into cinematic forms and to have substantially established the language of narrative cinema as we know it today.[2]

Naturally, as I suggested earlier, there is yet another influence on Griffith, one that also has links to melodrama, and that is the Victorian novel—more specifically, the Dickensian novel. It is no accident, I think, that when Eisenstein chose to write about the origin of the art of the film— to write, that is, about his own cinematic and literary precursors—he focused on Griffith in the context of his literary sources. In his essay, "Dickens, Griffith, and the Film Today" (1944), Eisenstein is at pains to insist that the cinema is, as he puts it, "no virgin birth," and it is obvious to his reader that one of his purposes in making this claim is to inspire pride, not anxiety; it is Eisenstein's intention to perform an act of legitimation in the service of his chosen medium. "For me personally," Eisenstein writes, "it is always pleasing to recognize again the fact that our cinema is not altogether without parents and without a pedigree, without a past, and without the traditions and rich cultural heritage of past epochs."[3] In tracing cinema's lineage, Eisenstein locates the technique of parallel action montage in the narrative methods of Dickens. Praising Dickens's "optical quality" and the plasticity and detail of his descriptions, and stressing the "close-up" in Dickens's descriptive technique and his sharply delineated point of view, Eisenstein literally reads Dickens's novels from a cinematic perspective. Indeed, the relationship between the Dickensian novel and the Griffith film is, as Eisenstein formulates it, "organic, and the 'genetic' line of descent is quite consistent."[4] In one sense, this move—that of calling Dickens Griffith's "montage ancestor"—enables Eisenstein to downplay Griffith's ingenuity in devising a cinematic language by claiming that the novels from which he derived it were cinematic in the first place. Not only does Eisenstein trace back to Dickens the parallel action montage organizing most Griffith films, he also carefully elucidates the advance from Griffith's more primitive, ideologically reactionary form of montage toward his own more complex and politically flexible dialectical montage. It is a strategically complex performance, but, details aside, Eisenstein's essay remains important to our concerns for the manner in which it constructs a family romance in order to account for the origins of early cinema.

MISCEGENATION AND THE SISTER ARTS:
GRIFFITH'S *BROKEN BLOSSOMS*

In actual practice, the question of cinematic parentage is posed intriguingly by Griffith's *Broken Blossoms* (1919), and once again the question of legitimizing cinema as an art form has a role to play.[5] In 1919, anxious to establish himself as a "film artist" on the European model, and spurred on by the worldwide success of *Birth of a Nation* and *Intolerance* (1916), Griffith set out to introduce the concept of an American art film to Hollywood.[6] To this end, Griffith planned to advertise *Broken Blossoms* as a film with so-called art values and as part of a "Griffith Repertory Season" that was to tour only cities that could produce an audience properly able to appreciate his work.[7] In keeping with this presentation of film as theater, Griffith made curtain calls at the premiere of *Broken Blossoms* and, during various interviews, he did not hesitate to compare his film to Dickens's novels.[8] Also in order to establish the film as an example of high art, the screening of *Broken Blossoms* was to take place in movie theaters resplendent with oriental decor and to be framed by other performances—notably a staged prologue, a one-act ballet ("The Dance of Life and Death," written by Griffith himself), and a musical score performed by a Russian balalaika orchestra.[9] It was, in fact, misguided events such as these that Kracauer was to scorn in his "Picture Palace" essay of 1926 as "the American style of a self-contained show which integrates the film as part of a greater whole. . . . a glittering, revue-like creature . . . *the total artwork of effects.*"[10]

While *Broken Blossoms* no doubt hinges on racist assumptions as crass as those of *Birth of a Nation*, it is nevertheless the case that the ideology of high art promoted by Griffith in his film had at least in part the function of distancing *Broken Blossoms* from the rampant anti-orientalism in American popular culture and the press in the late nineteenth and early twentieth centuries. As Vance Kepley has pointed out, during this period when the media was riddled with "Yellow Peril" sensationalism, and when Fu Manchu and other "inscrutable" oriental villains were well-known figures in popular literature, a whole series of anti-oriental films was made as well, films set in an American Chinatown fraught with melodramatic intrigue. And, as Kepley notes, it was miscegenation, or its threat, that shaped the plotting of this genre. Since he was hopeful that *Broken Blossoms* would be acclaimed as an art film, Griffith did not want his film to be categorized with these.

And yet, one characteristic that a Griffith film has in common with an "oriental film" of its time is that the whole thematic and narrative burden is placed on the body of the woman. Time and again, the twists and turns in Griffith's narratives exist in order to place the woman in the position of greatest possible danger: faced with many variants on the "fate worse than death"—with rape, with defloration, and even simply with the abstract threat to her purity—she chooses death. In *Broken Blossoms*, too, the purity of "the Girl," Lucy, is carefully preserved; she refuses the two narratives—marriage and prostitution—that would grant her freedom from her father's tyranny, though by doing so she must continue to allow her father to violate her body in yet another way—to serve, as Griffith's titles tell us, as Battling Burrows's punching bag. And, although Lucy is the object of the Yellow Man's love, it is obvious that the erotic aspect of this love must be downplayed, considering Griffith's intention to distance himself from the oriental films of Cecil B. DeMille, for instance, which feature the lascivious oriental. Thus, the male-female opposition so strikingly portrayed in the father-daughter relationship is rejected in favor of an identification of sorts between the Yellow Man and Lucy, and to this end he is feminized. It is clear, of course, that the racial ideology of this film, high art aside, conspires additionally to prevent a union between the Yellow Man and Lucy, the threat of miscegenation making such a union impossible. It goes without saying that incest is equally taboo. Although we might easily interpret the father's brutishly contemptuous violence against Lucy as a form of sublimated desire, at this point in film history a desire of this kind could never be expressed in overt eroticism or in rape. Lucy herself then becomes the battleground on which the conflict between the violent, active, male principle represented by Burrows, who is a prize fighter, and the passive, nearly static, and essentially female principle represented in the figure of the Yellow Man is enacted. It is Griffith's famous parallel-action montage that gives expression to this binary relationship, but there are visual echoes in the film that serve to remind the spectator of the essential relatedness of the two threats to which Lucy is exposed: when, for example, the Yellow Man approaches Lucy with worshipful eyes and lips poised to kiss her, she shrinks back with fear; a bit later in the film there occurs another scene, similarly composed, in which she responds with horror to her father, who approaches her with angry eyes and clenched fists. On both occasions, she is reclining on a bed. But the threat represented by the Yellow Man's signs of sexuality must be eliminated. To this end, it is sublimated, aestheticized, covered over with the values of high art.

The opening sequence of the film introduces this conflict between the active and the passive principles—between movement and stasis—by juxtaposing the Yellow Man with three swaggering American soldiers whose pugnacity characterizes them as "men of action," and who involve him in a fight against his will. But the Yellow Man's model of behavior is the statue of the Buddha that graces the temple where he has prayed and studied, and its serene passivity is his. An example of an artwork still sustaining its ritual function, this statue of the Buddha casts its aura over the series of tableaux with which the film begins and establishes the world of the Yellow Man as the world of static representation.

There is, of course, another obvious means by which Griffith is able to juxtapose narrative and motion with stasis and visual representation, and that is through the title cards on which silent cinema necessarily relies. It goes without saying that the title cards present the spectator with information regarding the narrative events of the film, and that they stitch together the action represented in the image track, providing the commentary of a narrative voice. Additionally, however, they have the function of interrupting the flow of the action, the movement of images that *is* the film's narrative, and the manner in which these static title cards interrupt and punctuate this narrative recalls the way in which Griffith uses tableaux evoking historical paintings in *Birth of a Nation* to just such an end.

Title cards in *Broken Blossoms* are of several kinds: one, the most common, is inscribed with Griffith's initials, an insignia of sorts, while another title card that occurs frequently features writing superimposed upon a pictorial background composed of flowers, a mountain, and a moon—a gathering of visual motifs commonly associated with Chinese art.[11] A third presents the written message over a variety of different graphic backgrounds (flowers, for example) that also evoke Chinese painting, and a fourth, which occurs only once and to which we will return, presents the message over a *cinematic* background, the blossoms of a fruit tree. Furthermore, these title cards distinguish between print and script: script is the graphic signal for poetry and is reserved for the haiku-like phrases such as "O lily flowers and plum blossoms!" that contribute to the tone of the Yellow Man's aestheticized world. The point, then, is that, whether by means of Griffith's personal insignia as emblem or graphic images, or whether signaled by the calligraphic aspect of writing, the title cards have the additional—and in some cases even primary—function of pointing, like the tableaux, to the static and composed visual image that film borrows from painting.

When, on the other hand, we examine those aspects of *Broken Blossoms* that represent action, the *moving* image, we approach an understanding of Griffith's attitude toward narrative. In 1919, the moving image is not produced by means of camera movement, but rather by means of montage that simulates movement. But film is nevertheless fascinated with the production of movement that enables narration. Although the conjunction of the visual with movement already intrigues the human imagination much earlier,[12] Comolli could easily say that "the second half of the nineteenth century lives in a sort of frenzy of the visible."[13] The best-known practitioner of series photography, Eadweard Muybridge, undertook motion studies that often featured the bodies of athletes mounted on glass-plate photographs. By projecting these on a screen with a magic lantern, he was able to reproduce action in a primitive way. Even more pertinent to our concerns, perhaps, is one of the most popular primitive films, the one made in Edison's Black Maria in 1894 entitled "Corbett and Courtney Before the Kinetograph," which records successive rounds of a boxing match. The boxing match is in fact one of the favored subjects of early American cinema; as one critic suggests, the real or staged boxing match provided an ideal framework for the representation of precise body movements: early audiences especially enjoyed "watching bodies subjected to various forces and disciplines."[14]

In *Broken Blossoms*, action, movement, and narration are tied to the figure of Battling Burrows. In fact, the film tends to linger over the scenes of Battling Burrows in the boxing ring, surrounded by spectators, in a manner that draws attention to itself and suggests a reference to other forms of spectatorship. It appears, indeed, to be the intention of the film to allude to proto- and early cinematic forms by representing Burrows as a boxer, and there is an evocative image that supports this contention: hanging on one of the walls in the room that Burrows and Lucy inhabit is a poster of Burrows that depicts him in various boxing poses, each one a separate photograph. This reference to series photography and its obsession with the *appearance* of motion is established when Burrows poses before the poster. Contained in this cinematic moment is the self-satisfaction of cinema, representing its moving figure liberated from the containment of the frame.[15] However, we should note that Griffith's highly negative representation of Burrows in this film, his correlation of action with aggressiveness and indeed with violence—a link that is established in the Yellow Man's encounter with the American soldiers—suggests a curious hostility toward narrative. In thus privileging visual representation over narrative, *Broken Blossoms* registers an attempt to impose distance between the film and Dickensian narrative, especially in view of the fact that this is the only Griffith film that has a Dickensian setting, the foggy Limehouse district of London. In this way, it becomes an allegory of the struggle between narrative and image for possession of, for control over, the cinematic text.

As Dudley Andrew has pointed out, for Griffith high art is pictorial; and certainly the static, pictorial world of the Yellow Man is the ideologically privileged aesthetic of this film.[16] But in *Broken Blossoms*, as in his other films, Griffith is at pains to create a genuinely cinematic discourse, and thus the visual image cannot remain tied to painting alone. If it is Griffith's project in *Broken Blossoms* to attach the values of so-called high art to cinema, then he does this most obviously by means of the title card with poetic apostrophes reading "O lily flowers and plum blossoms! / O silver streams and dim-starred skies!" against a filmed backdrop. It is here that he rejects the painted backdrop for the cinematic one—the blossoms sway gently in the breeze—replacing the motifs of Chinese painting with a cinematic image of the fruit-tree blossoms, obviously intact, unbroken, that refer to the film's title. Even for today's spectator the visual contrast between the painted background of the other titles and the dazzling reality of this natural scene is breathtaking; an earlier spectator would have felt this contrast even more acutely. Griffith's strategy here, then, is first to bind cinema to painting (note that the literary is privileged here only in the form of lyric evocation, not narrative) and then, as it were, to "outdo" painting by bringing it to life.

And yet, though this moment represents a tour de force of sorts for cinema, we can conclude that Griffith's successful troping of the static pictorial image by means of the moving one is not unaccompanied by anxiety. The question of the cinema's "parentage," as even Eisenstein had put it, the question of its origin posed as a family romance, brings with it an unease generated by the recognition that it is a heterogeneous form. This preoccupation with the hybrid status of cinema has an analogue in the narrative of the film, one that is attached to the body of the Girl. Typically for Griffith, again, the conflict between Burrows and the Yellow Man—between movement and narrativity in Burrows and stasis and visual representation in the Yellow Man—is enacted across the body of the woman.

Although Deleuze applies the term "organic montage" to Griffith's mode of converging parallel actions into a final unity, in *Broken Blossoms*, evident from the title, there is also a thematic and formal tendency toward fragmentation.[17] The topos that associates women with flowers (Shakespeare's Ophelia or Goethe's Gretchen) is well known: the plucked flower—or broken blossom—has traditionally been an emblem of a woman's loss of virginity, verbally cued in the term "deflowering." In Griffith's film, Lucy—the allegorical screen on which the film's self-image is projected—is repeatedly connected with flowers: she herself stares wistfully at flowers and longs to buy them, and the Yellow Man later buys them for her. There are, however, moments in the film that are ambivalent about this connection and seek to disrupt it. For instance, one of the title cards that describe the Yellow Man reads, "The spirit of beauty breaks her blossoms all about his chamber," and it is in the following shot that we see Lucy attempting to buy those blossoms. The spectator is meant to conclude, of course, that Lucy herself is the "spirit of beauty," thereby transforming the analogy between flower and body into that between flower and spirit. Other moments, however, are less circumspect in linking flowers to the body, as when, later in the film, Evil Eye picks up white blossoms and his gestures and expression suggest that it is Lucy he is symbolically holding. One title card refers to the girl's "bruised little body." In the narrative of this film the girl does not suffer the "fate worse than death" to which Griffith so often subjects his heroine, but is merely bruised, beaten, and killed. Nevertheless, there is in the metaphor of the broken blossom a lingering trace of the theme of defloration, potentially readmitting the theme of miscegenation that the oriental films of this period exploited so shamelessly. Clearly, however, the idea of miscegenation as a threat is not absent, but is rather displaced onto another order entirely in this film.

What is at issue for Griffith—and many other filmmakers—is nothing less than the fear that cinema as a hybrid form is, in fact, a kind of "monstrous birth," the fear that it is the offspring, as one might put it, of miscegenation. We can find the unease generated by a lack of formal unity and expressed in the trope of the monster as far back as the opening lines of Horace's *Art of Poetry* cited above. For that matter, anxiety concerning generic boundary crossings or the usurpation of one medium by another—as, for example, literature by painting or painting by literature—has also been with us since classical antiquity as well; it was notably given expression by Lessing in his *Laocoön*, where he presents Vergil as being in competition with the Laocoön sculptural group, and decries the so-called "painterly poetry" that was being practiced in the eighteenth century as a monstrous hybrid form. In fact, as W.J.T. Mitchell has pointed out:

> one thing [that Lessing] teaches us is that the relation of the genres like poetry and painting is not a purely theoretical matter, but something like a social relationship. . . . The relations of the arts are like those of countries, of clans, of neighbors, of members of the same family. They are thus related by sister- and brotherhood, maternity and paternity, marriage, incest and adultery; thus subject to versions of the laws, taboos, and rituals that regulate social forms of life.[18]

Arguably Griffith's anxiety about the heterogeneity of film is expressed in the narratives that do *not* take place in *Broken Blossoms*, as well as in the ones that do. As I have said, one might well read Battling Burrows' aggressive violence towards his daughter as the displacement of incestuous desires; incest does not take place, but the father beats her to death in an equally intense state of passion. No liaison takes place, either, between the Yellow Man and Lucy; but again, although the illicit contact is avoided, the possibility of miscegenation is signaled in the much-coveted doll that he gives her. Finally—and uncharacteristically for Griffith—not even the marriage of the two lines of parallel-action montage is effected in *Broken Blossoms*. As Deleuze puts it, "Admittedly, in Griffith, the junction does not always take place, and the innocent young girl is often condemned, almost sadistically, because she could only find her place and salvation in an 'inorganic' abnormal union: the Chinese opium addict arrives too late in *Broken Blossoms*."[19] Another fusion that does not take place, keeping in mind the connection of Battling Burrows with narrative

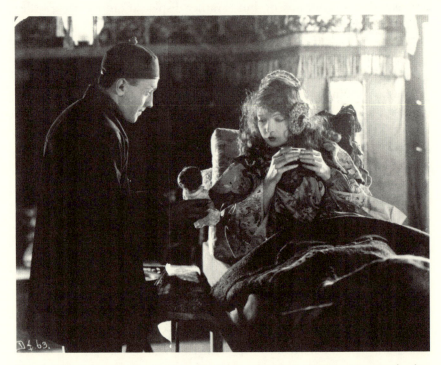

Fig. 5. The threat of miscegenation is displaced into the Yellow Man's gift of a doll.

and the male principle and the Yellow Man with pictorialism and the feminine, is the homoerotic union of what are, in fact, the two aspects of the cinematic image. In stabbing the Yellow Man with a knife, Battling Burrows signals another act that is not allowed to occur. As to the Girl and the feminized Yellow Man, everything they have in common (both are repeatedly allied with pictorial aesthetic values, their bodies covered by the same ornamental robe, and both, on the level of melodramatic narrative, are "broken blossoms"), makes it all the more important that their union be prevented. In *Broken Blossoms* the hybrid nature of film is repeatedly figured and denied in a series of illicit sexual relations—incest, miscegenation, homoerotic unions—that are first suggested and then blocked.

Griffith's eagerness to block the possibility of any union whatsoever is related to the discourse of unity and fragmentation in *Broken Blossoms*, and reflects the way in which the film sets up the narrative and the pictorial as a binary opposition on a collision course, thus guaranteeing its own fragmentation in the process. One of Griffith's title cards, prefacing a series of tableau-like scenes that provide glimpses into the Yellow Man's life in London, reads "broken bits of his new life in his new home" and thus verbally links the "broken" text with the bruised and broken body of the Girl. (In this example the title card as written text works, as one might expect, towards the production of a narrative coherence that is never actually achieved.)

While the work of art has been figured as a body ever since Aristotle, it may be most appropriate at this point once again to refer to Diderot who is, as Barthes has implied, in some sense the first theorist of film. Unity in Diderot's tableau, its "single point of view," according to Barthes, is anchored in the natural, *organic* wholeness of the body, a wholeness that in some sense can be said to generate the unity of all of the bodies within the composition.[20] Given Griffith's interest in establishing the place of his film among the arts, why does the parallel montage of *Broken Blossoms* not allow a so-called organic solution, but rather prohibits this and establishes it as transgressive (though obviously, on the level of the narrative, Griffith's racism in itself offers an explanation of the inexorably separate parallelism of the plot)? The answer would seem to be that the aesthetic of unity is not what he has in mind: his refusal to allow an organic resolution of the binary opposition in this film is symptomatic of his divided point of view, of the manner in which he suspends *Broken Blossoms* equidistantly between the narrative and the pictorial.

65

The sexualized anxiety of such a positioning is not just characteristic of Griffith, but actually contributes in a variety of ways to the self-definition of film as a medium. Very frequently in film, the relation of representational systems to one another—specifically, the anxiety concerning the adjacency of the literary and the painterly—are figured as sexual relations gone awry, producing the threat of a monstrous birth. Even the lines from Horace, with their "comely woman above" and their "grotesque fish below" contain a suggestion of this; although this thesis is paralleled within the territorial struggles of other arts, as a paradigm it has compositional implications that are specific to film.

An additional example, taken from Hitchcock, may help to clarify my argument. There is a scene in *Vertigo* (1958) that contains a painting not unlike that of the monster described by Horace. It is, significantly, a painting by a female character, Midge, who has copied a portrait identified with Kim Novak's character, with whom James Stewart's character, Scottie, is obsessed.[21] But on the body of that woman Midge has painted her own head, perhaps in an effort to suggest to Scottie, with whom she is in love, that she herself would be an adequate substitute for the inaccessible woman. The shock value of Midge's painting for the spectator is difficult to account for when one considers how accustomed we are to similar effects created in modernist painting. Indeed, Midge is a fashion designer who works in a studio full of examples of abstract sculpture and painting and whose current creation, a brassiere, mounted on a freestanding wire bust, she describes as working on the principle of the cantilever bridge. When Midge tells Scottie that she has "gone back to [her] first love, painting" (painting was Hitchcock's first love, too),[22] he asks whether she is painting a still life. "Not exactly," she replies, and in the irony of her reply lies a partial explanation for the shock that her painting occasions in us, the unnatural conjunction of body and head has rendered her representation inorganic, not even *like* nature and hence doubly lifeless. Additionally, of course, the fact that this is the work of a female artist, and that she has superimposed upon the portrait her own head complete with the spectacles that signify her access to the gaze, displacing the head a second time in that it looks back at itself knowingly, contributes to the sense of "unnaturalness" that we perceive in the painting. In *Vertigo*, this scene with its flaunting of fragmented and modernist works of art figures the hesitation created in the film by its multiplicity of perspectives, the splitting of point of view that finds its visual analogue in the fragmentation of the female body, displayed not only in the doubled portrait, but in the freestanding sculpture of the breast.

HITCHCOCK'S "HALF-CASTE"

The play of parts and wholes in Hitchcock's films is not confined to the bodies of the characters who populate them, but extends to the family romance that structures their narratives. Attenuated families with missing members—kidnapped children or dead parents—are the testing grounds of a marriage or the scene of "unnatural," incestuous relations. The Oedipal attachment of son to mother and the sexual ambiguity that accompanies it are of recurrent significance in Hitchcock, whether they occur as a passing allusion or a momentary image (as in *North by Northwest,* or in *Frenzy,* where it is nevertheless made to account for the psychotic behavior of the murderer), whether they strike a major chord (as in *Notorious* [1946], *Strangers on a Train* [1951], and *The Birds* [1963]), or whether they are displaced onto the relation of brother to sister (*The Man Who Knew Too Much* [1934]) or daughter to mother (*Marnie* [1964]). *Psycho* is, of course, the film in which the bond of son to mother takes its most astonishing form, both in the act of matricide provoked by the threat of replacement by another man and in the subsequent desire to *be* the mother in order to keep her alive symbolically. Linked to the problem of sexual ambiguity by way of the threat of castration, the relation to the mother has something to say about the generation of Hitchcock films as the repeated working through of this problematic. Sexual amibiguity in Hitchcock's characters, manifested both in male impotence and in a more general doubling between men and women, relates to the way in which film is understood as a hybrid medium comprised of image and narrative.[23]

Painting is present everywhere in Hitchcock's films, and it is related to his self-understanding as a filmmaker. For instance, when we look to the question of lineage in *Rebecca* (1940), which relies heavily on gothic romance, a genre noteworthy for its mystification of origin, we encounter in the heroine's father an artist who is said to have painted the same tree over and over again, having found in it his perfect subject. Likewise, in an interview with François Truffaut, Hitchcock speaks of making the same film over and over, comparing himself to the painter Rouault in the bargain. "Not that I'm comparing myself to him," Hitchcock said in a typical disclaimer, "but old Rouault was content with judges, clowns, a few women, and Christ on the Cross. That constituted his life's work."[24] And it is in Rouault's work, interestingly, that the paintings of Bruno Anthony's mother (*Strangers on a Train*) find their inspiration. Bruno says of his mother that she has long been unwell and gives as her reason for painting that it soothes her: notwithstanding that this remark parodies Freud's connection of neurosis with the production of art, it is meant to be taken seriously. Mrs. Anthony's portrait of her husband is one with which her son has sympathy, since it represents him as a king, as one who exerts despotic control over wife and son—the double allusion to the *Oedipus* and to *Hamlet* is not lost here. Although Bruno's psychotic aim—to arrange the murder of his father in order to claim his mother for himself—finds no sublimation in the visual arts, it does lead to a great deal of intricate plotting. Storytelling, painting, and parentage are linked in this film, suggesting that the art of film is the tainted offspring of dubious loves.

In Hitchcock, too, the space of painting is a female space, although *Rebecca*'s heroine, the second Mrs. de Winter, takes after her father in having a talent for sketching. When she sketches herself in a costume for an upcoming ball, she envisions herself as St. Joan;[25] the costume that she will actually choose, however, is based on an ancestral portrait of a gothic woman in white. Although this costume unleashes a destructive force, it will finally instate her as the "legitimate" wife: feminine and submissive, this second Mrs. de Winter, said to resemble physically the lady of the portrait, is aligned with the painting in this film, not Rebecca.[26] The dead Rebecca's name, on the contrary, haunts the film with gothic power in the form of the monogram "R" that appears as an inscription, sinister in its ubiquity, on everything in the house. As a device, the monogrammed "R" is no doubt borrowed from Lang, whose films abound with death-bringing writing, and whose *Woman in the Window*, released in the year following *Rebecca*, in turn featured a female portrait whose seductiveness leads to murder. The conjunction of painting and writing, nearly obscured by gothic motifs in Hitchcock's film, surfaces in the conflict between the "good" and the "bad" woman—joined as doubles through the painting that they both seek to embody—and in the conflict between feminine passivity (painting) and destructive action (the phallic power of writing) that they represent.[27] In *Rebecca*, painting's conflation with death is a secondary feature, and the anxiety concerning this connection is displaced into the opposite fear of the portrait's ghostly "life"; it is glossed over, that is, and assimilated into gothic conventions.

The feminine space of painting and death can be occupied by male figures in Hitchcock, especially the sexually ambiguous males in whom a murderous psychosis often resides.[28] Although as plotmaker Bruno is tied to the principle of narrative, he is also connected with visual representation: in *Strangers on a Train* there is a moment in which the composition of the frame pointedly connects him to a female portrait, Manet's "Bar at the Folies Bergères." This moment occurs during the tennis championship in which Guy, Bruno's double, is playing and Bruno sits staring directly into the camera, in marked contrast to the other spectators, whose heads follow the ball back and forth in synchronized engrossment in the action. Manet's barmaid, too, is surrounded by a crowd, reflected in the mirror behind her; as unwavering as that of the barmaid, Bruno's gaze similarly draws our own intent gaze into the cinematic frame. Naturally, this reference to painting reinforces the themes of mirroring and spectatorship (themes also present in the Patricia Highsmith novel on which the film is based), but its significance extends beyond this preoccupation. Bruno's stillness, accentuated by the other heads turning in unison, is notable within the context of the moving image, his pronounced lack of movement reinforcing his placement within a different kind of space, a painterly space within the cinematic one.[29] A related scene in the film presents Bruno in long shot as a small figure against the Washington Monument, his still body trapped within the architectural space of monument and tomb.

As Bruno's placement within the monument suggests, in *Strangers on a Train* the space of noncinematic visual representation is coterminous with the place of death. From this point of view, we might say that the portrait of Bruno's father painted by his mother places him under the sign of death in the eyes of his son. Similarly, and in ironic jest, the Mount Rushmore sequence in *North by Northwest* juxtaposes the gigantic, impassive presidential heads of stone—leading us momentarily to wonder where the Medusa is who has caused this calamity—with the specks of human figures moving across them, figures for whom this is the setting of a life and death struggle. Somewhat surprisingly, perhaps, this moment effects a triumph of sorts for cinematic representation: although cinema envies the three-dimensional quality of sculpture that guarantees its representational power, it affirms the power of the cinematic body in its capacity for movement that makes it lifelike. In *North by Northwest*, Cary Grant's character, having emerged from this feminine place of death a victor, will no longer be questioned about whether he is a "little boy" or a "big boy," will no longer be troubled about "the sizes things are," and will marry.[30]

Most ambiguous of Hitchcock's characters is Handel Fane, the perpetrator in *Murder!* (1930) and an actor who is a bisexual. Interesting here is what at first appears to be the displacement of sexual into racial ambiguity: Fane kills because the woman he has "dared to love" is about to be told the secret that he is a "half-caste." But Fane's specialty as an actor is female impersonation, and he appears on a stage in women's clothing, a costume foreshadowing, in fact, the outfit that Norman Bates wears in *Psycho*.[31] In the world of the theater, female impersonation is an acceptable convention, and a recurrent joke about performing Shakespeare underscores this assumption. Hitchcock, however, did not seem to feel the need to cloak this character's bisexuality under the cover of his mixed racial origin: the stage manager refers jokingly to Fane (played by Esmé Percy) as "one hundred percent he-woman," and Fane's alibi for the evening of the murder is that he was in the company of a young man. In view of the film's sexual openness, then, Fane's representation as a "half-caste" is at first puzzling. Whether as a bisexual or a "half-caste," however, the human figure so portrayed is notable for the manner in which it embodies the idea of heterogeneity. It would seem, then, that Hitchcock is interested in doubling Fane's heterogeneity, in marking its excess.

One of the subjects addressed by *Murder!* is the question of the relation of theater to film, and the film uses theatrical devices such as role playing and curtains to this end. As William Rothman puts it, "the invocations of theater are performed within the context of the film's declaration of its own decisive separation from theater, its declaration of itself as a film."[32] And certainly the noticeable presence of the camera and the film's preoccupation with framing substantiate this point. Its ending, however, suggests that the film is interested as well in incorporating the theatrical, just as it wants to allude visibly to painting and writing. The notable panning movement, for instance, with which the film opens, gradually reveals the space of *Murder!* in a motion that resembles a brushstroke. It is an opening typical of Hitchcock films that culminates, in *Sabotage* and *Notorious*, in signs covered with writing, thus making the *caméra stylo* effect of this gesture complete.

Even more centrally, the tableau scene that constitutes the scene of the crime points to the presence of painting as well. This tableau scene, complete with spectators, features a dead body, suspects, and the police; as these remain perfectly still, the scene resembles nothing so much as a tableau vivant—a theatrical embodiment of painting—across which the camera moves slowly and deliberately. In its searching movement, the camera reveals the faces and bodies of policeman and suspect, and then moves along the length of a phallic poker, the murder weapon, that points the way to the victim's corpse. It is not surprising that the dead female body is what the camera finally reveals at the end of the poker.

Nor is it surprising that death is at the center of the tableau constituted here, for the "death" of the body within representation is what has rendered this scene motionless, lifeless, and painterly. Once again the space of painting is the space of death, in this case a place where a woman has been symbolically violated and killed off into art.

Over and against this space and determined to penetrate it in his own way is the active inquisitiveness of Sir John Menier, noted playwright turned detective, who undertakes, as he puts it, to apply the techniques of his art to the problems of life. For Sir John, solving the case will also mean solving the problem of the woman, as he discovers that he has a romantic interest in the actress, Diana Baring, who is suspected of the murder. By writing a play based upon the real events of the case as he discovers them, and by asking Handel Fane to read the part of the murderer, Sir John hopes to lure Fane into revealing the last "act" and hence into revealing himself. Sir John, then, makes use of and represents the quest for knowledge as embodied in the active—and actively male—principle of narrative. But, although Fane realizes that Sir John has found him out, he does not give in to the momentum of Sir John's narrative and refuses to play it out. Instead, Fane chooses to perform and execute his own death.

The actual mystery of *Murder!* is the mystery of the woman only insofar as this also overlaps with the mystery of Fane. When, towards the end of the film, Sir John seeks Fane out, he is no longer working in the theater, but is performing in the circus as a trapeze artist. Arrayed in a feathered headdress, in leotards, and heavily made up, the costumed "one hundred percent he-woman" is now a poignant mixture of man, woman, and bird—a doomed hybrid resembling Horace's monstrous creature with its "many-colored feathers." In this astonishing scene, Hitchcock tropes the heterogeneity that Fane already represented as a bisexual, female imper-

Fig. 6. Handel Fane is represented as a hybrid figure comprised of man, woman, and bird.

71

sonator, and "half-caste" by imposing upon it the added otherness of the bird.[33]

In his circus performance, Fane the hybrid is presented first and foremost as a specifically cinematic spectacle: beginning in shadow, his entry allies him with an ever-increasing amount of light as he walks into the depths of the frame. In his aerial performance Fane intermittently enters and leaves the beams of two spotlights, his body casting shadows in the course of his rhythmic motion; at one point, in a reversal of this moment, Fane's body remains stationary in the frame, while the background moves back and forth. The play of light and shadow that Fane's moving body creates recalls the flickering light and shadow effects of cinema that *Psycho* represents in the light bulb that animates Norman Bates's mother.[34] The motion of Fane's body is reminiscent of nothing so much as the persistent motion of the camera during the course of the film. By these means, Fane's performance is explicitly connected with cinema, a connection that may very well have its origin in Dupont's *Variété* (1926), a popular film released during Hitchcock's stay in Germany. But in Dupont's film, the primary reason for identifying the trapeze act with cinema seems to reside more simply in the diegetic licence it gives to flashy camera technique and the representation of vertigo.

Fane's performance is cut with images shot from his point of view, with a series of personal visions featuring a close-up of Diana Baring—the "woman he dared to love"—and including Sir John's face, distorted into a "death's head grin" signifying the closure of narrative that will soon take place.[35] As Rothman points out, "the 'Diana' Fane envisions as bearing witness to this act and the 'Fane' who is possessed by this vision of Diana are not separate beings . . . for this Diana is also within Fane."[36] The same could be said of Sir John. As a total embodiment of the cinematic, Fane symbolically contains both Sir John as playwright and the female body of the tableau: a moving image displayed to the view, Fane performs a series of actions that will culminate in death.[37]

Encoded as cinema, Fane's extraordinary performance is also a sexual performance, a narcissistic self-display from which he visibly receives orgasmic pleasure. When it finally culminates in the tying of the noose and in his hanging, Fane's performance exceeds the boundaries normally placed upon spectacle, gravitating in the direction of performance artists who market photographs of self-inflicted bullet wounds, or in the direction of snuff movies that titillate their audiences by substituting real death for its representation.[38] Again the cinema emerges triumphant: death is a performance that cannot be outdone and cannot be repeated, save as a sequence in the mechanically reproduced and indefinitely replayable art of the cinema.

MURNAU

Cinematic Vampirism

Friedrich Murnau seems wholly self-conscious about the manner in which the discourses of painting and literature impinge upon his film-making. Trained in literature and the history of art, Murnau based the title of his first film, *The Blue Boy* (1919), on the painting by Gainsborough, and from this time on painting remained a presence in his films. Although Murnau's films are narrative, there is an abstracted stillness about them; in fact, Murnau's films sometimes give the impression of existing solely in order to dramatize the encounter between cinematic motion and static composition. Like Wegener, Murnau was fascinated by the "play of pure movement," with what he called,

> the fluid architecture of bodies with blood in their veins moving through mobile space: the interplay of lines rising, falling, disappearing; the encounter of surfaces, stimulation and its opposite, calm; construction and collapse; the formation and destruction of a hitherto almost unsuspected life; all this adds up to a symphony made up of the harmony of bodies and the rhythm of space; the *play of pure movement*, vigorous and abundant.[39]

Emphasized here are moving forms invested with cinematic, "hitherto almost unsuspected life." Both the balanced compositions that determine each of Murnau's carefully composed cinematic frames and the tendency to fixity that his painterly style implies are opposed—yet also subjected—to movement.[40]

At times Murnau quotes an entire painting, while at others he recalls famous paintings in piecemeal fashion. Often his use of painting is a strategy to undermine the power of literature, as when in *Faust* (1926), a film based on the most imposing literary work in the German tradition, he uses characteristically few titles to elaborate images that must stand in for Goethe's poetry. Omitting crucial scenes in which Goethe addresses the nature of the verbal sign, Murnau chooses instead to quote the work of Rembrandt and Vermeer: the scene of Faust in his study, for example, is based on the Rembrandt engraving Johann Heinrich Lips used as a frontispiece for his 1790 edition of Goethe's text.[41] But Murnau's allusions to the visual arts never suggest that he has fallen back on *mises-en-scène* that are ready to hand for want of imagination; his homage is always also critique, his troping pointed. In the Faust film, for instance, Murnau manages by means of movement to make the play of light more dazzling, more central to the composition than it is even in Rembrandt.

To cite another example, *Nosferatu* (1922), which has its literary source in Bram Stoker's *Dracula*,[42] takes its most vital inspiration from the style and imagery of Caspar David Friedrich; from Friedrich's paintings Murnau predictably borrows, among other things, the figure of the spectator viewed from behind, an index of mediation in Friedrich's work.[43] Although the graveyard by the sea in *Nosferatu* strongly evokes Friedrich's many churchyard scenes, and while Nosferatu's ship recalls the sketches and paintings of Friedrich's coastal period, Murnau's indebtedness to painting is not confined to quotation alone. Indeed, Eric Roh-

Fig. 7. The invasion of the static frame by narrative movement has a decidedly phallic cast in *Nosferatu*.

mer has argued that Murnau's pictorialism dominates his films to the degree that the composition and balance of each shot remains undisturbed despite being subjected to motion.[44] Yet there is an ambivalence towards painting in Murnau's films that is not accounted for by Rohmer's observation. Indeed, Murnau protects film from the encroachment of painting, not by suppressing its presence, but by placing it in the foreground and holding it open to question by the authority of the medium that incorporates it. Of necessity, but sometimes pointedly, Murnau also subsumes pictorial moments within the flow of his narrative, thereby challenging the claim to permanence of fixed representation.

In *Nosferatu*, as in *Broken Blossoms*, the relationship of the pictorial to narrative is sexualized. As a feature of Murnau's style, this is most readily discernible in the strategy that Alexandre Astruc has termed the "invasion of the frame," in which a moving object is represented as slowly and deliberately entering a static frame.[45] This invasion calls attention to the introduction of movement and narrative into the stasis of painting. Repeatedly in the Western tradition but preeminently in Murnau, painting as a spatial, atemporal art tied to the body, is coded as feminine, while writing and narrative are coded as sequential, temporal, and masculine.[46] In *Nosferatu*, for example, the prow of the Friedrich-like vampire ship as it enters the city's harbor, intensifies the phallic nature of this invasion, ironically in that Murnau uses an image taken from Friedrich to undermine static representation by setting it in motion. Nina, towards whom both her "natural" and "unnatural" vampire husbands journey,[47] can be seen as "representing and literally marking out the place (to) which the hero will cross," as Teresa de Lauretis asserts of the female position in narrative cinema.[48] In this respect Nina resembles the fixed space of painting, an observation that is confirmed especially in the frames in which she sits in the seaside graveyard—a Friedrich scene par excellence—with the strong vertical line created by her seated figure echoing that of the crosses in the sand around her. Within her painterly setting, Nina appears to be as rooted and immobile as the crosses—truly the conjunction of image, body, and landscape by means of which de Lauretis defines passive female identification in cinema.[49] Engaged in waiting for the husbands who are racing towards her, Nina is represented in terms that mirror the archetypal structure of Oedipal narrative as de Lauretis reads it, a structure in which the woman's body, "like Demeter's, has become her battlefield and, paradoxically, her only weapon and possession . . . a territory staked out by monsters and heroes."[50]

But the relations among the figures of this triangle are ambiguous and scrambled, even more so than they ultimately prove to be in *Broken Blossoms*. Framed in arched doorways that nevertheless fail ultimately to contain him, Nosferatu materializes, as Eisner has put it, "from the farthest depths of a shot";[51] in other words, like the ship that carries him, he introduces motion into a static composition and suggests a space outside the frame that, in Bazin's reading, is antithetical to painting but characteristic of film.[52] Although *Nosferatu*'s suspense is heightened by Murnau's parallel editing of the race between human husband and vampire, who both appear to be identified with narrative, the image track aestheticizes the human husband, it has been argued, hence feminizing him and rendering him, like his wife, an object of physical attraction for the vampire. Bergstrom's perceptive reading of *Nosferatu* stresses this relation, contending that desire is triangulated here, and that the image of Jonathan is nonnarrative, placing him in a feminine position. Via a series of observations concerning the nature of cinematic viewing in Weimar cinema, in particular that it is a kind of viewing associated with the fine arts, Bergstrom contends that Murnau's films reflect an "erotics of looking."[53] Reading the desire involved in looking at painting as having a passive sexual aim, Bergstrom concludes that the importance Murnau gives to landscape and to pictorial compositions that elicit a contemplative look covertly bespeaks a sexual identity (Murnau's largely inactive homosexuality) that could not be expressed directly in the narrative.[54]

Yet Nosferatu, while tied to the active principle of movement and narrative, cannot be said to occupy the male position exclusively. Not surprisingly in the genre of the monster film, all forms of sexual and narrative energy reside in the monster. As Williams argues, the monster's potency is not simply greater than that of the normal male, but rather of a different kind, a mesmerizing power that suggests, "the monster as double for women."[55] Indeed, Nosferatu is connected closely with coffins and the earth, and the ship on which he makes his voyage toward Nina is called the "Demeter," suggesting that the vampire is linked, as women are, to the cycles of nature. In the final scene, Nina's "unnatural" union with the vampire causes his image literally to dissolve on the screen and ends in her death. In this fatal attraction between woman and vampire, the male position is problematized, even rendered monstrous—or female—for Murnau by virtue of his homosexuality. Yet another ambiguity concerning the identity of the vampire has a role to play here: Nosferatu has rat-like features and soulful eyes, thus embodying a doubleness that is reflected both in his connection with the physical symptoms of the plague (the tooth marks on the necks of the victims) and also in the claim that he is a figment of the imagination. If the question is whether it is the body or mind that is monstrous, then Murnau's answer is that it is both, or each when acting as proxy for the other.

We can say, then, that the manner in which Murnau plays pictorial composition against narrative movement, against the literary, and, especially in the case of *Faust*, against the word, may have its origin not only in the desire to supersede literature, but also in a complex identification with the spatial art of painting that has come to be identified traditionally as female. The male narrative principle is a troubling presence in the text and provokes moments both of cinematic self-assertion and agonistic struggle. Predictably, then, reading and writing are problematized in Murnau films: in one sequence in *Nosferatu*, Nina, who has been forbidden by Jonathan to read *The Book of Vampires*, does so despite his injunction and "falls" as she reads. Even the exaggerated acting typical of cinema during this period cannot account for the actress's expressions: the woman has been seduced by the written text, much in the way that Rousseau and many another male writer has feared women readers would be. Viewed in the context of Murnau's complex attitude towards the high arts, Nina's seduction by reading appears to function additionally as an emblem for the filmmaker's seduction by literature.

Yet questions concerning the status of the cinematic in *Nosferatu* lead us to ask whether there is yet another ambiguity figured in the identity and place of the vampire in Murnau's film. Insofar as Nosferatu's domain—the magical, the fantastic—is recurrently connected with visual tricks, the vampire stands in for cinema as a hybrid text, a distorted formation produced by the overlap and disjunction of several art forms, which, in effect, it vampirizes. The overlay of identities located in the vampire parallels the diverse constitutive elements of cinematic discourse (a problem that, incidentally, affects this stunning film only in theory, as a presented allegory). Doors that move without apparent cause, the ride in the phantom coach for which Murnau used the negative, and the other "trick shots" for which the film was scorned by American audiences and which have been ignored by those who see Murnau's art as organic, and hence necessarily marred by "cheap shots" of this kind: these are tricks produced by means of the cinematic apparatus. Disruptive, distorting, as "unnatural" and fantastic as Nosferatu himself, these moments, in which the cinema itself is put on display, point to a underlying ambivalence concerning the medium, an uncertainty that reinforces Murnau's ambivalent attitude towards movement by concentrating and focusing it in an unnatural or supernatural phenomenon such as the magic door. The vampire's search for human blood, its longing to be a "body with blood in its veins," as Murnau writes concerning the ambition of cinematic movement, ends at last in his death, represented in a trick shot as a dissolving of the image, literally a bloodless fading from the screen.

The self-conscious display of the film medium itself both attracted Murnau—who took justifiable pride in his technical mastery—and disturbed him. The least painterly of Murnau's films, *The Last Laugh* (1924) features a working through of the Oedipal problems besetting relations among the rival arts. What results is an experimentally adopted cinematic narcissism capable of quite simply subsuming the other arts within its own display. In *Nosferatu*, technique had been expressed primarily through the trick photography that the film could not encompass as part of its mode of generalization; in *The Last Laugh*, technique generates a set as artificially constructed as that of *Caligari*, complete with forced perspective.[56] More importantly, technique is rendered palpable as a fetishistic obsession with camera movement.

The apparatus is not only prominent in *The Last Laugh*, it is a theme: its most compelling image is a revolving door whose various panels both reflect images and subject them to motion, recalling various protocinematic devices and emphasizing, as such films generally do, the transumption of the picture frame by the cinematic frame—all of this having to do, as we shall see, with Murnau's sense of urban phantasmagoria as an analogue of the cinema. The dream scene in this film opens with a distorted image of this revolving door, playing on connections between Weimar cinema and psychoanalysis and their joint claim to reveal the inner man; this, too, like the dizzying cityscape, is thematically justifiable. But the moving, doubled, or blurred images, the various subjective shots from the main character's point of view, though in turn carefully anchored in the film's narrative, finally do seem excessive.

Considered to have been the most technically innovative film of Weimar cinema, *The Last Laugh* features a ubiquitous camera that moves freely in all directions.[57] Its occasionally invasive and voyeuristic intrusions call into question its moments of mere aesthetic playfulness, and this aggressiveness renders it a powerful antagonist for the Emil Jannings character. Although the camera does also provide subjective shots from the porter's point of view, it remains essentially adversarial. Relentlessly, the motion of the camera underscores the increasing immobility of the porter; as a character he is left powerless by circumstances in the plot, and—as an image—he is rendered correspondingly motionless by the camera's penetrating gaze. By these means the porter is feminized, while the camera continues to display a remarkable sexual energy. Murnau's fascination with cinematic technique is apparent in the narrative of the camera's movement, in its space-creating motion, transposing visual interest from the movement of images across a pictorial surface to disembodied movement in a frenzied three-dimensional space.

Concerned to allow the images to do the work in his films, Murnau scrupulously avoided subtitles; in *The Last Laugh* the camera is also notoriously able to usurp sound, as when it traces the path traveled by music from a musical instrument to the ear. Even more importantly, by figuring so prominently in the film, the camera distracts the spectator's attention from the narrative by creating a blatant counternarrative of its own.[58] Thus cinema, in this film, subordinates other representational systems to itself. Though "anthropomorphized," as Elsaesser puts it,[59] yet invisible in the diegetic space of the film, the camera is itself in some sense a monster with supernatural powers, as well as a vehicle for the gratification of Murnau's visual pleasure.[60] An Austrian writer quoted by Eisner provides a metaphor for Murnau's obsession with the visual: he wrote of Murnau that he was "a new kind of being who thinks directly in photographs . . . a kind of modern centaur: he and the camera are joined together to form a single body."[61] This image of heterogeneity, of the film artist as a monstrous being—part man and part machine[62]—mirrors the monstrosity of his chosen medium, cinema, and resembles the traditional definition of the monster as "the product of a mixture of different species-types, the parts of which remain species-distinguishable and the whole of which is an anomaly."[63]

Painting and Repression

The Last Laugh notwithstanding, for Murnau cinematography and cinematographic space remain uncomfortably at odds with the prior claims of painting. Nowhere does this tension inform a film more directly than in *Sunrise* (1927), a film finally made in Hollywood though conceived in Germany. The project of this film seems to be to accommodate the painterly style of *Nosferatu* to the cinematic style of *Last Laugh*. If, as Robin Wood has insisted, *Sunrise* is the "most synthetic" of Murnau's films by virtue of the way in which it attempts to conciliate the arts with one another, nevertheless the marriage of cinematic motion to the stasis of painting that takes place here is a tentative one.[64]

The opening shots of the film illustrate the relation of still representation to that of the moving picture as a genealogical one in which the birth of cinema is recorded. In a moment that recalls the opening shots of *The Cabinet of Dr. Caligari*, a poster of a train station in what one critic has termed "Bauhaus-style . . . graphics" is suddenly animated and rendered cinematic as the train represented in the foreground begins to move.[65] That the train itself is emblematic of cinema as well as modernity is well established: filmmakers sensed an affinity between the landscape that unfolds before the gaze of the train passenger and the sequence of moving images presented to the spectator in the theater.[66] The glassed-in train station, emblem of the modern, also has a role to play in *Sunrise*'s evocation of cinema: by virtue of the frames that separate the glass into panes, it represents the manner in which cinema frames and composes reality, thereby addressing obliquely the question of what lies beyond these frames. Only one example of the many grids that Murnau repeatedly imposes upon the image, these frames both contain *and* are emblematic of the tension his films sustain between static composition and motion.[67] Appearing repeatedly throughout *Sunrise*, these divided glass walls contribute to the creation of cinematic space by allowing multiple actions and spaces to be portrayed simultaneously—stressing therefore cinema's claim to three-dimensional space—while providing a reflecting surface upon which lighting and mirror effects are displayed. More importantly, perhaps, the grid that they impose upon the image acts pointedly as a constraint, an effort at containment, thus uneasily reconciling painting and cinema to some degree. Thus the first few frames of *Sunrise* evoke *in nuce* the central aesthetic and theoretical preoccupations of Murnau texts. As Dudley Andrew has rightly pointed out, the obvious "visual surplus" of *Sunrise* and the "precision of the compositions suggests a second text and a second context for meaning."[68] This meaning has much to do with the conflict between pictorial and cinematic space already suggested by the film's opening shots.

Motion at cross purposes, expressed in the form of trains superimposed upon the equivalent of a page, is the subject of the next shot. Here images of trains exist in an extradiegetic space, suggesting that motion itself is at issue here (Hitchcock plays upon this shot in the image of the crossed trains in *Strangers on a Train*), as well as the trajectories of narrated conflict on their collision course. Dividing up the frame as though in a split-screen shot, the following shot, which graphically and thematically resembles a picture postcard, presents conflicting motion once more, but this time in a manner that seems to normalize it by placing it within a naturalistic context. Like the film's opening shot, this shot gives the impression of introducing movement into static visual representation by setting elements within the frame in motion: a steamer moves from the back to the front of the frame, and a man moves from the front toward the back, while the immobile body of a woman forms a strong vertical along the right-hand side. Finally, in the fourth shot, we find the kind of balanced "painterly" composition for which Murnau is noted. Involving the characteristic invasion of the frame by a boat, this shot looks ahead to the synthesis of styles that we will find in the film's concluding section.

In its first section, *Sunrise*, a film whose narrative leans heavily upon the juxtaposition of country and city typical of pastorals, associates the country with static visual representation (to the extent to which this is possible in a moving picture). Allusions to painting abound, but perhaps the most visually striking scene involves a painterly composition in which the wife feeds her chickens, hemmed in on both sides by the doorway and the thick walls that contain her graceful, minimal movements. Motion within the cinematic frame is very deliberate and controlled in the opening sequences; it is generally contained wholly within that frame, and reinforced by framing elements within the composition as well. In fact, in the early part of the film, movement itself can seem disturbing: one of the most ominous moments occurs when the husband's hulking upper body leans towards the wife he thinks he is about to drown (at this moment the spectator's point of view and hers converge) and his tie begins to billow out in the wind, creating movement within the center of the otherwise static frame. Movement in the first third of the film is linked thematically to the narrative and to the problematic expressed there concerning control and lack of control, issues whose origin lies in the libido. Though visually tinged by Expresssionism, what is pictorial about Murnau's compositions has little to do with Expressionist style; the diagonals and cross-diagonals of Expressionism are linked—like the crossed trains in the beginning—to the *narrative* impulse in Murnau, to movement and conflict, not to static representation.[69]

If the country—nature, landscape—is associated with the art of painting in *Sunrise*, it comes as no surprise that the second section of the film, which takes place in the city, is defined as the space of the cinema. Everything speaks for this linkage: as film historians have repeatedly pointed out, cinema is the art of the metropolis.[70] Both spaces converge in a visually surprising sequence as the pastoral space of the country is invaded by a tram moving through the woods. At this point in the film the theme that was briefly articulated in its opening shot is taken up again, this time with the obvious intention of cementing the connection between trains and the cinema, as the couple and the landscape are alternately framed in the train's windows, now subjects, now spectators.

Later, as traffic moving through the city streets converges from all directions upon the country couple, they are an island of immobility, effectively reversing the relation of stasis to movement delineated in the tightly controlled frames of the country scenes. During the course of their day, they enter a church and watch the performance of a marriage. As the bride and groom recite their vows, the man, seated with his wife in one of the pews of the darkened church, is moved to tears, much as the spectator of a movie melodrama might be. As the man and wife leave the church arm in arm under the watching eyes of the wedding guests lined up to receive the newlyweds, the boundaries between spectatorial identification and direct experience become blurred. Reconciliation is effected, as it were, by means of the cinema, but if the wedding ceremony has been experienced as though it were a film, it is a film that contradicts Benjamin's contention that it is in the nature of film to have severed its connection to the ritualistic origins of the work of art, and indeed Murnau's discomfort with the neatness of this plot shows how difficult it is to invalidate Benjamin's insight. Later on, the reconciled couple moves unharmed and unheeding through the same traffic-filled streets and, significantly, a *painted* set representing a country landscape briefly materializes around them. Despite the comic aspect of the sequence—the couple kisses and traffic comes to a halt—the film intends without frivolity to link the newly affirmed stability of the couple with control over motion and with static representation. After the reconciliation of man and wife has been effected, it is fixed by means of a photograph, transformed into what Andrew calls a physical object and icon.[71] Here still photography "embalms time," controlling and containing narrative flux and the unease that it implies for Murnau.[72]

Other moments of self-consciousness about the nature of cinema abound in *Sunrise*: we find them especially in the amusement-park episode, complete with fireworks, whose spectacle of lights and motion made it a favorite cinematic setting. Since this scene with its various rides and lights also recalls the opening shots of Lang's *Metropolis*, the icons of the city converge once again with those of the cinema, while shadow play on the walls recalls a protocinematic form, and gags such as a mysteriously moving sheet (there is a pig under it) allude to cinema's anxiety concerning the uncanniness of its moving images. This middle section of the film, then, takes pains to establish city and cinema as analogues, and to suggest that the more obviously cinematic style that Murnau employs here—a style that is no longer pictorial in its orientation, though it still plays upon the contrast of movement and stasis—produces merely ephemeral visual gags and easy effects. Earlier, the rhythmic motions of the amusement-park section of the film had been foreshadowed by the City Woman's gyrating dance, by means of which she had hoped to seduce the man into sexuality and city life; her swaying body had generated a vision of the city for the man, creating, as Andrew writes, another movie of which he is the sole spectator.[73] *Sunrise* seems to claim that frenetic camera movement and cinematic spectacle are to be rejected, along with the uncontrolled sexuality with which they are aligned.

Initially, the return to the country is signaled by a return to the flat, composed, painterly space that characterizes the first section of the film, but now it is a space that is more receptive to motion, and the couple's sailboat glides gracefully across a moonlit lake without "invading" the frame. In fact, however, the rest of this sequence works to problematize such seemingly effortless accommodation of movement to painterly composition: tranquillity is interrupted by the drama of the storm episode. Ultimately, however, even the chaotic, destructive movement occasioned by the storm serves as an integrating impulse that reconciles static, pictorial composition with a more cinematic style that nevertheless does not obsessively restrain movement. Unlawful sexuality and motion, with which the cinematic style is allied closely, must be accommodated within the controlled space of the frame. Significantly, this third section of *Sunrise* finally has recourse to the parallel montage that produces the dramatic tension of *Nosferatu*. Murnau's montage here alternates between the unfocused efforts of the rescue party to recover the body of the wife, and the body's persistent escape from the confines of the cinematic frame as it floats in and out of view. All is ultimately set to rights: the wife is rescued after the husband has been made to suffer her physical loss, having in the meantime finally repudiated the adulterous sexuality of the City Woman. When the living body of the wife is finally retrieved, the arrangement of the blanket around her head lends her the look of a Madonna, reassociating her with purity and with the subject matter and stasis of painting.

The blurring of sexual identity is rendered in *Nosferatu* through the body of the vampire-monster, who is likewise connected to the "unnatural," magical effects of which cinema is capable; in *The Last Laugh* these effects occur primarily in the camera (regarding itself and not the other media), which is usually said to "take on a life of its own" in this film, but which cannot, considering Murnau's mode of working, finally be said to exist separately from the directorial eye.[74] The apparent shift from the privileging of painting in *Nosferatu* to the flaunting of the apparatus in *The Last Laugh* is not so much an indication that a more cinematic style is being affirmed, but rather that the relation of the painterly to the cinematic is being framed in a new way: in *Nosferatu* it is mutually refractive, in *Last Laugh* it is simply nullified.[75] *Sunrise*, which rearticulates the problem posed by the other two films—likewise in sexual terms—first juxtaposes the two styles and then attempts to forge a more synthetic style from them. The controlled, repressive compositions of the first section of the film are finally loosened to accommodate movement more easily, whereas the chaotic motion and flashiness of its second section is radically restrained. Onto the generically typical contrast of country virtue and purity with urban decadence and sexuality, Murnau has superimposed the contrast of the pictorial with the cinematic, and he has done so by affixing these values to the bodies of the wife and the vamp. It is a commonplace of *Sunrise* criticism that the husband, when he is in the grips of passion, is represented as a monster;[76] Andrew suggests that the film postulates the husband's ethical task as purging himself of his adulterous passion and rechanneling his sexuality in a socially acceptable manner.[77] Yet one wonders about the stability of this situation, for in affirming his marriage to his Madonna-like wife, he seems to wholly repress the carnal desires that occasioned his "monstrosity," and not to convert from adulterous to conjugal desire. Although the heterosexual couple is reunited, just as pictorial and cinematic styles merge, the union is necessarily precarious, one that can only endure so long as controlled painterly compositions keep the upper hand.

As its title suggests, control and sexuality are also the theme of Murnau's last film, *Tabu* (1930), filmed on location in the South Sea islands.[78] While Murnau styled his journey to this site as a pilgrimage to an island paradise, it was an undertaking fraught with artifice. In an unpublished essay entitled "My Voyage to the Happy Isles," he seems to have been acutely aware that, though it was nature he was ostensibly seeking, that nature would for him be inevitably mediated by culture: by playing upon a literary trope, the very title of his essay is revelatory.[79] Just so, passages in Murnau's letters acknowledge his desire to see the Southern Cross because it is the constellation of Melville, Stevenson, and Conrad: "Soon, when we have crossed the Equator, it will shine down on our books and our dreams," he writes, "for it is towards our books and our dreams that we are voyaging."[80] During his stay in Tahiti, Murnau visited Gauguin's grave and the place where Melville was imprisoned, and there he also met and photographed Matisse.[81] Predictably, the South Sea islanders seemed "like pictures from Gauguin come to life."[82] Like Gauguin's, Murnau's view of the natives is shaped by the topos of the noble savage. Unlike Gauguin, however, Murnau does not "go native," but remains an aesthete and intellectual even in the midst of paradise: after his house in Tahiti was completed, Murnau arranged to have his entire library sent from Berlin.[83]

The mélange of cultural signs with which the experience of Tahiti is freighted for Murnau suggests the extent to which literary and painterly pressures must have informed the making of *Tabu*. Murnau does not in the least attempt to adapt his visual style to accommodate native art, as Gauguin did. Allusions to Western painting and to literary topoi are noticeable in *Tabu*, most conspicuously so in the scenes where one would most expect them to be absent, such as the film's idyllic opening section, intended to render the beauty of unspoiled native life as paradisiacal. All of the clichés involving the beauty of the tropics are deployed—the sparkling sunlight on the water, the lush foliage, the nearly naked bodies of the young Tahitian men—but the sheer beauty and rhythm of the images and the choreographed motion of this sequence make it in the final analysis a cinematic tour de force, not an evocation of paradise.

What is initially surprising, then, in this representation of the natural, is the way in which certain poses and groupings of bodies suggest works of art with which Western spectators are familiar: a young spear-thrower is posed in a manner reminiscent of Greek sculpture, and a group of girls bathing in a pool, unknowingly exposed to the voyeurism of young men, calls vividly to mind Poussin's mythological paintings as well as the biblical theme of Susannah and the Elders. Not only does *Tabu* lack documentary sequences (much to Flaherty's chagrin, for this had been his intention), not only does it remain uninfluenced by the approach to space and design of native art, but this film—like other Murnau films—imposes the perspective of European painting upon its images.[84] We might well ask why this is so, particularly when we consider that such allusions are not apparent in the later scenes—those that deal with a "fallen world," with the islands already tainted by the presence of white colonials and Chinese traders—and, in the narrative, with the conditions surrounding the declaration and violation of the taboo against the love between two young natives. As Murnau is said to have been sensitive to native culture, the question as to why European compositions are imposed upon the most visually exciting scenes—scenes in which moving bodies are on display and one shape relieves another in a series of dazzling movements—remains a puzzling one.[85] More striking even than *The Last Laugh*, *Tabu* does not, however, privilege camera movement: it is composition, light, and cutting that produce its effects.

Setting and subject matter—the consequences of tribal laws that govern sexuality even in a "sexually free" society—obviously have great significance for the style of *Tabu*. Hayden White calls attention to the fetishistic character of the noble-savage topos in European culture. Generated by a "pathological displacement of libidinal interest," it is "a projection of repressed desire onto the lives of the natives . . . but, if it is such, it is a desire tainted by horror and viewed with disgust."[86] A dialectical counterpart of the Wild Man, the noble-savage topos is associated with the double response that makes the native at once an object of desire and an object of disgust for indulging in taboo sexual practices such as incest within extended families. Given the evidence of the earlier films, it is tempting to read the imposition of painterliness in *Tabu* as a means of containing libidinal energies, of aestheticizing them and thereby imposing distance upon them.

It seems somewhat sordid to pry so intimately into the connection of life and work. And yet *Tabu* seems almost to strain to make these connections visible, certainly more so than Murnau's other films, even while it repeats and varies their themes and images.[87] Tahiti seems to have provided Murnau with an occasion to represent his conflicting attitudes toward sexuality, and also for acting out his ambivalence about interdiction and constraint. While the islands were associated with a relaxed attitude towards sexual practices, they nevertheless did have rigid prohibitions that Murnau almost compulsively violated: he knowingly and deliberately built his Polynesian house on the sacred site of temple ruins, choosing to live on a taboo site.[88] This violation of native cultural practices is particularly curious in light of Murnau's knowledge of and respect for Polynesian culture and law, but *Tabu* itself appears to shed some light upon it.[89]

Tellingly, in the film's narrative the notion of taboo occurs in two separate but finally conjoined events: in the plight of two lovers who flee from tribal law after the announcement that the young woman has been declared a tribal virgin and is now taboo, and in the issue of a rich oyster bed located on a reef, in a spot that tribal law has also rendered inviolable. (It should be noted that as thematic foci woman and place merge here, just as they do in *Nosferatu*.) Matahi, the young man, violates both taboos, the first because of his love for the woman, the second because the "fallen" island to which they flee has involved him in commercial transactions from which he attempts to extricate himself by diving for the large pearls to be found in the oyster bed. The implicit critique of capitalism is evident, but what is interesting about the second taboo is a subplot revealing its basis not only in tribal law but in common sense: the oyster bed is the home of a particularly fierce school of sharks and colonial law joins tribal law in prohibiting diving there. In this spot a sign is erected on which is written the word "tabu," the irony of course being the conflation of tribal and Western practices expressed by such a sign. Interestingly,

Murnau violated a taboo in a similar place: he set up his cameras on reefs where human sacrifices had been made.[90]

This episode also serves to introduce the notion that tribal law is not only grounded in religion or social practice but also has a "natural" origin (danger to the body). Since they reinforce tribal law and the status quo by implying that there is mortal, not only social, danger in transgression, ideas of this kind have ideological consquences. In particular, the manner in which the taboo on the place merges with the taboo on sexuality in this film suggests that laws regulating sexuality, too, have a meaning beyond the symbolic one, a "natural"—not culturally imposed—significance having to do with matters of life and death. This repressive suggestion, which has a tendency to diminish cultural difference, to undermine rather than to reinforce the contrast that at first appears to be set up between an idyllic native and a fallen colonial world, serves as an additional explanation for the presence of European compositions and topoi in the first section of the film. Not only do these compositions control and give shape to the sensuality of an idyllic world, they serve to underscore the insistence that sexual restraints are also operative in this world. It is noteworthy that Hitu, the tribal representative sent to pursue the fleeing couple, is rarely shown in motion, but is consistently associated with stasis.[91] Put reductively, the regulative presence of Western art shows that there *is* no idyll. It is here, I think, that biographical considerations come into play, and that if we knew more we could probably explain why Murnau chose to live in a taboo place without denying its status as forbidden.

From the perspective of the tribe, the taboo was upon Murnau, although they were said to have been favorably disposed toward him personally, and to have attempted to exorcise the house and Murnau as well.[92] As Eisner points out, Murnau's transgressions were uncharacteristic because he was very superstitious; he was interested in the supernatural and often consulted fortune-tellers. In this instance,

> misfortune then followed misfortune: as he approached a reef that was "tabu," in order to set up the camera there, an enormous wave arose, the canoes were flung against the rocks, two cameras sank to the bottom, and many feet of exposed film were spoiled. Some of the extras fell inexplicably ill, and even some of the principals. . . . The Chinese cook was drowned in mysterious circumstances.[93]

Finally, Murnau himself was killed in a car accident in Hollywood, shortly before *Tabu* was released in 1931.[94] Rational explanations, of course, come to mind for all of these events, but it does in general seem as though Murnau had embarked upon a suicide mission. When the tribal chief was later presented with a photograph of Murnau by his brother, he refused to take it because for him a photograph was a dead thing.[95] Motionless, composed, this photograph can be considered the final icon of a life and vision held under constraint.

HERZOG'S UNASSIMILABLE BODIES

Subject to repeated puncturing by nondiegetic material, by shots that exist for the sake of presenting images to our view, the sometimes enigmatic narratives of Werner Herzog's films have prompted a range of explanation for their peculiar textual status.[96] Following Elsaesser, Timothy Corrigan suggests that there is a discernible quality of resistance in Herzog's narratives, "which in themselves and as an opus consciously muddle that classic distinction between narrative and non-narrative form."[97] Though nonnarrative moments in cinema certainly need not be documentary, one explanation for such moments in Herzog's films resides in his predilection for documentary images. Indeed, while Herzog's "documentaries" are very much the product of authorial intervention at every conceivable level, including that of the profilmic, his fiction films— *Fitzcarraldo* (1982), for instance—contain material that has the characteristics of documentary footage.[98]

What appears to interest Herzog in his use of documentary material is what Kaja Silverman has called the "inarticulate real."[99] In contradistinction to Hollywood's illusions, Herzog speaks of his films as containing "unmediated life, filmed on the spot, without mediation," by which he also means to suggest that his films somehow take up the material world into the image.[100] Well publicized, too, is Herzog's preference for a "physical approach" to filmmaking, a procedure that is seemingly enhanced for him when it takes place under extreme conditions, preferably in a situation of some danger (again *Fitzcarraldo*, and *La Soufrière* [1976]).[101] *Of Walking on Ice*, a memoir of Herzog's trek from Munich to Paris in the winter of 1973–1974, records his indifference to—or relish of—physical and mental pain.[102] It is as though Herzog were convinced that his "physical approach" literally allows the body of the filmmaker to leave its traces upon the body of his texts, thus allowing him, too, to enter the films along with the images of his actors.

Taking up Silverman's suggestion concerning the inaccessibility of the "real" to language, Elsaesser has elaborated upon the manner in which "the question of the body" is central to Herzog's films because of its "resistance to discourse."[103] Herzog's characters tend to have an uneasy relation to language, whether they be Kaspar (*The Enigma of Kaspar Hauser* [1974]), who lives years of his life without language at all, Bruno (*Stroszek* [1976]) who, rather than explaining his emotions, builds a "schematic model" of his feelings, or Fini Straubinger (*Land of Silence and Darkness* [1970]), who cannot explain in words how it feels to be blind and deaf. Indeed, virtually all of Herzog's films are populated by marginal beings who resist language or who affirm its insufficiency to produce "true" meaning. For Herzog, their resistance to language is clearly a sign of their purity—the "purest of the pure" being those who are entirely silent.[104] More importantly, this resistance has the effect of rendering such figures opaque and image-like: in Herzog's films, this kind of image, an image that is visually striking but not wholly susceptible to verbal explanation, is coded as the genuinely "filmic" image.

It is their status as image that gives these characters their aura, the character of an unmediated sign: each has a body "which insists on the distance between itself and signification";[105] their opacity gives them the quality of an unassimilated image, an image that to some extent retards or actually interrupts the narrative flow with its nonnarrative effect. Presenting the visual and the filmic as privileged and beyond the purview of language, Herzog has repeatedly claimed that his films have their origin in images. "Seeing" a film is an act defined by its immediacy.[106] Despite the pronounced literary subtext in these films, the dismissal of writing as a secondary mediation in contrast with the immediacy of the image occurs persistently in Herzog. It is especially obvious when, in *The Enigma of Kaspar Hauser*, the words of Kaspar's name spring up as the watercress he has planted, becoming living things in a triumphant romantic gesture that recalls Hölderlin's longing, in *Bread and Wine*, for "words which spring up like flowers." By means of gestures such as these, Herzog has, in his view, redeemed language by transforming it first into a thing and then into an image. By infusing Kaspar's name with the corporeality and life that a name so conspicuously lacks, Herzog has reintroduced the materiality of the real into this sign in an act of collaboration that corresponds to his treatment of Kaspar as an unassimilable image.

Sharing the unmediated status of the image, these marginal figures nevertheless sometimes have a determining role in the narrative, indeed they are often the central character whose story the film tells. These beings figure both as images insusceptible of absorption into the narrative—

calling attention to their status *as* image—and as the bodies through and upon which the story is enacted. In this sense, they, too, can be said to be hybrid beings, images of the cinematic as well as cinematic images. Questions remain about the kind of narrative in which such figures are involved. The lack of erotic impulse in Herzog's narratives is pronounced: the sexualized body is not of interest to Herzog and in his characters libidinal impulses tend to be sublimated into an all-consuming vision or to disappear into interiority by some other means.[107] For this reason, perhaps, Herzog does not invest a great deal of energy in the representation of women: they are conspicuously absent from his films and, when they are present, they do not tend to function as the objects of desire towards which the narrative process moves (a notable exception in this regard is Lucy of *Nosferatu*, 1978, but she shares this position vis-à-vis the bisexual Nosferatu with her husband Jonathan).

As Silverman has pointed out in her reading of *The Enigma of Kaspar Hauser*, before his "fall" into a cultural order that he in fact never fully enters, Kaspar is "outside of language and outside of difference," and later resists the patriarchal narrative with which he is equipped.[108] No doubt one can account for the fluidity of gender identification among all of these characters on the grounds of their incomplete identification with the symbolic: we see a marked imperviousness to gender identification in Kaspar's enthusiasm for knitting that so shocks Lord Stanhope and in his general refusal to distinguish between male and female tasks. We see it also in Bruno's mothering impulse towards the prostitute Eva in *Stroszek*. More radically, we see it in *Even Dwarfs Started Small* (1970) in the wholly asexual, Beckett-like creatures who are seemingly blind, have no language, and are virtually indistinguishable from one another. Among Herzog's visionaries gender ambiguities as such are not an issue, though here, too, there are anomalies: although Fitzcarraldo has certainly entered the symbolic order, his all-consuming passion for music and specifically for opera suggest a displacement of libidinal interest that Herzog probably intended to counteract by the introduction of Claudia Cardinale into a film to which she is in nearly every other sense peripheral. While Aguirre's desire for the conquest of territory is certainly in keeping with traditional narrative desire, it is interesting to note that, as he falls more deeply into madness, he has incestuous designs upon his own daughter, thus suggesting a collapse of difference along another axis. We can say, then, that the peculiarly "filmic" nature of these characters is also linked to their ambiguous sexuality.

Conspicuous for their lack of erotic investment in the narrative process, Herzog's films displace the libido onto the image, generating an "erotics of looking" that relates them to the films of Murnau.[109] Herzog, who looks to Murnau's films with reverence, takes them as his model for the aestheticization of landscape, intensifying the process in so doing.[110] As I claimed above, for Murnau, the imposition of a static and painterly composition upon the cinematic frame is a means of containing libidinal energies and displacing them onto the image. Herzog's long and static takes hold the image longer than we expect them to. Sometimes, however, the characters escape the camera's gaze, as in a sequence involving the sideshow exhibits in *Kaspar Hauser*. As Paul Coates has observed, in such moments the camera seems to "round them up" again, containing the escaped characters once more within the frame in order, as Coates claims, "to dissolve the modern distinction between still photography, which presents fragments of a movement, and painting, where the ideality of the distilled moment justifies its fetish quality."[111]

Landscape is an emblem of the feminine in our culture, and insofar as Herzog wants to "direct" these landscapes—to control Mother Nature—he attempts to regulate the feminine under his directorial authority. Both the vehicle of an unattainable, visionary beauty and, as the sublime, the place of death, the natural landscape provides the images with which the imagination works (as in the example of Kaspar's dream of the Caucasus) as well as the setting within which characters are situated. In this displacement of an ambiguous feminine we can locate the way in which Herzog's films suggest an erotic narrative, at least for the filmmaker. Herzog's characters are very much "figures in a landscape," and must first be understood in their relation to this landscape;[112] like the figures in Murnau's *Nosferatu*, they are more particularly figures in landscape paintings, especially, again, those of Caspar David Friedrich. Although the feminine, then, is the aestheticized landscape into which Herzog's characters are placed, it must also be said that the marginal characters (especially Kaspar, Bruno, and the aborigines of *Where the Green Ants Dream* [1984]) as bodies acculturated only imperfectly through language, are to that extent "natural" and feminine as well. The continuity of these characters with the natural world—with the mother in a pre-Oedipal unity—is another aspect of their ambiguous gendering.

It is no accident that *Nosferatu* (1922), the Murnau film that alludes most pointedly to the paintings of Friedrich, should be the one which Herzog chose to remake, since it is from this film that Herzog derives the attitudes toward landscape that we find in so many of his other films. One can, of course, list specific visual allusions to Friedrich in both *Nosferatu* films: the seaside graveyard; the sailing ship; the figure of Jonathan as wanderer in long shot, a small figure against the sublime mountainscape; Jonathan as a halted traveler and spectator figure; the clouds and fog in the mountains, the gnarled Friedrich oak we see on Jonathan's ride. (Additionally, in Herzog, there is the seaside scene with Jonathan and Lucy that recalls "Monk by the Sea.") Further, both Murnau and Herzog use the technique of interpolating landscape shots in order to delay narrative movement, and both also use the opposite device of setting Friedrich's clouds in motion, thereby announcing their ability to release the static image into movement.

But specific borrowings are not at issue here. It is not surprising, when we recall the Romantic cast of Herzog's imagination, that he would turn to Friedrich as a model, especially given the mediation of Friedrich through Murnau. It is, in fact, precisely the issue of mediation itself that I take to be decisive here, an issue addressed overtly by Friedrich's famous *Rückenfigur*, the spectator figure with the averted gaze. As Joseph Koerner has pointed out, the function of this figure is paradoxical, as it is "site of both our identification with, and our isolation from the painted landscape."[113] Such figures are necessary to a representation of the Kantian sublime, considering that *The Critique of Judgment* locates sublimity as a subject effect: as figures for the gaze, they function as a point of entry into the painting and its landscape on the part of its beholder. Yet often the bodies of these spectator figures impede our view (as, for example, in "Woman in Front of the Setting Sun"), and the figure's absorbed viewing seems to create a fourth wall that excludes us from the space of the painting. The discomfort that we feel as beholders of Friedrich's paintings derives from the manner in which they invite us in and exclude us simultaneously: this effect constitutes Friedrich's mode of Romantic irony.

In Herzog's films there is a consuming interest in the image of a body whose availibility to the eye—but not to analysis—is what makes it filmic. Herzog is attempting to offer us, then, insofar as it is possible, an experience of an "unmediated vision" of the kind to which not even Friedrich, whose paintings are so clearly the "products of the mind's mediating vision," would aspire.[114] It is here that film promotes itself over painting: in the scene from Herzog's *Nosferatu* in which Jonathan is shot from behind as a seated traveler in a "sea of fog," the camera pans briefly to the right in order to reveal the object of his gaze, suggesting the flexibility of cinematic vision in contrast with painterly vision, and suggesting as well its easier access to the sublime. At the same time, however, Herzog wants to make us aware of the resistance that his figures offer to our penetrating gaze, thus setting up a paradoxical spectatorial relation that owes its structure to Friedrich after all. The final irony here involves the degree to which the cinematic text itself, precisely in the moment of its self-assertion, is mediated by painting.

But what of these characters as vehicles of a narrative impulse? Kaspar Hauser is perhaps the most interesting example in this regard, for he is literally dragged into the world of narrative after having been forcibly ejected from the cellar hole in which he had hitherto lived in an "oceanic" state.[115] The black-caped man who initiates Kaspar's entry into narrative, a symbolic father whose identity nevertheless remains enshrouded in mystery, resembles no one so much as Dr. Caligari in his black cape. As in some measure the "founding text" of German cinema and as an allegory of film per se, *The Cabinet of Dr. Caligari* would naturally speak to a filmmaker anxious to create a bridge between German films of the Weimar period and those of his own time.[116] If we take the mysterious black-cloaked man of *Kaspar Hauser* to be Kaspar's symbolic father, it seems likely that he functions here as the symbolic father of German cinema as well. Within the overall narrative of the film, it is the Caligari figure who intervenes with violence at various junctures in order, it would appear, to be able to direct its course. This violence, in turn, generates in the imagination of Kaspar a succession of visionary images that, like Herzog's films, begin with landscapes. When, in one dream sequence, Kaspar creates a mythical landscape of the Caucasus, a landscape with golden temples for which there has been no equivalent in his experience, Kaspar is creating with natural signs, like Herzog in hoping to bring "the real" into his filmmaking. It would seem, then, that Herzog understands his films (like Kaspar himself in this regard) not to conform wholly to the Oedipal narrative of *Caligari*. On the other hand, Herzog also understands them to have been generated by the pressures of an Oedipal cinema, much as Kaspar's visions are generated by the violence of his symbolic father.

In particular, it is the narrative structure of such films that Herzog resists but cannot entirely do without. A cinematic borrowing stands behind Kaspar's final vision foretelling and giving visual expression to death: the mountain in Fritz Lang's *Destiny*.[117] In Lang's film, Death himself functions both as a symbolic father who prevents the union of a pair of young lovers and as the closure in which every narrative act must culminate. There is a sense, then, that for Herzog "Papas Kino," as the

93

Oberhausen manifesto put it, is not dead, but must, in fact, provide the metaphorical blow on the head, the narrative closure that is necessary even for a film so relentlessly image-oriented as Herzog's.[118] Herzog's narratives are linear and episodic, quest romances that often culminate, however, in images of circular movement, like that of Aguirre's circling raft or Stroszek's ski lift.[119] Time and again in Herzog's films, the figure of the circle gives visual expression to the impeding effect of the image on the directedness of narrative movement; refusing to be indefinitely delayed, the fathers' stories sweep the resisting images along their paths.

WITCHCRAFT, VISION, AND INCEST:
DREYER'S DAY OF WRATH

In a review essay published in 1922, Carl Dreyer makes the following pronouncement concerning a newly released film by Benjamin Christensen, a fellow Dane: "It has long been an open secret that *The Witch* is based upon the medieval witch persecutions and from there draws parallels between the famous sexual excesses in the convents of that time—and modern female hysteria."[120] Though released in 1943 and welcomed by the Danes as a text that advocated resistance to the Nazi occupation, *Day of Wrath*, Dreyer's own film on the subject of witchcraft, speaks more directly to the topic of female sexuality and its containment than it does to any other form of oppression.[121]

Dreyer's psychological preoccupations seem hardly surprising when we consider that his filmmaking had its origins in the theater of Ibsen and that it had strong connections to German Expressionist cinema. Furthermore, Dreyer's noted "abstract" style—perhaps most pronounced in *The Passion of Joan of Arc* (1927)—was defined by Dreyer himself as "an expression for the perception of an art which demands that an artist shall abstract from reality in order to reinforce its spiritual content, whether this is of a psychological or purely aesthetic nature."[122] Women and female sexuality in particular are the focus of Dreyer's psychological explorations; the Dreyer heroine wields a sexual power that is "purely supernatural."[123] This is most obviously true of Anne in *Day of Wrath*, who is depicted simultaneously as desiring woman with access to the gaze, as artist, and as witch. In *Day of Wrath*, as I will argue, filmmaking allies itself with the visual arts and opposes itself to writing, while claiming that its "power of invocation," its "power to call up the Quick and the Dead"—together with its "evil eye"—are a form of "witch's work."

Once again cinema's territorial struggle is sexualized: in *Day of Wrath*, somewhat remarkably, cinema's ordinarily male-gendered power is problematized and figured as female.

Like Murnau, Dreyer was celebrated for his pictorialism, for exerting a control over the image that extended to the bodies of his actors, over whom he was said to "cast a spell,"[124] and whose movements often have the heaviness of people under hypnosis.[125] In *Joan of Arc*, the stillness of the human body and its arrangement within the frame lend it a sculptural quality. Visual detail for the film was based on illuminations in medieval manuscripts, and it is with undisguised self-consciousness that its compositions evoke these models.[126] In *Day of Wrath*, Dreyer makes frequent use of tableau scenes in which movement is deliberate and kept to a minimum, giving the effect of period vignettes frozen in time, like painting. The spaces of the film and their visual composition have been compared to the paintings of Vermeer and, as Kracauer puts it, other "Dutch Masters brought to life";[127] in more than one scene the configuration of the village notables strongly evokes the group portraits of Frans Hals. In an earlier film, *Michael* (1924), Dreyer addressed the relation of portraits to the bodies of their subjects as well as to those of the artists who painted them. Since its central character, a painter, is modeled upon Rodin, *Michael* establishes a triadic relationship among painting, sculpture, and filmmaking as it attempts to delineate the boundaries of visual representation and the erotic.[128] As in the case of Murnau, for whom the stasis represented by painting is a means of "fixing" desire, the painter in *Michael* hopes that his own painting will have this effect. But in one sense painting fails markedly: in *Michael* "the act of painting only finishes with the final tableau: [the painter's] death."[129] As we shall see, in *Day of Wrath*, it is visual representation—albeit played out within a literary context—that signifies female desire, but offers neither its fulfillment nor its attenuation.

Set in seventeenth-century Denmark, *Day of Wrath* tells the story of a young woman, Anne, who is married to a pastor, Absalon, old enough to be her father. When one day Absalon's son from his first marriage, Martin, returns home, he and Anne, who have never met, are strongly attracted to one another. Later, when Anne tells Absalon of her ensuing affair with Martin, Absalon dies, whereupon Absalon's mother Merete accuses Anne of witchcraft. Anne, who has learned that her own mother had been accused of witchcraft but had been saved from burning because the influential Absalon was determined to marry Anne, confesses to being a witch and is burned at the stake. Clearly, the theme of incest is overdetermined here: Absalon and his wife are of an age to be father and daughter (that their marriage has perhaps never been consummated, as the film suggests, only adds to the ambiguity of their relationship); Absalon is the spiritual father of his congregation, of which Anne is a member; Merete's disapproval of her son's young and beautiful wife is fraught with sexual jealousy; and finally, most importantly, though they are not related by blood, Anne and Martin are mother and son by marriage.[130] Oddly enough, the subject of incest, though central to the film and to its representational strategies, has not been a topic generally addressed by critics of Dreyer's film.

Earlier, it was suggested that witchcraft and sexuality are linked for Dreyer; and, of course, this connection has been claimed concerning witchcraft as an historical phenomenon: the witch, whose craft it is to conjure with hair and fingernail parings, with the things of the body, "ensures the survival of the pagan forces of desire."[131] Indeed, the link between sexuality and witchcraft is obvious in texts as diverse as Goethe's *Faust* and the movie versions of *The Hunchback of Notre Dame*. In being consigned to the flames, the witch is represented symbolically as consumed by her own passion and in her own element; her body is also burned so that the contagion it is thought to carry will not spread. In Dreyer's film where, as Raymond Durgnat has observed, "all the respectable bourgeois citizens . . . are clad in long black angular garments which encase their bodies like coffins," the sight of a witch's naked flesh during torture is doubly shocking.[132]

Somewhat predictably, both sexual behavior and witchcraft are presented in the context of nature in *Day of Wrath*, beginning with the herbs "from under the gallows" that the old witch, Herlof's Marte, sells to her female customer in the opening scene of Dreyer's film. In the horrifying scenes that follow Marte's capture, we hear an extraordinarily cat-like screech signaling the beginning of her torture, and more than once the shadows of leaves trace a pattern on Marte's and Anne's faces, as though marking them with the dark forces of nature. Signifying a release from the constraints of the social order that Dreyer's severe interiors reflect, nature is the scene of Anne and Martin's lovemaking. While the lovers run hand in hand through the fields, and while their bodies, later, disappear behind trees and beneath grasses, the always mobile camera, too, seems to have a new kind of freedom. Having escaped Dreyer's oppressive interiors, the camera's freedom expresses itself in a fascination with the wealth of newly available objects for scrutiny: trees and grasses shot from a variety of perspectives constitute stunning montage sequences, and the camera's pans to treetops stylize its enactment of the natural by the lovers below.

In Dreyer's film, desire and witchcraft are signified simultaneously by means of the look: as Anne becomes more and more consumed with desire for Martin, her look grows bolder—she no longer timidly averts her glance as in the opening scenes—until it virtually seems to smolder. Anne's eyes are read by each of the central characters in turn: only for Absalon are they "childlike and pure"; for Martin they are "fathomless" and have a "quivering flame" that, as Anne says to Martin, "you kindled"; while for Merete, who will finally denounce her as a witch, the flames in Anne's eyes are hellfire. Anne's eyes are linked to the camera as well, not by point-of-view shots (there are very few of these), but rather in a repeated similarity of movement between her body and the camera, as when, for instance, she surreptitiously enters the room and watches Absalon's interrogation of Marte, and when later, during the storm, Anne prowls around the room, staring fixedly, at exactly the same pace as the camera making its movements.[133]

Since *Day of Wrath* figures witchcraft as a negative aspect of nature's power, it is always able to provide a "natural" explanation for "supernatural" events by anchoring this power in the female body.[134] (Here is another point of correspondence with Murnau, whose *Nosferatu* imagistically compares the vampire with a jackal, and suggests, as Wood has argued, the connection of both with repressed sexuality, with the body's "animal instincts.")[135] It is fitting, then, that one of the recurrent images of the film is (Eve's) apple tree: occurring first in Martin's songbook, as the dominant image of a folksong in which a young woman falls out of an apple tree into her lover's arms, next in an erotic passage from the *Song of Songs* that Anne chooses to read aloud during family prayers, and finally in a stylized drawing created by Anne (a design, it would appear, for cross-stitch embroidery), of which she says pointedly to Martin, "my apple tree has only one blossom." Functioning in these contexts both as cultural construct and as emblem of nature, the apple tree with its religious and literary associations allows female sexuality likewise to be seen from this double perspective. And, while it is Absalon and Martin who read the folksong with its story of female seduction (Absalon begins the reading and Martin takes over in the middle, foreshadowing the way in which he will also appropriate his father's wife), in the latter examples of Bible reading and drawing it is Anne, affirming her desire, who revises the image positively and adopts it for herself.

While these narrative and imagistic strategies would not be surprising in the work of a feminist filmmaker, they take us aback when they occur in a film made by a man. Although various psychological explanations suggest themselves for Dreyer's persistent identification with women in his films—one critic refers to the "bisexual positioning" of the Dreyer text—these explanations would not further this discussion.[136] What is of interest is the manner in which—in accordance with tradition—the pictorial is once again conflated with the feminine, while writing and narrative so obviously belong to the male sphere. The film's diegesis, for instance, begins with the image of a hand writing a text that is dated and signed, a text stating that Herlof's Marte has been denounced as a witch and must be seized and stand trial. Two other official handwritten texts follow, one recording another Church decree concerning Marte, the other attesting to Marte's confession of guilt. In every sense emblems of male authority, these are writings that the remainder of the film—through plot and imagery—works to undermine. Marte's "confession," for instance, is obviously a compromised one, and Absalon's signature upon it both seals and covers over his own guilty acts. In this manner, the male appropriation of the signifier—we see the hand with its quill—as well as the process of writing a "story," the sequential telling of events that constitutes narration, are radically called into question as reliable, veridical acts.[137] Martin, who is virtually released from the male world during his affair with Anne, is at the beginning and end of the film reconnected to the written word: siding with the law represented in the written word, he will turn against Anne in the final moments.

The "female" perspective of *Day of Wrath* is apparent most literally in a remarkable moment in which Anne is also represented as an artist. Seated at her embroidery screen, she is stitching a design in which a woman is walking along a flower-strewn path; behind her screen, yet visible through it, is Martin, who stands watching her. As David Bordwell has astutely pointed out: "The images of Martin and Anne on both sides of the embroidery rack reproduce those replicas of artists sighting through grids in order to construct correct perspective upon a picture plane. The lovers are bound to each other in and through the relations of pictorial representation."[138] In his essay, Bordwell includes a reproduction of Albrecht Dürer's woodcut of a draftsman using a *lucinda* to draw a nude, the same woodcut used by Svetlana Alpers to represent the Albertian model of representation as that in which "the relationship of the male artist to the female observed, who offers her naked body to him to capture in his drawing, is part and parcel of the commanding attitude toward the world assumed by this model of representation."[139] What has been overlooked by Bordwell is the fact that this moment in Dreyer's film figures a strategic role reversal: gender roles are scrambled, for it is Martin upon whom the artist's grid is placed here. Martin is later shown to hold

Fig. 8. Anne and Martin are coupled with the incestuous Venus and Amor of Anne's unfinished tapestry.

the position within the space of the embroidered picture occupied in the finished embroidery by a little boy, who is represented holding the woman's hand. As Bordwell suggests, the affair between Anne and Martin occurs within the context of pictorial representation, a sphere that has repeatedly been identified in *Day of Wrath* as a female sphere. In a parallel episode evoking the camera, Anne is observed watching the spectacle of Marte's immolation through a leaded window that when shot from the inside—Anne's point of view—imposes a grid upon the spectacle and then, when shot from the outside, creates a grid upon her face. Dreyer's camera, positioning itself on both sides of the artist's grid, questions Albertian representation by seeing the female perspective as characteristically doubled, both looking and looked at.

Overlooked additionally in Bordwell's essay is the fact that the embroidery, quite clearly, depicts Venus and her son Amor, a mother and son pair about which mythology makes suggestions of incest. The representation of the sexual relationship between Anne and Martin as incestuous occurs among a series of other metaphorically incestuous relationships

99

between men and women. It finds expression, notably, in a reading produced by Anne—she is both a maker and a reader of images—concerning an image in nature: on one of their walks through the countryside, scene of their lovemaking, Anne and Martin come upon a willow tree overlooking a lake, of which Anne says that it "yearns for its own reflection." A variant on the Expressionist double, this image of narcissistic desire—the repudiation of otherness—is a mirror image of the lack of difference for which incest has long been a metaphor in the Romantic tradition. The notion of incest has a role to play in the history of witchcraft as well: according to tradition, the witch or sorceress is said to be the offspring of an incestuous union between mother and son.[140]

At this point in our analysis, we must turn to the nondiegetic opening images, the illuminated manuscript framing the narrative (with the exception of two images at the end, it opens and closes the film), by means of which the film self-consciously lays out its representational systems. As the soundtrack provides the traditional *dies irae* melody, the image track juxtaposes a pictorial with a written text: the manuscript that gradually unwinds on the screen presents a series of woodcuts depicting, on the left, events that will take place on the Day of Judgment, while on the right it presents the text of a poem.[141] As each stanza of the poem is accompanied by a woodcut that illustrates it, and since both image and word are used to tell the same story, their relation seems defined initially as mutually supportive. But this definition, as we have seen, is what Dreyer's film works to undermine. Even here, in fact, the visual impression of imagistic and verbal text side by side is one that suggests lockstep juxtaposition rather than the integrative harmony of differences. And, when we examine the relationship of the texts to one another more closely, we see that it is necessarily oblique. The shadow of the Cross constantly superimposed upon the manuscript as it unwinds functions as the stamp of ideological authority—the Christian system of belief enforced by the authority of the Church—an authorization binding these two representational systems together in regimentation rather than in fusion. Likewise, the fateful and familiar *dies irae* melody—the only nondiegetic sound used in this film—attempts to minimize their difference by locating the manuscript more firmly within the security of a familiar cultural context, but this melody is later disrupted by human screams.[142]

Rather than presenting the spectator with a harmonious whole, then, the opening frames of the film isolate cinematic discourse into its component parts, locked together only under the aegis of cultural violence, and display the heterogeneity of the cinematic medium to our view.[143] As we have seen, *Day of Wrath* increases the initial tension between the systems of images and writing by stressing repeatedly the manner in which—as in Griffith's *Broken Blossoms*—they are sexualized, the one allied with the feminine position and the other with the masculine. Dreyer, very much a visually oriented filmmaker, appears repeatedly in his films not only to privilege the pictorialism with which he connects female expression, but also to identify with the female position in a patriarchal system that monitors the expression of sexuality. In the textual system of *Day of Wrath*, the woman who expresses desire is both a witch and a woman who commits incest. (As the daughter of a witch, she is coded as the offspring of incest as well.) Tellingly, Anne does not contend the accusation of witchcraft with which the narrative closes: her confession, the film implies, is a first and final assertion of identity with her mother. Similarly, Dreyer identifies his art with witchcraft and with incest, and the concluding images of the film confirm this identification.[144] As one might expect, the final woodcut of the illuminated manuscript represents the crucified Christ. Persisting beyond this image is the shadow of the Cross, now in isolation upon a white background. In the final image, the Cross is transformed by means of two bars into the witch's sign: the sphere of visual representation is reclaimed as female and transgressive.

We can now return to the quotation from Dreyer with which we began our reading, in which Dreyer establishes a connection between witchcraft and sexual excess on the one hand, and "modern female hysteria" on the other. In her essay "Sorceress and Hysteric," Catherine Clément convincingly reads the cultural positions of witch and hysteric as mirror opposites: the hysteric, insofar as she internalizes the erotic and expresses it in symptoms, is "the witch in reverse, turned back within herself."[145] Perhaps it is no accident, then, that critics of Dreyer's films have used the term "hysterical discourse,"[146] in which they see a "displacement away from the inherent emotionality of the action," onto the mise-en-scène and into "the chaste form of photographic compositions."[147] The witch's expression of desire in the diegesis of *Day of Wrath* is mirrored, then, by the repression of desire that is exemplified by the pictorialism of its style.

THE PHANTOM OF THE CINEMA: BODY AND VOICE

I have been concerned with the way in which the self-understanding of cinema is defined in relation to the sister arts of literature and painting and with the manner in which this self-understanding is psychoanalytically and metaphorically grounded in the human body. In confronting the knowledge that it is not an organic but a heterogeneous medium comprised of several representational systems, film may figure itself as a wounded, mutilated, or castrated body, or, alternatively, as a monstrous hybrid, produced by a mixture of different species that retain their own characteristics. In the figuration of film as the offspring of unorthodox conjunctions between more traditional art forms, the relations among film's representational systems are rendered ambiguous. With the addition of sound, this situation can be more complex, yet is often rendered similarly.

After all, the introduction of sound does not necessarily ease or smooth over the relations among film's other representational systems. Brecht built on this idea in devising the songs that disrupt epic theater. As Mary Ann Doane has pointed out, following Hanns Eisler and Theodor Adorno, sound does not necessarily contribute to the semblance of a more unified filmic body (the notion of this body remaining phantasmatic in any case) but rather "carries with it the potential risk of exposing the material heterogeneity of the medium."[148] I have suggested already that sound contributes to the impression of disjunction in *Day of Wrath*. Using Rupert Julian's classic horror film, *The Phantom of the Opera* (1925), I will conclude this chapter on hybrid conjunctions by sketching out briefly the manner in which silent cinema, in a defensive reaction to the uncanniness it perceives in its lack of voice—perhaps precisely because so often accompanied by live music not of its own production— may figure the body that houses voice as monstrous.

Central to this variant on the "Beauty and the Beast" story is the representation of the "phantom" as a malevolent being but also as a kind of *genius loci*, or presiding spirit, of the Paris Opera, whose cellar and underground passages he inhabits. Though conflicting stories circulate concerning the phantom's appearance, he does not allow himself to be seen, but appears, rather, to the young opera singer with whom he is in love as a melodious and seductive voice—so seductive, in fact, that she agrees to leave her noble lover to descend into the depths with him in return for the immortal singing voice with which he promises to endow her. We learn that he is both a musician—he plays the organ as well as sings—and a practitioner of the black arts, and that, instead of being ghostly, a mere phantom, he is indeed corporeal, a man behind whose mask is the misshapen face of a monster. He is also a man who desires and is determined to possess the singer, whose beautiful body alone can redeem him.

Despite the fact that *Phantom of the Opera* is loosely linked to the genre of the opera film, what remains curious about it is the fact that its setting and its subject matter are nevertheless innately antithetical to the silent cinema. We watch the ballerinas dance and we watch the enactment of brief scenes from Gounod's *Faust*, but we hear nothing: all is spectacle and visual surface, for in this setting *Faust* cannot be rendered either in music or in words. Unlike Murnau's slightly later *Faust* (1926), this film makes no attempt to usurp the opera by means of the cinematic medium: it simply omits music and song. When the phantom, who represents the spirit of music and the power of voice, appears in public, it is only during a masked ball, where he is costumed as the "Red Death." Not only, then, does voice appear as death—silent cinema's inversion of the anxiety concerning the uncanniness of silent bodies, including its own—but it appears in the context of a work of literature, Poe's *Masque of the Red Death*, a gothic tale that can be seen as a generic precursor. Sound and voice in this silent film, then, are thus doubly burdened in belonging to the domain of literature, towards which the cinema takes such conflicting positions. To put it schematically, *Phantom of the Opera* identifies its own visual surface with the beautiful body of the female singer and claims that its images would be desecrated by a monstrous conjunction with sound, just as sound, it suggests, is "defaced"—and necessarily masked—when it is embodied in the image.

Incorporation: Images and the Real

> Oh, Chardin! It is not white, or red or black you mix
> on your palette, it is the very substance of
> things themselves.
> —*Diderot*[1]

> A man who concentrates before a work of art is
> absorbed by it. He enters into this work of art the way
> legend tells of the Chinese painter when he viewed
> his finished painting.
> —*Benjamin*[2]

TROMPE L'OEIL EFFECTS

As a preoccupation of the literary imagination, the tantalizing gap between signified and signifier has a long history, which suggests that the desire to merge the "real" and representation has been one of the aims of writing from its beginnings. An awareness of the disjunction between the factuality of the real in general and the inability of language not only to represent it but somehow to cross over into its domain informs fiction and poetry alike. This desire may surface in fiction, for example, as the desire to write upon the body—seductive epistles are written on a lover's backside in Laclos' *Liaisons dangereuses*—or, in a more radical form, actually to inscribe the body, this being the function of the gnomic, sadistic writing machine in Kafka's *Penal Colony*. Poetry's earliest history points to a relation between object and text: the epigrams of the Greek Anthology make use of the fiction of being inscribed upon urns and statues, a device on which ecphrastic poetry sometimes relies today. The frequently cited passage from Hölderlin, desiring that poetic language might originate as flowers do suggests concern with this problem in Romanticism. In the twentieth century, so-called concrete poetry, as the term implies, records the struggle of language to *be* an actual object—for example, in the poem, "au pair girl," where these words are arranged repeatedly on the page in the shape of pear.[3]

Ontological boundary crossing is an aim that trompe l'oeil in the visual arts has in common with the moments in which writing aspires to invade, incorporate, or be a thing. In painting, the desire to join the realm of the real with that of representation engenders trompe l'oeil, among other effects, and the Zeuxis and Parrhasios story recounted in Pliny's *Natural History*, cited through the centuries, attests to a parallel fascination with this problem on the part of the visual arts and the writing about them.[4] During this contest, the painter Zeuxis is said to have created a picture of a bunch of grapes so true to nature that it lures a flock of birds into approaching the painted surface in order to eat from the image of the vine.[5] It is not the realism of Zeuxis's painting that is intriguing about this narrated incident, and not simply the fact that this anecdote launches an attitude toward painting that Norman Bryson has called "the natural attitude," a point of view that stresses painting's "reduplicative mission."[6] Rather, Pliny's narrative is so fascinating because it provides us with an early instance of one of the drives that fuels the visual and the verbal arts: the drive to bring "the real" into the space of representation. Most obviously operative in theater, which uses the living human body as the vehicle of dramatic performance, this drive is more intriguingly (because less obviously) present in a wide variety of visual representations and in the narratives about them. It finds its satisfaction in the frisson generated when life and art or, more broadly, reality and art, purport to be continuous. One familiar and grotesque example of such continuity exists in Poe's tale, "The Oval Portrait," where at the precise moment when the artist achieves his goal of rendering a portrait so realistic as to resemble life itself, his subject is discovered to be dead. A variety of texts—visual and verbal—play on the continuity between the image and reality and, in particular, on the manner in which this play is figured in the opposition between movement and stasis. Through these texts, we can lay out the theoretical parameters of a discussion within which cinema can be ontologically situated.

We can locate a continuity between images and the real in the seventeenth- and eighteenth-century fascination with the Quattrocento camera obscura when used for aesthetic ends rather than as an optical instrument. In the 1620s, the Dutch painter Huygens, for instance, made a rather typical claim when he said of the images produced with a camera obscura that "all painting is dead in comparison, for here is life itself," or even "something more noble."[7] In part, of course, it is the camera obscura's capacity to generate *moving* images that evokes the response that these images are "life itself."[8] Subsequent centuries saw the invention of a number of "machines of the visible" that featured motion, such as the painter de Loutherbourg's "Eidophusikon" in 1781, advertised as producing "Various Imitations of Natural Phenomena, Represented by Moving Pictures."[9] "Transparencies," precursors of the magic lantern, passing before a lamp, revealed images of figures in landscape settings.[10] Earlier in the eighteenth century, Addison's *Pleasures of the Imagination*, like many other eighteenth-century writings, speaks of the fascination that the moving image holds for the spectator, and suggests a "something more" such as that intuited by Huygens.

"The prettiest landscape I ever saw," writes Addison,

> was one drawn on the walls of a dark room [a camera obscura] which stood opposite on one side to a navigable river, and on the other to a park. . . . Here you might discover the waves and fluctuations of the water in strong and proper colours, with the picture of the ship entering at one end, and sailing by degrees through the whole piece. On another there appeared the green shadows of trees, waving to and fro in the wind, and herds of deer among them in miniature, leaping about upon the wall.[11]

Addison admits to a sense of visual pleasure brought about by the close resemblance of this protocinematic scene to reality, a resemblance heightened by its capacity for motion. But he also understands the picturesque scene to be an optical effect, hence actually to incorporate the real: the landscape produced by the camera obscura is intriguing in part because it is a representation that can truly be said to make use of natural signs, in this case rays of light. In much the same way, a fine natural prospect pleases Addison all the more when it is framed by an arch—that is, when the natural is selected and shaped by art. So, too, the images produced by the camera obscura are all the more appealing because they are a heterogeneous combination of art and nature.[12]

Although the effects of the camera obscura as described by Addison are fleeting, more often than not its images were captured on paper, creating a drawing whose indeterminate status—art or nature?—was broadly intriguing to the eighteenth-century sensibility. Here I would take issue with Crary's contention that the camera obscura abolishes the "interlacing of nature and its representation" and that it is "inseparable from a certain metaphysic of interiority."[13] Rather, I would suggest that it is the ambiguous or indeterminate status of the images generated by the camera obscura, enhanced by their three-dimensionality, that governs their appeal.[14] The location of the spectator within the chamber—far from disembodying him or her—produces the uncanny and pleasurable effect of being physically present within a "natural" space and the space of representation at one and the same time. This effect, similar to the play between reality and the represented that we find in the trompe l'oeil, overrides, I think, that produced by the darkness of the room.[15]

This effect also seems to dominate the aesthetic pleasure produced by the panorama, whose static images were usually created with the help of a camera obscura.[16] Although Kepler's experiments with the camera obscura in 1620 were optical and epistemological, the landscape images he produced—a series of little drawings of the landscape surrounding him as he turned 360 degrees—point to the role that the camera obscura would later play in creating the panorama, which was constructed from a series of such pictures mounted side by side to create a whole.[17] Invented and patented by the portrait painter Robert Barker in 1793 or 1794, the panorama was usually a cityscape or seascape located within a special rotunda whose design ensured that the painting was viewed under the highest possible degree of illusion. The beholder entered the panorama from the center and viewed it from a platform that often resembled a stage set and whose props contributed to the illusion of the painting. In the case of Barker's first panorama, which represented a naval battle, the platform was built to resemble the deck of a frigate, a ploy that contributed significantly to the *"illusion totale"* experienced by the beholder.[18] By this means, as in the trompe l'oeil of Baroque churches, the two-dimensional images of the panoramic painting proclaim their extension into the three-dimensional world of objects. Hence, the space of a peculiarly "natural" form of representation—whose images were "traced," as it were, from nature—was extended to include the aesthetic space of the viewing platform. The beholder, then, was located within the extended representational space itself. In this way, the panorama objectified and troped the principles of realism in painterly composition—the shifting of forms between two and three dimensions, between the planar and the sculptural, on which realism is based.[19]

Conversely yet similarly, the walk through nature—taken by Addison's spectator and recorded in countless eighteenth-century topographical poems and travel texts—was of interest because it situated the spectator within a natural space that was perceived as an aesthetic one. While visual devices such as the fashionable Claude glass obviously aestheticized natural scenes for the spectator, such devices in themselves were not felt necessary for the "man of sensibility" whose response to the natural scene was inherently picturesque, who would naturally see in pictures.[20]

Because such pictures were produced by nature, visual experience of this sort was not arranged in a particular sequence, as would be the case in the landscape gardens that became a focus of aesthetic attention during the same century. Since the scenes of the landscape gardener's art were arranged to be perceived sequentially, the spectator who strolled through the "improved" natural setting experienced a gradual unfolding of scenes and frequent changes of perspective, with the doctrine of Associationism assuring that perceptions and their accompanying emotions could be determined in advance.

The introduction of motion into the experience of landscape, is stressed as the landscape garden's primary advantage over painting by theorists such as Shenstone and Lord Kames in Britain and Hirschfeld in Germany.[21] We can read in this claim both an acceptance of Lessing's dictum in the *Laocoön* that painting is static and atemporal, and an attempt to expand the territory of the visual arts, more broadly understood, to include movement. Here, too, the introduction of movement suggests a protocinematic viewing experience, although the multiple perspectives available to the spectator simply through the turn of the head enable spectatorial participation that is more on a par with interactive video than with cinema.[22]

Of course, insofar as it is natural, the garden itself is subject to temporality; it changes with the time of day and the season. Indeed, the landscape garden has an additional advantage over painting precisely because it is created largely from natural signs. Hence, during this period we find Girardin's much-cited claim that the art of landscape gardening is higher than that of painting because it is to painting (and to poetry) as reality is to description and the "original to the copy."[23] Although Girardin has recourse to the rhetoric of realism, the landscape garden exists in an aesthetically arranged form from which there are expectations of heightened visual pleasure. Interestingly, paintings were sometimes strategically placed within such gardens, even occasionally framed by actual cliffs, and served in part to play upon the parallels and differences between original and copy, between the three-dimensional arranged landscape and the two-dimensional images of painting.[24] In the landscape garden, then, we have at once a natural and an aesthetic space that may be entered by the spectator, into which he or she may be incorporated as a moving or halted "figure in the landscape."

As we might imagine, the experience of the cityscape conveyed by the panorama, no matter how realistic, brought with it a different kind of pleasure than that occasioned by a real view. In the case of the panorama it was precisely the beholder's awareness of artifice pushed as far as possible in the direction of the real that seems to have been so compelling. Conversely, in the case of the landscape garden, it was the manner in which the real was subjected to aesthetic shaping that was appealing. At the same time, these visual experiences can be said to produce related pleasures deriving from the contrived opposition and joining of reality and illusion. Finally, in the experience of both the landscape garden and the panorama, the spectator's location within the scene—not simply as a disembodied eye but as a material presence—seems to have intensified visual pleasure. Once again, it is the heterogeneous status of each medium, one that allows spectatorial entry into the realm of aesthetic representation, that produces this pleasure.

Diderot's *Salons* provide us with the clearest examples of the beholder's imagined entry into the text. Michael Fried has pointed to the manner in which Diderot projects himself into the genre paintings he describes by using the fiction of "physically entering" them.[25] Sometimes Diderot's descriptions narrativize the paintings he describes, turning them into dramatic sketches: the imagination animates these paintings, and Diderot describes them as actual scenes complete with sounds, gentle breezes, and odors that evoke the myth of total cinema. Repeatedly, Diderot represents himself as entering the space of genre paintings, walking along the paths of a landscape or seducing a pretty girl.

On another occasion, in describing a painting by Vernet, Diderot effects a double exchange between the real and the represented: "Go out into the countryside, turn your eyes upward to the vaulted heavens, observe exactly what is to be seen there at that moment and you will swear that a piece of the great, glowing canvas that is lighted by the sun has been cut out and carried back to the artist's easel."[26] Further, in the Salon of 1763, most notably in his writing concerning the still lifes of Chardin, Diderot imagines himself as bringing a concretized image into the space of beholding, removing a piece of fruit, say, from the space of the painting and eating it, no doubt in allusion to Pliny's story of Zeuxis. Diderot writes: "You have only to put out your hand and you can pick up those biscuits and eat them, that orange and cut it and squeeze it, that glass of wine and drink it, those fruits and peel them."[27]

Diderot particularly admired the texture of Chardin's paintings, their areas of thick layering or impasto, by means of which painting struggles toward the three-dimensional. It is as though, Diderot continues, the still lifes were painted with the material of the represented objects themselves: "Oh, Chardin! It is not white or red or black you mix on your palette, it is the very substance of things themselves."[28] Clearly what is at issue in this description, as in the story of Zeuxis, is not merely the question of realism, of tricking the eye, but the *materiality* of painting and the possibility of painting in natural signs. Diderot's rhetorical assertion redeems these *natures mortes* by claiming that they are not mere dead representations of natural objects, but natural objects—existing, if not alive—themselves.[29] What is figured in this narrative is the very threshold, the liminal point, that separates representation from the real. Today, Eric Cameron's "Food Related Thick Paintings" (1990), which he produced by applying many coats of gesso to food items found in the refrigerator, provide a postmodern allusion to this problem.[30]

Diderot's conceit that the beholder of Chardin's still life might remove, cut, and squeeze the orange is related to the more familiar trope of the work of art that comes to life, a trope figured most obviously in the Pygmalion story. This issue of the visual work of art brought *to* life, as in the case of Pygmalion's statue of Galatea, and art brought *into* life—in the above example, eaten—exists in a dialectical relation to Diderot's rhetorical gesture of entering the space of representation, of bringing the living body into art. It is telling that the Pygmalion myth enjoyed renewed popularity in the eighteenth century, inspiring Rousseau's monodrama of that title as well as Herder's essay on sculpture. Subtitled "From Pygmalion's Creative Dream," Herder's essay (1778) draws upon both Diderot and Winckelmann in privileging sculpture over painting. Following Winckelmann, whose ecphrastic descriptions of sculptures such as the Belvedere Apollo bring them to life and emphasize their movement, Herder claims that sculpture speaks through action and must represent the body in motion. But it is the materiality of sculpture that is also at issue. Expanding upon Lessing's contention that painting cannot represent an action, Herder suggests that painting runs the danger not only of rendering the human body inanimate, but also of "flattening" the body by its two-dimensionality.[31] Indeed, for Herder, painting's single perspective seems to pin its subject to the canvas, much as one might display a butterfly, thus rendering it inanimate and dead.

Notably, in the 1780s it became fashionable to visit Italian art galleries at night, because the torchlight was felt to generate the illusion of movement in sculptures, producing "living statues."[32] Other art forms that played upon the relation of the living body to the represented one flourished during this period as well. Notable among these were the exotic performances of Emma Hart, the future Lady Hamilton, witnessed and written about by Goethe and numerous other travelers to Naples. Her so-called "attitudes"—representations of classical works of art—held her spectators spellbound, as did her poses inside a life-size black box framed in gold by means of which she evoked ancient and contemporary painting.[33] Spectatorial interest in "attitudes," referred to as "mimoplastic" art, was no doubt fed by the widespread enthusiasm for "body language" in theater, as evinced by Diderot's writings on gesture and pantomime. Hart's achieved effect in representing sculpture played upon Galatea's coming to life, for her spectators were acutely aware that at any time her living body could break out of its sculptural contours and cast off its self-imposed immobility. On the other hand, by framing the body as an aesthetic object and placing it against a funereal backdrop of black velvet, she played upon the killing off of the body of which Herder accuses painting. Interestingly, the figures that she most often reproduced by these means were said to be from Pompeiian murals, doubly connected with death, embalming time.[34]

As Goethe notes in a letter of 1787, Hart even represented the Belvedere Apollo, Winckelmann's favorite sculpture, and in general confined herself to classical subjects. Arrayed in a white tunic, hair flowing, and with the aid of a variety of shawls, she arranged her body in a series of poses, thus creating shifting—not moving—three-dimensional pictures. Characteristic of Hart's attitudes was the alternation between prolonged immobility (each pose seems to have been held for about ten minutes)[35] and sudden movement, an alternation that emphasized the tension between the painterly subject of each representation and its human vehicle. In the 1790s, another performer of attitudes, Henriette Hendel-Schütz, stressed picturesque movement in her performances and created a special lighting device to enhance its effect.[36] Her pantomimed performances took place before a canvas of black or gray material that recalled the *toile* of Diderot's dramatic tableaux and emphasized the manner in which attitudes combined theater and painting. Once again the body is the site of a mode of representation that juxtaposes the three-dimensional with the two-dimensional—the living, suggested by the capacity for movement, with the dead or static.

Attitudes, pantomime, and Diderot's dramatic theories were among the sources for tableaux vivants, a genre involving the static embodiment of paintings by human actors for which Goethe's *Elective Affinities*, published in 1808, is said to have established the fashion.[37] In Goethe's novel, a rather telling pantomime precedes the staging of the tableaux vivants. In this pantomime, accompanied by the mournful strains of a funeral dirge, a young woman represents Artimisia carrying an urn containing the ashes of her husband Mausolus, the king for whom the first mausoleum was built and named. Behind her walks an architect carrying a blackboard, on which he is expected to draw the mausoleum that is to house the funeral urn with its ashes, the remains of the body. After he has sketched the mausoleum, Artimisia gestures to him to "place" the urn on top of the monument by drawing it there. As a prop in the pantomime, the urn, already an artifact, is raised to a higher level of artifice in the aesthetic space of the stage upon which this performance takes place. The urn then symbolically "enters" yet another aesthetic space and another ontological level when it is transposed into a chalk drawing on the blackboard, achieving a still greater degree of aestheticization and an increased distance from the body.

Tableau vivant, as a staging of painting, achieves the effect that the drawing within Goethe's pantomime strives for, but cannot attain: it successfully brings the living body into painting, collapsing as far as possible the distance between signifier and signified suggested by the chalk image of the mausoleum. In so doing, tableau vivant plays on two related uncanny effects: the arrested motion or freezing—hence death—of the human body on the one hand, and the embodiment or bringing to life of the inanimate image on the other. Not surprisingly, Goethe's narrator comments on the uncanny effect these tableaux have upon the spectators: "The figures corresponded so well to their originals, the colours were so happily chosen, the lighting so artistic, you thought you had been transported to another world, the only disturbing factor being *a sort of anxiety produced by the presence of real figures instead of painted ones*"[38] [italics mine].

In his short-lived journal on art, the *Propyläen* (1798–1800), Goethe sketched the fictional portrait of the type of sensibility he understands by the term "Imitator," or realist. His novelette, "The Collector and His Circle," humorously recounts the story of a collector who shows "peculiar pleasure in a particular kind of art"—in "the faithful imitation of natural objects."[39] His passion for mimesis begins with precise sketches of objects from garden and kitchen, a cross between naturalists' studies and still lifes: all objects of significance are said to have been "fixed" on paper. The collector's desire for exact copies expands to include first portraits of family and friends and then life-size representations of them. Next, his obsession leads him to commission a trompe l'oeil portrait of himself and his wife behind a false door, executed in accordance with all the rules of perspective.[40] Finally, the collector's "blind drive" culminates in the commission of a life-size wax figure of himself derived from a plaster cast of his living face, clothed in wig and dressing gown. His son, the narrator of the tale, says, "the old boy is still sitting here behind a curtain which I did not dare draw back for you."[41] Goethe's "Imitator," in his obsession with the preservation of life through lifelike representation, is well on his way to creating the automatons that populate Hoffmann's tales. In so doing, he evokes in his son the response that Freud associates with the Uncanny. From Goethe's point of view, the trompe l'oeil painting behind the door and the wax figure are disturbing in part because they reduce art to its function as memorial and because, in so doing, they lay bare the desperation with which we seek to sustain life. Further, Goethe suggests in this allegorical narrative that the passion for mimesis is at bottom a desire to bring the body into the space of representation. The motivation of this desire is paradoxical: it lies, of course, in the need to memorialize life through art, but it also involves the attempt to create an intimate relation between sign and object, to bridge the gap between representation and things-in-themselves.

The introduction of temporality into the visual arts by way of movement, the opening up of what Lessing called the spatial arts by the introduction of time—whether effected by an optical device or human motion—introduces death more obviously into the framework of aesthetic discussion. The eighteenth-century discussion of the picturesque confirms this thesis, as the emblematizing of death forms an integral part of its power. There is a concern with natural process that lurks in descriptions of picturesque natural and painterly scenes, a concern specifically with "the effects of age and decay" that establishes the temporal axis of the picturesque.[42] It is in part their connections with decay and process that explains the overwhelming fascination of the picturesque with ruins, structures upon which time has wrought its texture-creating effects. Tellingly, the movement back and forth between representation and the real is also a characteristic of picturesque aesthetics; as a focus of interest for the picturesque sensibility, inanimate object and person are often interchangeable: Uvedale Price writes with equal fervor concerning incrustations on the surface of ruins[43] and of potential incrustations on the teeth of a parson's daughter.[44]

The interest generated by texture and "incrustations" is not only an index of the preoccupation with temporality and natural process: it is a determining feature of picturesque aesthetics in general. Especially through the writings of Price, the picturesque comes to be defined by its tactility. In part, this has to do with its dependence on variegated textures as the greatest source of visual interest: frequently cited examples are the rough and shaggy coats of goats or of shedding cows.[45] Texture is, of course, a quality that we tend to associate with objecthood. As a consequence, when the insistence on texture is carried over into painting by way of impasto—as in the work of Chardin and of painters in the picturesque mode such as de Loutherbourg—we can read in this technique the unrealizable desire of painting, a two-dimensional medium, to become three-dimensional and to take on the quality of an object.

At bottom, then, the juxtaposition of the image with the real that so often occurs in representation derives from a desire to construct an identity between the two that covers over the abyss between life and death, hence reassuringly mystifying the latter. With this understanding, Jean Baudrillard calls the real "a simulacrum of accumulation against death."[46] The seductiveness of the juxtaposition of life and death arises from the ease with which an exchange is accomplished between living bodies and things and their images, and with which either and both can be said metaphorically to enter another ontological plane. The real, when introduced into the space of representation, is secure from decay within that space, and the image, when brought into the space of the real, seems to impart to that space its own imperviousness to time.

CINEMA AND THE REAL

In the opening passsage of his essay on the *flâneur*, Walter Benjamin describes Baudelaire's experience of entering a marketplace as though it were a panorama, thus aestheticizing the real in a manner that recalls Addison's reading of landscape in the *Pleasures of the Imagination*. Indeed, Addison's spectator walking through the English countryside has something in common with Benjamin's and Baudelaire's flâneur in the French cityscape, despite the obvious difference in psychosocial perspective. At the end of the eighteenth century, the specifically visual and motor relation to landscape in which a topographical literature had been grounded produced texts as different from one another as Wordsworth's poetry and Goethe's *Elective Affinities*. As the ninteenth century advanced, it produced a visual and mobile apprehension of the city that informed texts as diverse as Baudelaire's poetry, French panoramic literature, and Dickens's novels. While all topographical writing situates the eye in an ambulatory body, there is a predictable shift of emphasis from the eighteenth century to the nineteenth whereby the univocal point of view loses its distinctness. In Baudelaire, for instance, the self is "an 'I' with an insatiable appetite for the 'non-I,' "—a "man of the crowd."[47]

While Addison's spectator is a master of all he surveys, Baudelaire's man of the crowd responds to and reproduces what he sees, and Benjamin's flâneur is in a state of distracted attention, "shocked" by the sensory perceptions that impinge upon him. Baudelaire's description of the "painter of modern life" turns the man of the crowd himself into a machine of the visible. "We might liken him," Baudelaire writes, "to a mirror as vast as the crowd itself; or to a kaleidoscope gifted with consciousness, responding to each one of its movements and reproducing the multiplicity of life and the flickering grace of all the elements of life."[48] Like the mimetic mirror and the kaleidoscope of moving images, a conjunction of images that calls cinema to mind, Baudelaire's flâneur as painter is capable of recording what he sees "in pictures more living than life itself," "a phantasmagoria distilled from nature."[49] Since in rendering the painter of modern life Baudelaire relies on tropes that evoke the moving images of the camera obscura and prefigure the cinema, it is interesting to note that his "passionate spectator" has an excessive desire not only for the visible, but also for "tangible things, condensed to their plastic state."[50]

More predictably than Baudelaire's, Benjamin's flâneur also experiences the city as phantasmagoria, as cinematic spectacle. Benjamin quotes Dickens's confession that his characters seem to want to stand still when he does not have the "magic lantern" that is London as inspiration before him.[51] As a perceiver, Benjamin's flâneur on his stroll has much in common with the spectator of a film, for whom the cinematic "shock effect" resides in the ceaseless and sudden changes that the film's images undergo.[52] Moreover, as with the spectator of Dada art and performances, they are assaulted by visual images: in the "Artwork" essay, Benjamin notes that "the work of art of the Dadaists became an instrument of ballistics . . . it hit the spectator like a bullet, it happened to him."[53] For Benjamin, its quality of violent assault makes the art of the Dadaists tactile (the idea of its tactility, the plasticity of the word, is held by the Dadaists themselves) and promotes "a demand for the film, the distracting element of which is also primarily tactile, being based on changes of place and focus which periodically assail the spectator."[54] Like Baudelaire's spectator, whose scopic desire is accompanied by an obsession with the tangible material object, Benjamin is concerned with the image in its relation to tactility.

Benjamin's materialism ensures that the optical regime will not lose its grounding in the body. From Benjamin's point of view, the spectator of a film responds not only emotionally but viscerally—as one might respond to a punch—to the cinematic medium. In reading the art of the Dadaists and of film as tactile media, Benjamin has recourse, just as Baudelaire does, to a boundary crossing between the image and the real. Further, he effects the connection between the represented and the real via the human body, not in terms of its spectatorial position with regard to the work of art—its placement, say, within the panorama—but in terms, rather, of its somatic responsiveness. In focusing on the tactility of visual representation, Benjamin plays upon a perceptual shift between the two-dimensional and the three-dimensional that is, as Bryson has said of painting, "*the* underlying compositional figure of the realist tradition."[55] Aware of the flatness of its own image, cinema nevertheless plays its effects of spatial depth against the two-dimensionality that it reads in painting; a perceptual shift back and forth between these two dimensions shapes the point of view of the cinematic spectator.

In an image that recalls both the flâneur and Addison's spectator, Adorno describes Kracauer as a traveler, a "strange realist" with "a mode of seeing that represents everything to itself as if on a journey, [that sees] even the gray everyday as though it were a colorful object of wonder."[56] Kracauer's essays on visual culture, such as "The Mass Ornament" and "Cult of Distraction," demonstrate abundantly that Kracauer is skilled in topographical readings, in transforming the environment into "the site of figural play."[57] But in these early essays by Kracauer there is no reciprocal gesture that locates the real within the text in terms other than the sociopolitical. In "Cult of Distraction" (1926) Kracauer stresses the two-dimensional quality of the cinematic image as properly illusionistic, bemoaning the manner in which three-dimensional theatrical presentations framed the screening of films. By blending "the events of the three-dimensional stage imperceptibly into two-dimensional illusions," the false claim is made that these images are reality.[58]

In *Theory of Film* (1960), Kracauer develops his idea that "films come into their own when they record and reveal physical reality," articulating a material aesthetics in the process.[59] In this work Kracauer is no longer as intent upon maintaining boundaries between the mass media and high culture, and stresses the "gain in spatial depth" that characterizes cinematic representation and that is particularly observable when realistic paintings are shown on the screen. When the camera lingers on parts of bodies represented in a painting—a Rubens head, for example—this filmed body part, he argues, seems to participate in the "indeterminacy of real-life phenomena" and hence seems lifelike.[60] Pointing out that there are no films on art in which the movement of the camera is not featured, Kracauer suggests that a so-called "resonance effect" causes the film's spectator to incorporate the experience of space created by camera movement into his perception of the picture surface, "so he will attribute natural fullness to a group of figures or fancy himself—like Diderot—meandering through a painted valley."[61] Kracauer explains this effect in terms of our partiality for the three-dimensional, arguing that this perception of three-dimensionality lingers even when the camera is at rest. In the context of camera movement, the static moments that result from its cessation seem like natural lulls rather than still shots. On the other hand, Kracauer maintains, when the camera approaches or retreats from a painting the spectator is convinced that the painting has changed position: this kind of camera movement is especially suited to "breathe life into a painting" and to suggest that "painted people are on the point of moving about like real people, or just now stop moving to compose a *tableau vivant*."[62]

It is Bazin who, elaborating on Aristotle in "The Ontology of the Photographic Image," recognizes that the desire to duplicate the real world through representation is a drive, an "appetite" for illusion and a "proclivity of the mind."[63] For Bazin, the "psychological ambition" of painting to render three-dimensional space and movement, most eloquently expressed in the "convulsive catalepsy" of Baroque art, is realized in cinema.[64] By taking on the burden of this "resemblance complex," in Bazin's view cinema frees the plastic arts from their obsession with likeness. In order to assume this burden adequately, however, the cinematic image "must have the spatial density of something real."[65] Christian Metz, following Kracauer, suggests that it is motion that causes filmed objects to appear more "materialized"; for Metz "it is often the criterion of touch, that of 'materiality,' confusedly present in our mind, that divides the world into objects and copies."[66] For Jean-Louis Comolli, too, it is movement and—following Bazin on this point—depth of field that produce the effect of relief in cinema and promote the identification of the cinematic image "with life itself."[67]

In another essay, Comolli suggests that it was the trompe l'oeil dioramas, the "perfect illusion of reality," that provoked Daguerre "to research the possibilities of 'a new method of fixing the views found in nature without recourse to an artist.'"[68] Since the diorama must ultimately stand revealed as a trompe l'oeil effect, however, it provides the spectator with evidence that the eye can be fooled; thus, Comolli argues, the camera was invented as a replacement for the eye and as an ideological guarantor of the epistemological certainty that the eye had relinquished. Continuing where Comolli leaves off, Doane reads cinema as a means of stabilizing and controlling the visual field and as an "institutionalized control of the trompe l'oeil."[69] Trompe l'oeil poses a threat, then, because it promotes the "subject's lack of presence to itself by fore-grounding the image's potential to mislead."[70] Within the terms of Doane's Lacanian reading, the function of trompe l'oeil is opposite that of the fetish. Rather than defending against the threat of castration and the splitting of the subject, it exposes the subject's vulnerability to these threats. In this reading, then, it is precisely its "closeness to the real" that makes the image so threatening.[71] Doane's view of trompe l'oeil does not seem to include the element of ontological play upon which I base my understanding, nor does it see the possibility that trompe l'oeil can be a defense against death.

It may be that cinema is interested in trompe l'oeil effects and in appro-priating the real because it has a certain degree of self-consciousness con-cerning its institutional role in controlling the threat of illusion. There seems, in any case, to be a lure in trompe l'oeil's uncanniness that makes cinema unable to repress it completely. Like painting, cinema plays upon trompe l'oeil effects of various kinds despite—or because of—its aware-ness that this kind of illusion will not fool the eye for very long. Indeed, Lacan has suggested that trompe l'oeil is most attractive precisely at the moment when we recognize it as such.[72] Edwin Porter's *Uncle Josh at the Moving Picture Show* (1902), for instance, which records the anxiety of early audiences as to whether the train on the screen will enter the space of the theater, as well as the sexual jealousy provoked by a screen kiss, wants ultimately to demystify these images by exposing them as pro-jected.[73] But it wants also to entertain the possibility, if only for a few moments, that the space of the real will be invaded by the image become thing, or that it might be possible to enter the diegetic space of the screen. It is this confusion between the real and the image that is recorded in the mirror shots of Expressionist cinema and thematized when a character shoots his mirror image only to fall down "dead" himself, much as the portrait in Oscar Wilde's famous novel is made to suffer the ravages of time in place of Dorian Gray, who finally stabs the portrait and dies. (Such moments have *their* mirror image, in turn, in the moment of trompe l'oeil related by Freud in a footnote to his essay on the Uncanny—the anecdote of catching sight of a disagreeable man on a train who turns out to be none other than his own mirror image.)[74] To cite another, rather different, example, the deliberately visceral impact of special effects in contemporary science-fiction films contributes to the ambiguity concern-ing the relation of the real to the cinematic on which science fiction thrives. Ontological boundary crossings in cinema tend to rely on perceptual shifts in the spectator, shifts produced by visual effects such as camera movement, color, lighting, and especially, as Comolli points out, "effects of relief, effects of depth."[75] The following readings, then, focus on films that figure and theorize the struggle to bring the real, often in the form of the body, into textuality and, in so doing, position themselves with respect to painting, writing, and theater. They focus as well on the ontological claims of problematic images, on the perceptual shifts that render them so, and, where appropriate, on the nature of our spectatorial response.

BODY LANGUAGE: KLEIST'S AND ROHMER'S *MARQUISE*

Two months after the famous letters of March 1801 that Kleist scholars use to document his so-called "Kant crisis," Kleist returned to Dresden and wrote another letter that still bears traces of this struggle.[76] He wrote with relief about the restorative effects of his visits to the Dresden art galleries, where the beholder of the works of art housed there could take pleasure in them without the necessity of understanding, because they act only upon the senses and emotions. Since Kleist had visited these galleries on an earlier occasion, it is evident that this "world of beauty so new to him," as he puts it, is new only because he sees it with new eyes. He envies painters, he goes on to say, because they are not given to doubts about Truth, living as they do exclusively within the Beautiful. Kleist's response, however, is not unambiguous, and to some extent he shares the suspicion Rousseau expresses towards the visual work of art precisely because it speaks to the senses.[77]

The only painting Kleist mentions specifically in this letter is Raphael's Sistine Madonna—then in Dresden—before which he says he stood for hours. Although his response to this painting is expressed largely in the Neoclassical parlance made popular by Winckelmann's "noble simplicity and serene greatness," Kleist also implies that one aspect of its charm for him is the resemblance the Madonna bears to his fiancée and his sister. A few months later in Paris, Kleist remembers this Madonna with intense longing. Now openly acknowledging the erotic basis of his exalted response, he writes that the painting enchains him with the power of an adored woman.[78] In this same letter, which was almost certainly known to Eric Rohmer (who studied German for years in preparing to film *The Marquise*),[79] Kleist mentions Raphael's "St. Michael Vanquishing the Devil," which depicts an archangel as he triumphs over a devil.[80]

119

The enthusiasm for Raphael was shared by Neoclassicist and Romantic writers and painters, and it is not surprising that Kleist was caught up in the general current. The Sistine Madonna especially evoked Kleist's idealized sensuality. Later, he elevated the seeming anomaly of his response into a creative principle. Among his essays in his journal, the *Berliner Abendblätter*, there is a fictive "Letter of a Painter to His Son," in which the father, an experienced artist, reassures his novice son that the lust he feels toward the model posing for his painting of a Madonna will spur on his creation. Not only is the imagination not sullied by the sexuality from which it arises, but, on the contrary—and here the father enlists a figure for the work of art that must have raised many an eyebrow—this union of body and mind can bring forth a son, a vigorous child whose climbing about between heaven and earth will give the philosophers "a good deal of trouble,"—which is to say, sustaining Kleist's paradox concerning this hybrid text, food for thought.[81] Kleist's *Marquise of O. . . . ,* begun in 1805, midway between these actual letters and the fictive ones, is itself just such a daughter, a text that dramatizes the gap between mind and body, signifier and signified. The points of connection between Kleist's novella and his mode of admiring the Raphael paintings are numerous and apparent. Raphael's themes are prominent in Kleist's figural texture, as when the Marquise tries recurrently to interpret her embarrassment as a virgin conception, once with an irony beyond her control when, to her immense discomfort, the Count forces his way into her garden and tries to declare himself in a scene that iconographically recalls the Annunciation.[82] By the same token, the polarities of angel and devil that condition the Marquise's struggle to locate her conception of the Count reconstruct one aspect of Kleist's fascination with Raphael's St. Michael. As recent criticism has emphasized, Kleist situates his theme of paternity and generation so as to condition the production of the narrative itself. According to this cogent argument, the "unnarrated center" of the text, the moment in which, as the narrative allows us to realize with increasing certainty, the Count has raped the Marquise, is the moment that generates her "interesting condition" and the interest of her story, "pregnant with meaning" as it is.[83]

This leap from the emotional and physical response to the work of art to the way in which the text is generated metaphorically by rape forms a background to what will be problematized here. Kleist's juxtaposition of writing and speech with the unwriteable or unspeakable evinces a deftly qualified envy of those forms of cognition that are more sensuous and immediate than language, an envy that is at the same time a critique of ideology—of the encodedness of mediated knowledge. From this standpoint, which reveals a tendency to masculinize the arbitrary codes of language and honor—both personal and social—while feminizing the domain of sensuous intuition, we can understand the celebrated equilibrium of Kleist's sympathies as a play of irony in which the arbitrary is never understood to be unnecessary and the natural, precisely in being represented semiotically as "body language," is never as natural as it seems. In his adaptation of Kleist's text, Rohmer inverts Kleist's duality between the arts, associating the visual with the restrictive encodedness of ideology and language with the possibility of a more flexible and nuanced expression.

The Marquise of O. . . . begins with the narrator's account of a text so controversial, so clearly a violation of good form, that it would seem to contradict the hypothesis of restricted language in Kleist. This is the advertisement that the Marquise has written and placed in the newspapers to the effect that "she had, without knowledge of the cause, come to find herself in a certain situation, that she would like the father of the child she was expecting to disclose his identity to her; and that she was resolved, out of consideration for her family, to marry him."[84] The simplicity of the text masks the complexity of its motivation and function, a complexity very much in keeping with the instinct for paradox Kleist inherits from French classical drama. By making the most intimate fact of her life a matter of public knowledge, the Marquise denies intimate knowledge of the act that has shamed her, and thus by publicizing her shame she proclaims her innocence. From this perspective, her text is not transgressive after all. Despite its daring as a gesture and the apathetic fatalism that engenders that daring, the Marquise's want ad still in effect promotes the social order by legitimizing illegitimacy and preserving the family at all costs. The marriage this text envisions is purely a matter of social contract. But what the Marquise's ad cannot and indeed will not do, except by reasserting in public view the failure to meet the unsavory either/or questions that have so scandalized her family (if not hysterical pregnancy, then real pregnancy, and if real pregnancy, then if not parthenogenesis, complicity!), is to get beyond the binarism of linguistic forms and thereby bring to light that third something, the intuitive knowledge ("Gefühl," feeling, or emotional knowledge) that the Marquise's not quite fully socialized nature intermittently fails to repress.

For Kleist, language, even at its most risk taking, is inescapably ideological, and the Marquise's advertisement comes first in his text because it points to this belief and constitutes a trial experience for reading the

121

novella as a whole. Kleist promotes the ideal of mimetic adequacy in his subtitle, with its claim to be drawn from "a real incident," but his title has already acknowledged the unnameable with the first of the many marks and horizontal lines that replace, or rather displace, words, the most famous of which is of course the phallic dash that stands in place of the unrepresentable factuality of rape. The text incorporates its mimetic shortcomings as a system of graphic signals. The Kleistian character likewise systematically "loses consciousness," whether by fainting or by persisting in ignorance, whenever it becomes impossible to come to terms, literally—such are the conjunctive and unitary rules of language—with the unaccountability of the actual.

The problem of language is typically linked in Kleist with the problem of knowledge. He plays on the Biblical meaning of *wissen*—"to know"—and significantly uses *Bewusstsein*—"consciousness"—where *Gewissen*—"conscience"—might have seemed more appropriate, as for instance in the oft-quoted exclamation of the Marquise's mother—"ein reines Bewusstsein und eine Hebamme!"—which should be (but rarely is) translated, "a pure *consciousness* and yet a midwife!"[85] What the Marquise knows and what it is right for her to know and what she wishes to know are all subtly at odds with one another. The text frequently insinuates that she has fallen in love with the Count, and the slight margin of doubt registered in her initial vision of him as an angel—the kind of doubt that surfaces in the masculine rationalization of rape—would suggest that indeed it was love at first sight: love not for a man but for the heroic figure who protected her from degradation and who must henceforth himself be protected by the most strenuous sustained effort of repression and protected from the awareness that he himself is the contaminant, even if that means keeping him in every sense out of view. The Marquise's ambivalence toward the Count is itself the only sign of a feeling that must be expressed as a binary contrast. During the first onslaught of the Count's courtship she confides to her parents that she finds him "both attractive and unattractive," anticipating fully—yet no doubt at least partly unawares—her ultimate realization that she would not have treated him like a devil if she had not at first believed him to be an angel.[86]

The intimation that the Count is the father of her child, which is what she is never willing to hear in words, is closely related to what she calls, referring to her possible pregnancy, her inner feeling or sensation, an expression she repeatedly uses, appropriately in the context of female discourse, in conversation with her mother. In *The Marquise of O. . . .* , language corresponds to the sphere of consciousness, while the real is virtually unavailable to it. In this system, feeling, the kind of flickering perception entertained somewhere between intuition and the will to certainty and moral integrity, is an intermediate area that can be brought only partially and imperfectly into expression. It is feeling that attempts a mediation between consciousness and the real, and Kleist continuously presents feeling, both to its credit and its detriment, as a kind of body language. The Marquise acquires certain knowledge from her changing body, but this very certainty makes the body thus far inauthentic, a signifier displacing and objectifying the novella's "unnarrated center." It is precisely the translatability of her body's language into the thinkable and sayable that displaces her attention backward from the body's present, knowable condition and precipitates her crisis of consciousness. It is the carnal aspect of this crisis of knowledge that the Marquise's text, her advertisement, cannot record.

The many blushes and sudden fits of pallor to which Kleist's characters, both male and female, are subject belong also to the realm of body language.[87] Here also we should locate the studied pose of their gestures, the most telling of these being the Count's encircling of the pregnant Marquise's waist, affirming its beauty and taking possession of it in a single gesture of legitimation. The imperfect reconciliation and concretization

Fig. 9. The Count's body language—the gesture with which he encircles the body of the Marquise—is contrasted with the written word.

123

effected by body language recurs everywhere in Kleist, as in the figure of the mestizzo Toni, the young woman who embodies the conflict between black and white in *The Engagement in Santo Domingo*, and it acts itself out most startlingly in the figure of Penthesilea, whose refusal to accept the figurativity of language causes her to take literally the expression whose contemporary equivalent is "I love you so much I could eat you up." She says she despises the kind of woman who would merely say this sort of thing, and accordingly she cannibalizes the corpse of her lover Achilles, as she puts it, "word for word."[88] It is the theme of body language, finally, that provides a supplementary explanation for the Oedipal reunion of father and daughter in Kleist's *Marquise*.[89] The father, who refused to speak and is called a "doubting Thomas" by his wife, is now discovered still speechless but repeatedly kissing his daughter on the mouth, not only rejoining the world of women through the medium of touch but more pointedly attempting to fuse the language of tactility with the very organ that produces the language of division and separation. The imperfection, the inadequacy, of this and other such gestures in Kleist— like that of Penthesilea—can be inferred from the grotesque exaggeration that carries them beyond the desired moment of harmony and into the mania of erotic introjection.

Because it remains language after all, the inner feeling that gives the Marquise the knowledge that she is pregnant is more plausibly linked to the idea of artistic conception. When her mother jokingly suggests that she will no doubt give birth to the god of fantasy, the Marquise replies "that at any rate Morpheus or one of his attendant dreams must be the father."[90] Later her mother warns her of the consequences if she should be inventing "a fable about the overturning of the whole order of nature," and she tells the midwife that her daughter is suffering from a *Vorstellung*—an image within the mind.[91] There is comfort in the internal logic of fable, even though it would overturn the order of nature, because even when it is subversive it offers explanations. Language first and last in Kleist's novella, even when it is stretched to its limit in the service of disrupting existing orders, simply shifts from one level to another within an ideological structure from which it can never escape. Moreover, Kleist's intricate thematization of his medium confirms the submission to the arbitrary with which he and his text self-consciously take up their position in society.

When film critics refer to the "literariness" of Rohmer's films, they ordinarily have in mind his reliance on spoken language, on the conversations that insinuate themselves with more intellectual charm than the restrained elegance of his visual technique. Acknowledging this tendency, Rohmer has said that he has wanted "to portray in film what seemed most alien" to it.[92] Given his declared emphasis on language, it is hardly surprising that Rohmer claims not merely to have wanted to adapt Kleist's novella for film, but actually to "use the text . . . as if Kleist himself had put it directly on screen, as if he were making a movie."[93] Rohmer's measure of submission to the medium of writing is so great that he intermittently literalizes the gesture of putting himself in Kleist's place by retaining his author's text on title cards and by "signing" the film in Kleist's name. The newspaper text of the Marquise's ad, which the spectator sees twice and also watches being written in a lingering shot composed entirely of hand, quill, paper, and inkwell, turns even Rohmer's characters into readers of Kleist. Where he cannot avoid using cinematic equivalents of writing, Rohmer is still rigorously deferential: he devises a rhythmic alternation of cuts and fades to parallel the alternately fluent and obstructive Kleistian syntax, and he acknowledges (even as he mutes and softens) the insistent bipolarities of his author's medium by adopting a two-color palette of grayish reds and greens. Imitating the customary unobtrusiveness of Kleist's narrator, Rohmer's rather static camera moves most notably during conversations, contrary to classical cinematic syntax, when the camera is held on a character who has finished speaking, thus drawing attention to the language of the off-camera speaker. In addition, the acting style used in the film suggests a familiarity with the eighteenth-century theater's interest in gesture and pantomime.[94]

Alongside the homage to language, both in its spoken and written forms, that parallels Kleist's admiration for the sensuous directness of the visual artist's medium, Rohmer pursues a running critique of the ideological conditioning imposed by the medium with which he is primarily engaged, thus imitating Kleist most attentively in the very process of inverting his representational values. Apart from the ways in which Rohmer's images themselves resemble Kleistian language, he focuses attention on the ways in which images as such condition perception. His interiors perform diverse functions of this sort even beyond the theme of environmental conditioning that their historical accuracy keeps continuously before us. There are paintings everywhere, and their subject matter is for the most part not accidental. The public rooms of the town house feature paintings representing classical architecture—a domed temple, a villa with a viaduct, and, most crucially, a large painting of a monumental ruin that appears, frequently amid the debris of furniture, in every scene marking the transition of the Commandant's family from the invaded citadel to the town house, and before which the Marquise stands more than once as an unknowingly ruined woman. All such images, including Rohmer's point-of-view analysis of domestic interiors, impose a cultural interpretation on the female body as a dwelling honored by traditional association that can only be perceived—and lived in or away from—as a structure that is either intact or ruined. Kleist sets the cue for this theme when he says "the Count seemed to be accustomed to taking ladies' hearts, like fortresses, by storm."[95]

Additionally, painting mediates the consciousness of each of the central characters. The Marquise's country house is decorated not with historical or civic but with comparatively personal subjects—portraits and floral paintings—while her room in her father's house contains a small print of what looks like one of the Vermeer "letter" paintings, with an ambiguously full-figured woman standing near a half-curtained window, a print positioned suggestively over a vanity mirror. This print is visible twice in the film, first at the moment when the Marquise and her mother can no longer doubt that she is pregnant, and second when she sits with her mother waiting to be reconciled with her father; the print, in other words, both is and contains a signifier of ineluctable knowledge, marking the beginning and the end of the Marquise's rift with the social order. The study of the Commandant, the Marquise's father, notably contains objectifications of the violence that sustains his convictions: a battle scene and a portrait of the Marquise that he takes off the wall when his interpretation of her infamy attains its most lurid proportions. The Count, finally, who has good reason not to doubt the Marquise's innocence, hears of her pregnancy with equanimity while standing next to a serenely immutable marble bust, a little larger than life, which looks very much like the Marquise.

Yet more central than these static objectifications is Rohmer's emphasis on the visual conditioning of the rape itself and of its imperfect repression by the Marquise. At three crucial moments in the narrative—the moment when the Marquise first sees the Count, the moment preceding the rape, and the occasion of their marriage ceremony—the film's images themselves allude pointedly to painting. The white-clad Count in his cloak, dramatically backlit and shot from below—from the Marquise's point of view—evokes Renaissance paintings of avenging angels (Raphael's, for example)—and Rohmer thereby suggests that the Marquise would not have ennobled his heroism with such adamance had she not associated it with images of this kind. We are given similarly to understand that the Count might not have raped the woman he had, after all, just saved from rape if his inflamed imagination had not associated her body, draped in satin and limbs akimbo under the influence of the sleeping potion, with paintings of reclining female bodies. Both the color contrast of this scene and the posture of the Marquise are based on the first version of Henry Fuseli's immensely popular erotic painting called "The Nightmare" (1781),[96] which vividly confirms the argument that woman is "the central motif and possession of the European painter's art."[97] Finally, there is the marriage scene in the cathedral where, as if to confirm the tendency of these readings, the camera takes another shot from the point of view of the Marquise, who refuses to look at the Count and instead "stare[s] rigidly at the painting behind the altar."[98]

Kleist says no more than this about the painting, but Rohmer shows it to us, focusing the Marquise's gaze on a depiction of Lucifer's banishment from Heaven. Rohmer had almost certainly read the letter of Kleist mentioning Raphael's "St. Michael Vanquishing the Devil," implying that there are creative advantages in visual seduction. While the painting in this scene is not "St. Michael," it resembles it quite closely. Rohmer also undoubtedly had Kleist's letter in mind not only here but at the point of the Marquise's first glimpse of the Count, which is recalled by the lighting of the cathedral painting, which is more dramatic than in Raphael. A slow pan downward from angel to devil, one of the very few pans in the film, links these two moments somewhat obtrusively. What is problematic for Rohmer is the implication of the spectator in the language of painting. To revert to the Fuseli-inspired image of the Marquise draped across the bed, it is the Count who is the spectator the first time the image is shown, and the camera fades his voyeuristic look to black out the rape, the unnarrated center of the story. But there is a second shot of the Marquise in a similar erotic posture, this time when she wakes up, and the only voyeur on this occasion is the spectator, who is thus placed morally as well as spatially in the position of the Count. For Rohmer as for Kleist, painting—and film through its agency—speaks directly to the body.

There is another moment in the film that dramatizes the problem of visual representation with a positively Dutch intricacy. Here the Marquise at the easel is at once a maker and an object of representation, and the curtained windows suggest that nature cannot be admitted within any of the frames in view. The Marquise is not painting from life but from a sketch, probably of another painting. (Her sketchbook is on a daybed in the foreground next to a closed book.) In the film it is possible to see the outlines of buildings roughed in on her canvas, a scene similar to those in

127

the drawing room of this, her father's house. If this is so, then both in recalling unconsciously the equivalency of body and building introduced by Kleist and by perpetuating rather than looking beyond the cultural iconography that surrounds her, the Marquise sketches herself within the ideology that in turn objectifies her.

The Marquise is positioned in the frame in an unusual way. For the most part in this film Rohmer centers his characters in a manner that recalls the style of Neoclassical painting.[99] But the Marquise is not centered here: a mirror stands in the center of the frame, and within the mirror one sees the bust of a woman's head, apparently at a great distance, rather than the Marquise's head, which is truncated. As seen by the unreflecting spectator foregrounded in the mirror of art, then, the Marquise is as much a marble image belittled as she is a larger-than-life image in the mind of the somewhat melodramatically repentant Count. In the sequence that follows these frames, the Marquise's two daughters and her serving women, women of all ages and classes, pass to and fro in awkwardly flurrying succession before the mirror, suggesting that the reduction to self-conscious objecthood by the gaze is gender specific.[100]

To return to the frame in which the Marquise stands at her easel, a surprising depth of field seems to be established by the diminution of the bust in the mirror, and in this subtle way Rohmer shows not only that woman's body is inscribed within cultural frames but that the grandeur of depth in the dwelling places (especially of the affluent) is shaped in turn by the female anatomy. Rohmer also introduces by this means the suggestion that the concept and manipulation of perspective itself can be understood as a patriarchal mode of perception.[101] In giving special prominence to the Neoclassical corridor framed by pillars or doorways, Rohmer's interiors are organized for a centrally located, unselfconsciously authoritative spectatorial eye, which gauges the depth of interior space with the confidence of a frontal perspective. If the house is a body, it must be said that in this film dangerous entries are made from deep space, typically from the far end of the corridors or passageways that the spectator penetrates. Beginning with a tableau vivant, the film represents itself as a painting come to life in which, with the women in the foreground bound to the defining frame of the pillars, the father, amid the smoke and sounds of battle, bursts through a door made more distant than it is by tunnel perspective. As one might expect, the film is a more or less continuous representation of its unnarrated center: more entries are effected than any mise-en-scène could possibly require. The Count especially, when he is not trespassing on the Marquise's estate, is viewed from both directions passing through door after door. Frequently he rushes to the foreground through the corridor in the town house, the door at the far end of which opens upon the father's study. In short, men control and patrol both ends of the perspectival tunnel. It is in affirmation of the patriarchal order, indeed, that the Marquise is united to the Count in the deep space of the cathedral, flanked by pillars, in a scene that recalls closely the moment at which the father bursts through the door in the citadel.

In returning one last time to the Marquise at her easel, we are now in a position to see that this frame places a false perspective at its center: the deep space we think we see, diminished as a sign of the control we think we have gained over it, exists authentically not in the distance but on the plane we suppose ourselves to occupy, the foreground that far from being defined by our gaze in fact defines a fourth wall—as though in accordance with Diderot's requirements for the bourgeois drama[102]—and displaces our presence from the room altogether. Or rather, insofar as any human form remains in the position of the spectator, it is the head of a woman. Here fully delineated, then, is an emblem of this film's critique of visual perspective.

But Rohmer's representation of the Marquise as an artist is not an attempt to offer a female prototype in preference to the standard image of the visual artist. The Marquise's painting is culturally conditioned, as much merely a well-bred young woman's "accomplishment" as the needlework on which she and her mother are engaged. One of her small daughters interrupts the Marquise at her easel in order to show her a page full of the letters she is learning to form, but these letters are pointedly not writing: they are a conventionally formed calligraphy, and the Marquise responds appropriately by saying "beautiful" (an appropriate response to visual representation) and placing the page on her easel. Clearly, throughout this scene there is a running commentary on the transmission of culture by rote, on the unwitting conspiracy against creative independence that gathers strength in eras of cultural homogeneity such as that of post-Revolutionary Europe—a conspiracy for which the pervasiveness of visual norms bears no small part of the responsibility. Ultimately, the *empire* "look" of this film carries the theme of ideology forward most effectively.

It is language, both voice and writing, that holds out the possibility of unconditioned expression. At the moment when the Marquise accepts her situation and thereby overcomes it, her thoughts become audible in a voice-over imposed upon the image. As the voice-over soon gives way to her actual speaking aloud, Rohmer suggests that in this moment she becomes the narrator of her own story. Similarly, in honor of verbal expression, the film places the Marquise at a writing desk that has dozens of little drawers—a richness of hidden possibility—at the precise moment when she speaks to her mother of her "inner sensations" or feelings. But when writing is in any sense subjected to coercion, as when the Marquise writes her ad and loses the chance to be released from the social order, Rohmer points to its status as a visual artifact, recalling her daughter's calligraphic penmanship. The status of the letter that banishes the Marquise from her father's house is complex in this regard. That it has been dictated makes it all the more notable and more chilling that it has not been said, but rather passed along in the form of a visible signifier produced by a scribe, the mother, who is at least to some extent the unwilling executor of autocratic authority.

Kleist, too, insistently identifies the father at this juncture as a "dictator," and makes it clear that his dictation of this letter is what leads the mother in the long run to defy him and go to the Marquise's country estate. Indeed, it cannot be said that Rohmer significantly revises Kleist's implicit analysis of texts and letters; the difference is that Rohmer places voice, script, and print against a backdrop that—even more pervasively than language—coerces and shapes consciousness, understanding this backdrop to be most subtly and profoundly, a female body atavistically inhabited by those for whom the transmission of the signifier consists, as it does for the Commandant and the Count, in the respective surrender and appropriation of a sword.

Whereas for Kleist, then, the body is potentially the site of the sensuous immediacy he admires in painting and thus far an escape from the languages of culture—the irony being that body language remains one of these—for Rohmer the body as visual field, at once vulnerable citadel, object for the voyeur, and the cinematic frame itself, is a battleground over which ideology rages—the irony being that it is *not* discourse (which is Kleist's discourse in any case) but the liberation of the visual itself that signals a release from ideology. Seen neither as chiaroscuro nor as a tunnel (the two forms of visual constraint) but rather as a *field* resembling the grounds of the Marquise's estate, the screen of vision, like the Marquise, proclaims its innocence in the very moment of being violated.

HITCHCOCK AS PYGMALION

Hitchcock, like Kleist, is concerned with the place of the body in relation to textuality, and he indulges in countless sleights of hand that blur the boundaries between illusion and reality. With typical irony, *Stage Fright*

(1950), for instance, begins with the opening of a theater's safety curtain and ends when that curtain kills the murderer in the film. Playacting is the central metaphor of *Stage Fright*: the premises on which its narrative is based originate in a story that is only revealed to be a lie at the film's conclusion. Like *Murder!* (1930) in this regard, *Stage Fright* uses a myriad of theatrical conventions to stage the repeated intersection of life and art that ultimately produce a solution to the question of whodunit.

The juxtaposition of illusion with reality, given *Stage Fright*'s theatrical setting, naturally involves the attempt to delineate further the boundary between theater and film that *Murder!* had set out to discover in seeking to give shape to the cinematic. In theater, illusion is anchored in presence, and the filmmaker's envy of the corporeality of theater—of its access to the living body as a vehicle of representation—often provokes the counterassertion of cinema's superiority as a medium.[103] But another source of motivation for cinematic moments that play havoc with character and spectator point of view concerning reality and illusion is more deep-seated than that of envy. At bottom, it is the fear of death—Bazin's "mummy complex"—that produces the many fictions enacting death.[104] By proclaiming these fictions *as* fictions, Hitchcock reminds us that no actual death has taken place; alternatively, he introduces the real into textuality in order to protect it within the safely "unreal" status of the image. As we shall see later, these strategies have an erotic dimension as well.

It is in the context of a system of substitutions of this kind that we can read Hitchcock's self-representation in his films and television movies. The famous cameo appearances in his films, his role in the promotional trailers of these films and in the episodes of *Alfred Hitchcock Presents* framed by his personal appearances are all of interest in this regard. In the sequences framing the television episodes, Hitchcock's shadow enters and fills the famous silhoutte drawing of himself (the same silhouette that was turned into a jigsaw puzzle and distributed as a Christmas card).[105] Then, a moment later, an act of materialization takes place as the shadow becomes the filmic image of Hitchcock himself. This visual joke, recalling the magic tricks of a Méliès, makes a statement concerning the manner in which the "flatness" of drawing is both inspirited and animated (signified by the arrival of the shadow) and then fleshed out by the filmic image. Having once materialized, Hitchcock functions as the impresario whose job it is to introduce his own "magic trick," the show itself.

In the promotional trailers to *Psycho* (1960) and *The Birds* (1963), Hitchcock no longer serves simply as commentator, but also to some extent enters the world of each film as he takes the audience on a tour of the Bates Motel or announces a lecture that he will give on the subject of birds.[106] In both examples, the humor that is generated by these gestures nevertheless involves an uneasiness concerning the boundary between reality and representation. Hitchcock then plays upon this uneasiness by cutting directly from himself to a scene from the film in question, drawing back a shower curtain, for instance, to reveal Janet Leigh screaming, or matching his off-camera look to a shot of Tippi Hedren shouting "They're coming!"[107] The trailer to *Frenzy* (1972) cuts from Hitchcock as commentator to several different scenes in the film, presenting "the director as a naif who has wandered into his own movie."[108] These amusing examples substantiate Hitchcock's interest in "doing it with scissors," in cutting and editing, while pointing also to the constructed, synthetic nature of film in general. As a gloss on this point, we might point to a moment in the trailer for *Frenzy* in which a model of Hitchcock's head, mounted upon a dummy, is shown floating down the Thames. Such gestures represent more than authorial self-consciousness concerning cinema as a medium. In the case of the framing material for the television shows, the body is "placed" into the text as Hitchcock materializes. Similarly, in the trailers for the films, Hitchcock deliberately and repeatedly enters into his text.

Both more puzzling and more revealing than textual play of this kind are Hitchcock's cameo shots. Present in his films since *The Lodger*, these signature shots are clearly more than simple self-advertising,[109] and their function would seem to extend beyond providing a vehicle for authorial recognition that promotes spectatorial pleasure.[110] What is problematic in the ontological status of such shots is that Hitchcock appears in them in costume, but none of his actions—usually he is a passerby of sorts—are integral to the narrative. Insofar as such shots are extradiegetic, this has to do with the principle of recognition: the spectator's awareness of the double status of the image—Hitchcock as character and Hitchcock as Hitchcock—thus placing these shots in a different context from the others that constitute the narrative.[111]

But what of the mechanism that triggers the cameo? Raymond Bellour has suggested that it is closely linked to the Imaginary of the films, interpreting Hitchcock's authorial signatures as functioning according to the logic of the Freudian pun, which, through the mechanisms of displacement and metaphor, acts as a point of crystallization for the biography of the subject. Bellour reads the cameos, then, as constituting the "imaginary body-symbol which engenders the film."[112] This is a persuasive in-

Fig. 10. Hitchcock's cameos—this one from *Vertigo*—suggest the introduction of the "real" into the space of representation.

sight, but it neglects the issue of their problematic ontology. Against the backdrop of the framing sequences and of the trailers, in which the body and the body's placement within the text are central, it would seem that another aspect of the cameo's significance lies in the way it, too, effects the gesture of placing the "real" body—Hitchcock as Hitchcock—into the text. From this point of view, the extradiegetic aspect of these images is precisely their point.

Hitchcock's films do not rehearse the exchange between real and fictional or living and dead on the thematic level alone (*Murder, Stage Fright*) or even—although this is perhaps its most telling manifestation—exclusively by means of the introduction of Hitchcock's own body. In *Vertigo* (1958), to which the story of Pygmalion and Galatea is central, this exchange is revealed to be no less than an obsession: the film's eroticism lies in its hesitation between reality and the image. A film about a painting brought to life, this is at the same time a text in which the relation of visual representation to the feminine and to death is expertly probed.[113]

133

Vertigo's famous credit sequence sets up an opposition between reality and image, image and text, while emphasizing the camera's ability to fragment the body by revealing a female face (Kim Novak's) in close-up, piecemeal. In this sequence, the image of the "real" eye generates a drawing of a vortex, thus stressing the colors, shapes, and movements of an abstract cinema whose primary effect is located in the changing shape of the image in time. Yet it is this same eye from which the word "vertigo" proceeds, suggesting that the writing (story) as well as the images that constitute the film itself have their origin in the female body. Significantly, the name "James Stewart," positioned over a shot of Novak's mouth in close-up, links the organ of speech and of narration with the male. The first two scenes of the film reinforce this opposition between static image and narrative movement: the opening scene on the rooftop establishes the domain of action as male and detective work as a narrative activity, while the second scene in Midge's studio connects visual representation with the female body and space.[114] "Vertigo" is the subject that unites both scenes.

The woman with whom Scottie, the James Stewart character, becomes obsessed is first presented to the spectator as an image: at Ernie's restaurant, Madeleine Elster (or the character "Judy" who impersonates her, and in actuality Kim Novak, who plays both) is briefly framed by the tracking camera in a composition that has a painting at its center. Moving in on her from behind, the camera lingers on her motionless and painterly image, surrounded by the draperies of stole and dress, and focuses on the blank, white space of her naked back as if to suggest that it is a screen for the projection of fantasy. When, from the point of view of Scottie, the camera centers Madeleine within the frame of a doorway, she begins to move, creating the effect of a painting brought to life, and creating at the same time a space that is clearly three-dimensional, though this "movement" is interspersed with static shots that present her face in cameo-like profile.[115] Later, when the "re-created" Madeleine walks towards Scottie along a long corridor, she is framed again and her moving image again emerges from a two-dimensional space, coming alive into a space that is three-dimensional.

Shortly thereafter, when Scottie is launched upon his detective work, Madeleine leads him through a series of scenes in and through which she defines her body and her "story." The first of these is a flower shop that she has approached via an alleyway and a service entrance. By means of this dark and clandestine approach, the brightly lit flower shop becomes a kind of "secret garden" within which Madeleine poses as a static image, a feminine interior space that itself represents her body and within which she initiates the connection between her body and a flower. The shot from Scottie's point of view by means of which we first see her is a "brush-stroke" shot that generates the image in one sweep from left to right, filling the blank space with the colored image, and suggesting that the connection between Madeleine and a painting has already been effected in Scottie's imagination.

The second scene is also a space that is entered by means of a darkened place, a chapel through which Madeleine passes into the bright and sunny graveyard beyond. Here we see Madeleine posed in long shot, in her gray suit resembling graveyard statuary amongst the tombstones, aligning herself with the grave and headstone of Carlotta Valdes. The third and most significant space takes us into a museum, a cultural edifice in which the exchange between "real" body and painterly image is finalized. Again Scottie pauses in a darkened anteroom; from this vantage point he looks at Madeleine seated still as a statue before a female portrait. Twice the camera's motion, standing in for Scottie's glance, traces a connection between the real world and that of the painting, focusing first on the bouquet purchased at the flower shop (now lying on the bench upon which Madeleine is sitting) and then on an identical one in the portrait. Next the camera fixes on the whorl into which Madeleine's hair is sculpted in order to point to that same figure—the figure for vertigo—in the painting. Although Madeleine is seated before the painting as its beholder, this scene implies that her space is continuous with it.

Each of the interiors defined by Madeleine's silent performances figure an essentially vaginal space that is entered hesitantly by Scottie, a space variously connected with flowers, death, and art. (The fourth space, that of the hotel, makes the connection to sexuality explicit.) The flowers function as an image of the female body: later, when Madeleine stages her attempted suicide by drowning, she first tears up the bouquet and tosses it into the water. Here Hitchcock is knowingly alluding to cultural tropes: death by drowning, which Gaston Bachelard calls the feminine form of death, evokes the image of a flower-bedecked, mad Ophelia, another instance of continuity between woman and flower.[116] (Madeleine's symbolic fragmentation of her body as she tears up her bouquet has another literary analogue as well: Gretchen in Goethe's *Faust I*.) As their romance develops, Madeleine tells Scottie what she experiences when she "goes away"—what happens, that is, when she becomes an image for Scottie:

135

she tells him that she feels as though she were walking down a long corridor at the end of which are darkness, a room, and an open grave.

It is not my object to analyze the role of scopophilia in this film, but rather to focus on the way in which *Vertigo* figures the collapse of the real into the representational.[117] Perceived by Scottie in Madeleine's act of spectatorship, this collapse is present also in the moment of Madeleine's "rebirth" by the agency of Scottie as Pygmalion, a sequence that narrates the collapse itself. Tellingly, the film visualizes this moment as the reverse of the walk down a corridor towards death: Judy as Madeleine walks along a hallway towards Scottie, who has been awaiting her nervously, like an anxious father awaiting the birth of his child. When, finally, Judy's hair is arranged as that of Madeleine had been, her transformation into a soft-focus "vision" is complete. If "Madeleine" can be said to have collapsed into the portrait of Carlotta, a moment refigured by her "death," then Judy brings the painting to life once more. While Scottie feels deeply betrayed by Judy because she was never the original but always only played Madeleine—"You were the copy; you were the counterfeit!"—the film nevertheless suggests that for Scottie, though not for Pygmalion, desire is essentially necrophilic and is directed, therefore, toward the image alone.

The metaphorical movement between three and two dimensions in *Vertigo*,[118] between the body's "life" in cinema and its "death" in painting, has a sexual dimension that has to do with desire for the image (of the actress) by Hitchcock himself.[119] But desire is located precisely in the hesitation between the image and the real. Repeatedly in *Vertigo*, the experience of vertigo is connected with the perceptual shift that accompanies the collapse into the two-dimensionality of the image as well as the reverse movement from flatness into the three-dimensional.[120] Similarly, the vertigo moment is represented visually by two simultaneous camera movements: a tracking out, on a single plane, and a zooming in through several planes. As Raymond Durgnat has pointed out, although Hitchcock has commented upon the flatness of the cinematic image and its restriction to two-dimensional effects, "*Vertigo* plays implications of depth off against its devious spiral inroads . . . in the astonishing combination of approach and retreat whose complex confusions of perspective briefly induce all the sensations of nausea in the spectator."[121] The approach and retreat of the camera has its obvious model in the body. By producing physical as well as emotional reactions in the spectator, Hitchcock initiates another instance of circulation between reality and the image, one which brings the body into aesthetic response.

WINGS OF DESIRE: REALITY, TEXT, EMBODIMENT

In *Wings of Desire* (1987), Wim Wenders takes up cinema's relation to the real from a perspective quite different from Hitchcock's. With its gestures toward semidocumentary status, *Wings of Desire* takes an almost Bazinian attitude toward the real in cinema, suggesting that cinema bears an "ontogenetic" relation to the real.[122] Though obviously not a documentary in any strict sense, *Wings of Desire* draws upon the genre of the city symphony in carrying out its complex project. A somewhat lyricized image of an as-yet-divided Berlin forms the backdrop for this film's meditations on a variety of representational systems, that of cinema among them. The film's ubiquitous and intrusive camera reveals a strong urge to present a cross-section of Berlin's populace: it pursues a young girl half-heartedly playing at prostitution, artists contemplating their work, an alienated youth for whom rock music functions as a lifeline, aging workers, a Turkish woman doing her laundry, streams of pedestrians and, everywhere, the city's children. Wenders's probing camera with its aerial perspectives invades the spaces of Berlin and lays them open to the spectatorial view, voyeuristically pursuing pedestrians into the private spaces of their apartments with what resembles an erotic fervor. Like other films of its genre, the film presents its vision as totalizing: shots of a woman in labor complement shots of a dying motorcyclist. Also, like Ruttmann's *Berlin: Symphony of a City* (1927), *Wings of Desire* presents a suicide to our view. But the camera records a reality that remains in some sense impenetrable, *Wings of Desire* suggests. Perhaps it is for this reason that the film exhibits traces of a directorial desire to incorporate that reality, to penetrate it, and even to merge with it in the space of the text.

As though to usurp the real by aesthetic means, both Berlin films impose formalist techniques upon the images of the city. But if *Wings of Desire* appears to emulate the earlier film in its fascination with movement, in Wenders this fascination derives only in part from a preoccupation with cinematography, with the production of moving images.[123] In this regard, Wenders' film seems to support Metz's dictum that "because movement is never material but *always* visual, to reproduce its appearance is to duplicate reality."[124] If Wenders represents his characters in every conceivable mode of transportation, it is also because these vehicles connect the various spaces of the city to one another, and evoke Wenders's typical manner of experiencing reality cinematically: a city for Wenders is a gridwork between landmarks. In *Wings of Desire*, there is a movement away from the internationalized world of *The American Friend* (1977), whose cities visually merge into one indistinguishable metropolis. The Kaiser Wilhelm Gedächtnis Kirche, the Siegessäule, the Brandenburger Tor, the Kurfürstendamm, the Staatsbibliothek, and the Wall: images of Berlin's representative spaces mark the body of this text with the texture of reality. The problem of identity is central to the narratives constructed by Wenders and Peter Handke, his frequent collaborator, and their sustained interest in material reality, derived from the insistence on surface in the nouveau roman, relates to this concern.[125] Objects mediate between reality and the perceiving subject, both displacing and augmenting the search for personal identity. Photos—which Wenders refers to as "monuments of moments"[126]—are particularly privileged objects in that they link the problem of identity to that of perception and memory, an idea that also originates in the theoretical underpinnings of the nouveau roman. For Wenders, polaroids as "instant objects" that arrest the flow of time—or "embalm" it, as Bazin puts it—are thus of special interest.[127]

As though in an effort to frame and control the reality that the camera admits into *Wings of Desire*, the body of Wenders's cinematic narrative is bracketed by images of writing, as the angel Damiel's writing hand that opens and closes the film. Since the film begins in black and white and only gradually acquires color, the initial black and white images are the more obviously presented as cinematic writing, as though to counteract a Bazinian realism with an allusion to the nouvelle vague's "caméra stylo." Connected with secondariness and absence, writing is doubly coded as fallen: Damiel is only capable of writing after he has literally fallen—after, that is, he has acquired a body and a history. The film's narrative, the whole of which exists as a flashback of sorts, is punctuated by Damiel's poetic evocation of an unfallen past, the repetition of which—"when the child was a child"—suggests that Damiel's written text, a product of experience like other stories, is governed by an elegiac desire for immediacy that the film represents as available only to the camera.

Wings of Desire contains a figuration of the narrative impulse in the character of Homer, "the storyteller," as he is usually called, in whom stories are said to "well up." This old man is presented both as an allegorical, ahistorical figure who has existed through the ages—whose listeners gradually became his readers at the point at which the oral tradition is superseded by the written one—and also as a man with a specific German past dating from the early part of this century. Not surprisingly, one of the spaces in which the storyteller appears is the library, and in the delineation of this space allegiance is also divided between reference and self-reference: it is at once quite obviously Berlin's *Staatsbibliothek* and also a kind of Borgesian, allegorical Library. As the storyteller ponders a book of photographs of Berlin, these photos are "animated" by actual wartime documentary footage of the destroyed city with its dead—footage that, in the narrative of the film, is represented as constituting the storyteller's personal memories. As in the opening sequence of the film, where hand-writing and the "writing" of the camera occur in concert with the narrating voice, in this moment the sense of the real conveyed in a genuinely documentary cinema is undermined by being represented as the product of narrative desire and personal memory. On another occasion, the storyteller looks for the remembered places of a destroyed city, for the Potsdamer Platz, site of the Café Josti where he had sat and of the tobacconist he had frequented. As the storyteller wanders aimlessly within a transformed cityscape, his fading voice mourns and is unable to evoke the places we do not see. In the meantime, the camera exposes the rubble and rubbish of Berlin's no-man's-land to view.

Wings of Desire is a far cry indeed from the documentary without a voice that Ruttmann's Berlin film was originally intended to be, the kind of film that, according to Doane, "promotes the illusion that reality speaks and is not spoken."[128] Montage is the dominant structuring principle of Ruttmann's Berlin film and, given its historical moment, this is necessarily a voiceless montage, a montage of images alone that renders human bodies as mechanisms continuous with their surroundings. In contrast, what is notable about Wenders's film is the montage of voices of which it is comprised: its montage of interior monologues, so extensive as to dominate the fabric of the film and to comprise its network, is unusual in film history.[129] Presented as voice-overs, this montage of sound constitutes an aural equivalent of the film's montage of images, thus fulfilling what Lacan calls the invocatory drive, the spectator's drive to hear as well as to see.[130] By imposing voice-overs upon the images of characters' bodies—rather than simply allowing them to speak their lines of dialogue—the film acts out its desire to penetrate the opacity of their bodily presence.

When the cinematic voice is not anchored or grounded in an imaged body, this detachment of sound from its source threatens simultaneously to reveal the voice as a signifier and the heterogeneity of film as a medium.[131] In the case of the interior monologue, as Doane points out, "the voice and the body are represented simultaneously, but the voice, far from being an extension of the body, manifests its inner lining. The voice displays what is inacessible to the image, what exceeds the visible: the 'inner life' of the character. The voice here is the privileged mark of interiority, turning the body 'inside out.'"[132] In *Berlin: Symphony of a City*, the absence of an overarching narrative other than that of its own formalizing impulse suggests that this film is to some extent *about* the unavailability of personal narratives in an urban setting. Wenders's interior monologues, in contrast, impose personal narratives upon the characters that are more intimate than any that the spectatorial gaze alone can afford. But Wenders's control over the image is short-lived: through the separation of speech from its source in the speaking subject, a rupture is created between the revealed body—whose mouth does not move—and the personal voice of the interior monologue. This rupture, slight as it is, produces a split in point of view on the part of the spectator, who cannot wholly reconcile image track with sound track.

Elsaesser has called the cinema "an apparatus designed by a Kantian epistemologist," basing this claim on Baudry's discussion of that "hidden third term" of the cinematic apparatus—the camera—that necessarily sets up "an unbridgeable subject/object division that renders the object forever unknowable."[133] In the films of Herzog, Fassbinder, and Wenders alike, Elsaesser has noted, both the place of the self and that of the spectator are effectively "empty," and the camera is both unlocalizable and omnipresent. Indeed, *Wings of Desire*, like Ruttmann's film, is characterized at times by flashily subjective camerawork from a character's point of view, while at other times the camera is invasive and "disembodied." Unsuccessful though it may be, the use of interior monologue is one way in which *Wings of Desire* gestures toward a bridging of the gap between subject and object necessarily set up by cinema.

Most obviously, perhaps, the collapse of subject into object occurs on the level of the narrative, for Wenders's film allegorizes its desire for access to the seen. The narrative proper begins with a shot of clouds followed by a shot of a great "transcendental eye" that cues a preoccupation with vision. It tells the story of the angel Damiel's desire to leave the realm of the spiritual for that of the material and for bodily sensations: Damiel wants to feel pain, to take off his shoes under the table, to feed the cat, "like Philip Marlowe." Damiel wants an existence governed by temporality; he wants a story. A frustrated observer of life, Damiel is distanced by virtue of his spectatorial relation to the world: he can see and hear, but he cannot be seen or be heard in turn and hence cannot participate in the narrative of life that unfolds before him. Although Damiel is necessarily visible to the film's spectator, within its diegesis he is visible only to children who, like him, are as yet unfallen.

During the course of the narrative, Damiel's desire for embodiment is fired by the female trapeze artist Marion who, as a circus performer, offers a lure for the eye. Although Damiel feels desire for Marion, she cannot feel his touch and he cannot be touched; the frustration provoked by Marion as spectacle motivates Damiel to abandon his voyeuristic relation to the city and its inhabitants and to participate in its life. We might say, then, that Damiel's position closely parallels that of both the male spectator and the director of a film: he is caught up in narratives in which he cannot participate, which he must watch from a distance, and to which he exists in a relation of desire. Insofar as Marion is connected with the camera as well, Damiel's desire for her also figures the directorial preoccupation with the apparatus.[134] Wenders's coup in this film is to have narrativized the spectatorial and, somewhat more obliquely, the directorial position. During the course of *Wings of Desire*, Damiel materializes—is rendered "real" in the context of the narrative—and thus metaphorically realizes the spectator's and director's entry into the text.

Wenders signals Damiel's embodiment through an ingenious use of color: before his fall, Damiel had been able to see only in black and white. After his fall deposits him near the Berlin Wall, his head bleeding slightly, the scene gradually becomes suffused with color—the film is now "in living Technicolor," as it were—and the Wall is revealed to be decorated with multiply reproduced images of cartoon men, graffiti by the artist Thierry Noir, featuring the color red.[135] Almost immediately, Damiel touches his wound, says of his blood "it is red," and tastes it, learning colors and physical sensations at one and the same time. Lest we should forget, however, that color retains the representational force that had been the exclusive province of black and white, the paint on the Wall is there to remind us of this, ironizing the success of Damiel's descent into the real. It also suggests, less ironically, a similarity between red paint and red blood, pointing thereby to a mode of representation that seeks to collapse the distance between body and sign, despite remaining irreducibly a sign. (Here Wenders's film most clearly shows its Kleistian preoccupations, giving expression to the position delineated in the "Letter of a Painter to His Son," in which the work of art is seen as the vigorous offspring of body and mind whose climbing about between Heaven and Earth will perplex aestheticians.) By means of this scene, the film gestures toward actualization, toward the attainment of the real, and in this way metaphorically infuses contemporary—reproducible, cinematic— representations with new life. As a gesture toward the real, it exists in opposition to a trompe l'oeil moment in Wenders's *Paris, Texas* (1984), in which the camera pulls back to reveal that the blue sky against which the Dean Stockwell character had been posed is actually a commercial, reproducible, billboard representation.[136] In this moment, the irrefutably textual status of reality is gestured toward; *Wings of Desire* wants instead to focus its materiality.

In *Wings of Desire*, Wenders is fascinated with an impenetrable "reality" that enters film via the camera, and this fascination explains his concern with quasidocumentary images. Finding this reality to be inaccessible, Wenders inverts the problem by composing a narrative around the real by means of which he can then fictionally enter what has obviously become a text. By suggesting that he can be absorbed into the spectacle before him, Wenders stages a collapse of the subject/object relation implicit in cinema, attempting thus to resolve the narrative of desire at its most basic level. Wenders narrativizes this collapse in the sexual and spiritual union of Damiel with Marion, concerning which Damiel's voice-over claims, "I was in her and she was around me."[137] Tellingly, the desire for fusion with the film is figured not only as a desire for sexual union, but also as the regressive desire, not fully conscious in the film, to return to the womb. Nevertheless, from a cinematic perspective, Wenders's film effects a metaphorical collapse with the real, a collapse that is figured as a "becoming real" within the narrative and as an act of erotic appropriation. This strategy, which we might call Wenders's "solution" to the subject/object gap in cinema, is an "authentically" postmodern solution.

A brief look at Godard's *Two or Three Things I Know About Her* (1966), a film that conflates city and woman, may serve to bring Wenders' film into relief. In *Two or Three Things*, it is the director's voice— Godard's voice-over—that unites the various representational systems that are carefully separated and juxtaposed by the film's modernism. It is Godard's subjective, often whispering and intimate voice that binds the systems he has deliberately taken apart into a new whole. Indeed, his voice-over, unanchored by any visible body, suggests the presence of a muted but insinuating authority, and the controlling power of this voice, given the subject matter of the film (the city as prostitute), is connected with sexual control—over the woman whose story is told, over the city whose story the woman indirectly tells, and over the body of the film itself. Wenders's film, on the other hand, is marked by an even higher degree of self-consciousness about this directorial power to dominate the material of film than Godard's, a mode of self-consciousness (not without its own attendant blindness) that substitutes fusion for dominance.

The rhetoric of the postmodern aside, however, Wenders's allegory of fusion ultimately remains just that. Damiel, though granted a body and plunged into the city to which he had existed previously in the relation of voyeur, is nevertheless left ultimately and ironically in the position of writer and narrator. Distanced in the act of writing, at the end of the film Damiel's body is figured only in a gesture of loss as the writing hand that frames the film. While *Wings of Desire* does seem to suggest that cinema "embodies"—gives immediacy, life, and color to—the hopelessly distanced signs of the writer's medium, in its final frames the various subjectivities that the film had been at such pains to evoke collapse into the subjectivity of its authors after all and its voice-overs stand revealed as Handke's text. Its "documentary" images acknowledged to have been shaped by human perception, Berlin itself stands revealed as the product of the authors' constructing view.

KLEIST, TABLEAU VIVANT, AND THE PORNOGRAPHIC

Understood both as a moment of suspended action in the drama and as the interface between theater and painting, Diderot's concept of the dramatic tableau no doubt provided a model for tableau vivant.[138] As a dramatist well acquainted with French literature, Kleist would have been familiar with the tableau in Diderot's sense; and, because tableau vivant struggles to bridge the gap between the body and representation, a gap to which Kleist seems to recur compulsively, it comes as no surprise that tableau vivant would hold an interest for him.[139] Perhaps it was, therefore, in response to Diderot, to the tableaux vivant of Goethe's *Elective Affinities*, or to Goethe's writings on art, that in 1811 Kleist wrote and published *The Foundling*, a novella in which he explores the tension between living body and visual representation that structures tableau vivant. Kleist's text establishes a relation between tableau vivant and eighteenth-century conventions of pornography, a connection that proves to be instructive concerning the manner in which cinema sometimes incorporates tableau vivant.

In *The Foundling*, Kleist is concerned with the consequences of replacing an original with images and doubles, and he sets up a seemingly endless set of substitutions to this end. Rendering *The Foundling* unlike *The*

143

Marquise of O. . . . in this regard, language and written texts in their relation to the real have a less important role to play in this novella than painting and theater, although they do not disappear from view altogether. *The Foundling* features Piachi, a murderer who refuses to take communion, to eat the body of Christ in order to save his soul, and thus enacts Kleist's perplexity concerning the symbolic relation of the wafer to Christ's body and towards the Christian doctine of the "Word made Flesh." In the letters that spell "Colino," to cite another example, Piachi's adopted son Nicolo mistakenly reads an anagram of his own name, an error that reinforces the tenuous connection between sign and signified and provokes a chain of disastrous consequences.

But the manner in which visual representation and the situation of beholding are presented in Kleist's text are of greater significance here than the gap between the *verbal* signifier and the signified. Pertinent to these concerns are two scenes in particular: the first involves a male voyeur's view through a keyhole of a woman kneeling before a painting, the second a tableau vivant enacted consequently by the voyeur for the benefit of the woman. Kleist's narrative contextualizes these scenes as follows: the woman, Elvira, had in her youth been rescued by a young Genoese nobleman who lay near death for years as a result of his heroism and eventually died. Now married to another, the much older Piachi, Elvira keeps a life-size painting of the nobleman in an alcove of her bedroom, "behind a silk curtain, lit by a special lamp."[140] It is not necessary to be familiar with the keyhole and candle situation of eighteenth-century pornography on which this scene relies, or with the erotic nature of Kleist's response to the visual arts in general to perceive the sexual significance of this scenario.[141] At the same time, by means of the curtain, special lighting, and the tableau vivant later staged in this space by Nicolo, Elvira and Piachi's adopted son, this scene also points to conventions of theatrical staging,[142] suggesting that Kleist is experimenting with Rousseau's attitude concerning the morally corrupting effect of the visual arts and theater.[143]

The complexity of the spectatorial relations suggested in Nicolo's surreptitious observation of Elvira's ritual through the keyhole, deserves attention. The scene involves a relay of looks: not only does the reader observe Elvira and her lover through Nicolo's eyes, but the reader is privy to Nicolo's voyeuristic pose outside the door. Not surprisingly at this point, seen through the peephole that reduces depth vision, the full-length portrait of the young nobleman is not recognizable to either Nicolo or the reader as a portrait. It is important to the frisson that the novella generates later that Elvira appears to be having a tryst with a living man: "What should he see but Elvira lying in an attitude of swooning ecstasy at someone's feet."[144] As the narrative later reveals, Elvira sometimes presents herself naked to the portrait's "view." In these moments, Elvira is at once a beholder and imagines herself beheld, enacting an erotic spectacle over which she has complete control: she pulls the curtain to reveal the portrait at will.

From a representational point of view, Kleist's rather daring idea of the beholder as spectacle for an image is unthinkable without the intervention of Diderot's *Salons*;[145] in this scene, Kleist plays both upon the trope of the portrait come to life (ironized by the reader's awareness that this is the portrait of a dead man) and on Diderot's fiction of the beholder's entry into the space of the painting.[146] It is on the trope of the portrait come to life, too, that Nicolo plays when he stages the tableau vivant by means of which he hopes to seduce and to punish Elvira. Draping the portrait in black cloth as a background for himself in costume—like the future Lady Hamilton in her picture frame—Nicolo assumes the posture of the portrait with the intention of acting out the scenario that Elvira has presumably fantasized. The appearance of Nicolo's three-dimensional, living body in place of the two-dimensional portrait has the predictable result that Elvira, Kleistian character that she is, falls unconscious to the floor.

Let us turn for a moment to another spectacle of some importance to this novella, one that is staged by Piachi, Elvira's husband, for the benefit of Nicolo. By resorting to ruses of various kinds, Piachi contrives to make Nicolo believe that a funeral procession he witnesses is that of his mistress rather than his wife.[147] The dead body displayed in the coffin—a *tableau mort* of sorts—is rendered even more "spectacular" by virtue of the fact that Nicolo believes it to belong to someone else. By creating a fiction around the body, Piachi as dramatist has imposed another level of artifice upon the body on display.

While this incident involving a corpse reinforces by contrast the uncanniness of tableau vivant, its motionless "fixing" of the living human body that is akin to death, the source of its power does not lie in this connection. Instead, it lies in the erotic pull of the woman in the coffin upon Nicolo as spectator. This scene, then, together with Nicolo's tableau vivant, give narrative expression to Lyotard's claim that tableau vivant exerts a strong libidinal pull on the spectator.[148] The necrophilic aspect of Elvira's ritual before the portrait—her desire for a dead man—is supplemented by the erotically "fascinating paralysis" of his image in the portrait. Lyotard also glosses the subject of arrested movement: there are parallels between Nicolo's pose and the Swedish institution called *posering*, in which young girls assume and hold poses for clients who may only look, not touch. Apparently it is not merely the nature of the particular pose assumed that is of erotic interest to spectators, but also the fact that the pose is held and the body is immobilized.[149]

Elvira's fascination with arrested movement is interrupted when Nicolo supplants the image with his living body, rendering the image "real." In Baudrillard's terms this is the genuinely pornographic moment of the scenario, since "the only phantasy in pornography, if there is one . . . is not a phantasy of sex, but of the real."[150] As a "simulacrum of accumulation against death," the real in Baudrillard's reading sheds light upon the tableau vivant at once as an erotic spectacle and as a defense against death.[151] Kleist, then, narrativizes the two most compelling characteristics of tableau vivant: the erotic fascination that its confusion between persons and objects sometimes elicits, and its ability to evoke the uncanny boundary between life and death. Since both of these relations are based upon substitutions, the suitability of tableau vivant as a vehicle for the playing out of Kleist's crisis of signification (his so-called "Kant crisis") is confirmed as tableau vivant nearly succeeds in producing the collapse of the signifier into the signified that so much preoccupies him.

It is tempting to read *The Foundling* not only as an effort to take Rousseau's side against Diderot in the matter of the seductiveness of the visual arts and theater but, more specifically, as a warning against "entering the painting" and exposing oneself to the tableau's lure. The potentially pernicious binding force of the tableau vivant, recognized by Kleist, is also addressed by cinema, for which the arrested motion of tableau vivant is also a matter of compelling interest. As Pascal Bonitzer sees it, tableau vivant in cinema is "un monstre composite, un sphinx" that stops the moving image and poses an "enigma."[152] Seen in the context of film's own essentially hybrid nature, tableau vivant in film suggests a troping of this heterogeneity. In Fassbinder, tableau vivant's essential generic heterogeneity—its fusion of theater with painting—provides a model, alongside its ontological heterogeneity, for cinematic efforts to situate the body within a variety of representational modes. For Fassbinder, perhaps, it is tableau vivant's pornographic interest in Baudrillard's extended sense, its "maniacal obsession with the real" in relation to representation, that is ultimately of greatest consequence.[153]

Fassbinder's Cinema of Mixed Modes:
Tableau Vivant and the Real

For Rainer Werner Fassbinder, the heterogeneous nature of the cinematic text at times seems simply to be a given, at other times more fraught with difficulty, but it is never a matter about which his films sustain illusions. Characteristic of Fassbinder's style are his unusually long, embedded narratives—stories characters tell one another that are not, contrary to usual cinematic practice, illustrated by the camera. This foregrounding of narrative, though vocal, is nevertheless a reminder of film's relation to written texts that tell their story only in words, as one of Fassbinder's literary adaptations, *Fontane Effi Briest* (1974) makes abundantly clear. In this film the literary, Fontane's novel, remains the vocal—a voice-over of passages from the novel read by Fassbinder himself—while the sequence of images on the screen largely concerns mundane events that the novel either treats in passing or does not mention at all. The film seems meant to complement the novel, and thus to offer a more complete and answerable texture of reality than the novel alone could offer, calling attention to its limits simply by quoting it in a context beyond its scope.

Fassbinder's *Despair* (1978), on the other hand, carries out in shockingly literal fashion the wish that Nabokov with great irony allows his deluded narrator to utter: "An author's fondest dream is to turn the reader into a spectator."[154] By doing just that, by turning the novel into a film, Fassbinder exposes the naiveté of the narrator's wish and exalts film as a simultaneous mode of creation and interpretation. In Fassbinder's film, the struggle between Hermann, Nabokov's narrator and quasi filmmaker figure, and Ardalion, the red-bearded painter, is staged as a struggle for the body of Hermann's wife, Lydia. The film, like the novel in this regard, works to found Hermann's desire for his wife upon a desire for his mother, and incest is also suggested in the affair between his wife and Ardalion, who are cousins. By these means a triadic relation is established through which painting and cinema are linked, once again, in their struggle for the body of the woman over which the painter—as "father" here—has greater control. Fittingly, perhaps, Fassbinder dedicates his adaptation of Nabokov to Van Gogh and to another writer who was fascinated by this painter, Antonin Artaud.[155]

Fassbinder has recourse to painting most obviously in *The Bitter Tears of Petra von Kant* (1972), in which one entire wall of the room where

147

most of the film's action takes place is covered with a huge, frameless reproduction of Poussin's "Midas and Dionysos." Dionysos in this cropped version of the painting now occupies its center, a position that accentuates his mediating function between a reclining bacchante and King Midas; this position, as Lynne Kirby has argued, serves to accentuate Dionysos's bisexuality, his "status as a figure of mixed modes."[156] Sexual ambiguity, rendered acceptable by its embodiment in the Greek god and hence represented by Poussin as anything other than "monstrous," can be said to be emblematic of Fassbinder's commitment to an art that typically transgresses boundaries of gender and genre, that insists on blurring the arts in a heterogeneous text in which literature and painting both have their—sometimes disputed—place. On the whole, then, we can recognize in Fassbinder an open allegorization of the themes whereby film willingly embraces its status as a hybrid text. Very often in Fassbinder there is a layering of painting, sculpture, theater, and the cinematic by means of which his films explore the place of the body within representation.

This is not to imply, however, that there is in any sense a diminishment of the sexual tension marking the interaction of image and narrative in Fassbinder's films. Indeed, what might be called the impulse toward tableau vivant plays a crucial structuring role in Fassbinder's work. Critics have often noted the frequency of the tableau shot in Fassbinder's films, the static compositions of his frames and the frozen attitudes of his actors, elements of Fassbinder's style that characterize all of his films to a greater or lesser degree from *Love is Colder Than Death* (1969), the first, to *Querelle* (1982), the last. In these films, then, painting has a role to play not only as a static, essentially two-dimensional mode of visual representation that interrupts narrative, but also in its merger with theater as painting's embodied form, the tableau vivant. In Fassbinder's films, the double effect of the tableau vivant comes into play: its evocation of mortification or a kind of "death in life" at once supplements and offsets the erotic pull exerted by its suspended action.

The reciprocity between theater and film in Fassbinder's work is well documented: avant-garde theater practices informed his films from the beginning, much as the cinema shaped his dramatic productions.[157] *The American Soldier* (1970), for instance, a film made by Fassbinder's *anti-theater* ensemble, juxtaposes the generic conventions that originate in an archetypal theater with the conventions of the gangster film, thus pitting the conventions of high and low art against one another in the act of ironizing both.[158] Repeatedly in Fassbinder's plays and films, Brechtian analysis is countered by melodramatic catharsis, and frequently the astonishing corporeality of Artaud's theater is called upon as a model for the staging of the "real."[159]

Theater, along with painting, is one of the representational systems that Fassbinder harnesses in *The Bitter Tears of Petra von Kant*. Produced both as a play and as a film, *Petra von Kant* appropriates the Neoclassical conventions of theatrical staging as an ironic backdrop for bathos and melodrama: unity of place is reflected in the womb-like prison of the studio, division into acts reduced to periodic changes of wig and costume, the oppressive closure of the plot reinforced by a sense of its infinite repetition. But the theatrical resides not only in these parodied structures and in the exaggerated costumes worn by the actresses. It may also be located in the studied poses and ritualized movements of their bodies on display. In *Petra von Kant*, Fassbinder resorts to pantomime and gesture in a manner worthy of the eighteenth-century stage. The mask-like expression and muteness of one of its characters, Marlene, points to the influence of pantomime. What appears to interest Fassbinder most about theater—and he is like the early German commentators on cinema in this respect—is the presence of the body on stage. One of the ways in which Fassbinder seeks to retain the sense of the body's physical presence for cinema is, somewhat ironically, by discarding "natural" movement in favor of choreography: exaggerated gestures emphasize the body's corporeality as well as its ability to move.

The mannequins that are variously deployed within the spaces of *Petra von Kant* are central to a discussion of the body in the film. The position of these figures changes from scene to scene in a manner that at once echoes and comments upon the actions of the actresses: posed in an embrace, they mirror the lovers Petra and Karin; as models for Marlene's sketches their blank eyes appear to be watching her. Though corrupted by their commercial function in dressmaking and design, these mannequins inhabit the place of sculpture in *Petra von Kant*. As naked and sightless as Winckelmann's classical statues, their female figures nevertheless point to themselves as three-dimensional representations of the body, especially when, for instance, they are placed near the depth- and space-creating rafters of the set.[160] While the actual inability of these figures to move suggests a stasis more profound than that of the actresses in their arrested poses—suggesting that these are *not* living bodies—a uncanny impression of "life" is evoked by their appearance in a variety of postures. Both in their limitation—not actually possessing the "life" of the theatrical body played and played upon by the actresses—and in their strength—their three-dimensional corporeality—these sculptural figures stand in for the cinematic body with its lack of "presence" and its simultaneous claim to materiality.[161]

In their obvious three-dimensionality, the mannequins are distinguished from the naked figures of Bacchus and the bacchante in Poussin's painting, whose lavishly displayed bodies, accentuated by spotlights, attain a painterly version of corporeality that is doubly "flattened" by the spectator's awareness that the painting has been reproduced and reduced to a wallpaper of sorts. In Fassbinder's film Poussin's painting is cropped but enlarged, and the frame that would emphasize Poussin's composition and concentrate its power inward has been discarded, as if in specific reference to Bazin's view that the function of the picture frame is to enforce a "discontinuity between the painting and the wall, that is to say between the painting and reality."[162] For Bazin, this discontinuity distinguishes it from the cinematic frame whose outer edges he reads as "the edges of a piece of masking that shows only a portion of reality."[163] Fassbinder's gesture of removing the painting from the frame, as it were, and of actually covering the entire wall with an image of it suggests a comment concerning, on the one hand, the cinematic frame as reproducible image rather than Bazin's slice of reality and, on the other, the extension of the representational space of painting into those of theater and film. As Timothy Corrigan has suggested, one aesthetic objective of *Petra von Kant* lies in its juxtaposition of various planar surfaces, of which the mural is one.[164] As Corrigan points out, Petra, situated between the Poussin and the mannequins, exists within a dialectic of sorts. But the nature of the interplay between her body, coded as theatrical, the bodies in the painting, and the sculptural bodies of the mannequins may be of a different kind than Corrigan suggests. Moving among the various representational systems upon which this film plays, Fassbinder seems to probe the nature of cinema's "reality effect."[165] At the center of these juxtapositions is a struggle for identity that has to do not only with character and narrative, but with ontological issues concerning the mode of existence of cinema as well. The conclusion of *Despair* addresses these issues most obviously when it narrativizes the movement from representation into the real in a moment that recalls *Uncle Josh at the Moving Picture Show*. With the words "I am coming out. Don't look at the camera," Hermann "leaves" the text in an act of "literalization."[166]

As we shall see later, questions of artifice and reality also intersect with a variety of psychoanalytic scenarios that play themselves out repeatedly in Fassbinder's films. It is the camera itself, with its ostentatious move-

Fig. 11. Fassbinder plays upon the layering of painted and "theatrical" bodies.

ment so typical of his films, that stands in for the cinematic in *Petra von Kant*. At the beginning of the film the camera's movements call attention to themselves by the manner in which they virtually generate space through an enigmatic floor-level tracking shot that is retraced backwards and forwards until the spectator understands the continuity that it has constructed. In making these movements from the foreground into another space, the camera has a function in addition to that of representing the spectator's voyeuristic eye: the camera is not merely an observer or even a participant in the action. By retracing its movements, the camera underlines the manner in which it is able to create depth while gesturing toward the three-dimensionality of cinematic space as such in the process. The effectiveness of this gesture is enhanced because it is made outside the conventions of spatial continuity, thus enabling the spectator to see camera movement in and of itself, in its most basic function.

Strikingly mobile, the camera forms a pronounced contrast both to the studied movements of the actors as theatrical bodies and to their actual immobility in the shots that suggest tableaux vivants. The camera zooms in and moves in circles, tracking around the actors as though to expose the painterly stasis in which they are entrapped. As one critic notes of *In a Year of Thirteen Moons* (1978), this film's gruesome slaughterhouse scene presents the dismemberment of animals by means of a moving camera whose flow reveals a still life, "a kind of *nature morte*."[167] Indeed, Fassbinder seems to refer almost intentionally to the mixed nature of tableau vivant when he says of similar moments in *Chinese Roulette* (1976) that "when the camera moves a great deal around something that's dead, it's shown to be dead. Then you can create a longing for something that's alive."[168] Fassbinder's project in *Chinese Roulette* is to take artificiality to its limits in order to examine the place where death and life, the artificial and the real, meet.

Fassbinder's last film, *Querelle*, indulges in just such moments of artificiality, perhaps the most notable being the vertiginous sequences during which the camera inscribes two 360 degree circles or in which it follows Querelle and Lysiane as they dance slowly in circles. These moments undoubtedly point, on the narrative level, to various kinds of entrapment experienced by the characters, but they point also to the camera's participation in an erotic scenario.[169] Sometimes camera movement seems to elicit a character's look, as when it lingers, in *Petra von Kant*, on the back of an actress who then turns around to meet its gaze, as though prodded or awakened by the camera. In other ways, too, camera motion is linked to the erotic, both by revealing posed bodies to the gaze and by actually creating an eroticized space. As Kaja Silverman points out, in *Beware of a Holy Whore* (1970) "the camera meanders from person to person, and group to group, sometimes by means of a cut, and at other times through some aleatory movement which parallels the libidinal 'drift.'"[170]

It is in conjunction with the immobility of the characters that camera movement is most libidinous. The camera presents these figures to the view as though "elaborating their formal arrangement for the pleasure of the spectator."[171] This is where the erotic—or, indeed, pornographic—aspect of the arrested movement of the tableau comes into play. Writing about Freud's reading of *Gradiva*, Barthes observes the power of such moments: "What Hanold falls in love with is a woman walking (*Gradiva*: the one who comes toward him), and furthermore glimpsed within the frame of a bas-relief. What fascinates, what ravishes me is the image of a body *in situation*."[172] Although Barthes does not stress the entrapment of the figure in motion within the bas-relief, it is surely this that renders her "in situ" and captures his erotic imagination. In Fassbinder films such as *Beware of a Holy Whore* or *Petra von Kant*, the "formal suspense" implicit in suspended action is heightened by camera movement—a slow pan or a tracking shot—over the tableaux. Here the fetishization of the apparatus that Fassbinder's mobile camera represents mirrors the fetishized images of the tableaux vivants. As I have suggested above, the tableau expresses a hesitation concerning the development of narrative that has its origin in masochism.[173] Formal suspense proceeds at once from a desire to arrest narrative development in order to defer and fetishistically to cover over the threat of castration *and* from the fact that death—or the stasis that stands in for it—can be read as the fantasy fulfillment of masochistic desire. It is for this reason that in films such as *Querelle* both sex and murder scenes are choreographed and sets are so obviously artificial. By such formal means, a counterpoint is set up to the reality of the body. At times, this body is subsumed by or "killed off" into representation, while at others artifice causes the body's corporeality to stand out in sharp relief.

While artifice and formal arrangements can be understood as erotic display in Fassbinder's films, the artificial, as Fassbinder himself is quoted above as suggesting, is very much tied to the "real." One of the tableau scenes in *Ali: Fear Eats the Soul* (1974) is telling in this regard. In this scene, a theatrical space is created by a stage-like bed placed in front of a window framed with curtains. Both the layering of representational systems and the voyeuristic position inhabited by the spectator call Kleist's *Foundling* to mind.[174] Although both Ali's and Barbara's naked bodies are on view here, this scene does not derive its power exclusively from the specularization and eroticizing of the image.[175] Rather, it is the conjunction of the signs of theater and of painting (suggested by means of the doorway that occasionally frames the scene) with the corporeality of the body that engenders the pornographic effect of this notably silent scene: its power derives from an excess of reality—the naked body—within a context of pure artifice.

Satan's Brew (1976) explores the dialectic between the artificial and the real from another perspective, and within a preposterous plot that nevertheless displays a few twists and turns worthy of Hitchcock, most notably in the scene in which a murder enacted within a sado-masochistic sexual relationship is revealed to have been staged. The poet has not killed his mistress after all, nor has the supposed murder in actuality released him from his writer's block: he has not really composed a poem at all, merely "written" a Stefan George poem that George himself had translated from Baudelaire. The poet's self-stylization as the dead George (the German poet most closely associated with aestheticism and homosexuality) is supported financially by a woman who prostitutes herself on his behalf. At every conceivable point in this film the body, as the representative of the real, is juxtaposed with textuality and artifice; bodies (usually of women) are subjected to violent sex, beating, illness, and

153

death. Difficult to watch as it is, this violence toward the body should not be read only as a misogynist act of "punishment" or an aspect of sado-masochistic sexuality, but also as a symptom of an even more overwhelming need to signify the real. In *Satan's Brew* orgiastic sex and violence are interchangeable because they assert—insofar as representation is able—the materiality of the body through its sensations of pleasure and pain.

In his use of violence to suggest physicality, Fassbinder owes a great deal to Artaud.[176] In essays such as "Theater and the Plague," the manifesto of his "Theater of Cruelty," and in the "Letters on Cruelty," Artaud delineates his desire to find a "physical language. . . . a solid, material language by which theater can be distinguished from words."[177] Artaud calls for a "visual and plastic representation of speech," one that Derrida compares to dreamwork in its desire to find the word that lends itself best to plastic representation.[178] According to Artaud—and here we recall Fassbinder's strategy of representational layering in *Petra von Kant*—one way of creating such a language is to use all available expressive means together, so that they will interact and subvert one another. Although Artaud does not explain precisely how the mutual subversion of various representational systems will produce the effect of a material language, he no doubt feels that it is this excess of representation that will create a foil for the body's physical reality. Naturally, gesture and mime also serve the physical and plastic ends of theater.[179] For Artaud, theatrical gesture in itself is violent but "disinterested,"[180] and cruelty is not understood as exclusively physical, but as "a pure and detached feeling, a veritable movement of the mind."[181]

It may have been Artaud who piqued Fassbinder's interest in Hieronymus Bosch, the middle panel of whose "Garden of Earthly Delights" forms the backdrop for Franz's crucifixion in the dream scene of *Berlin Alexanderplatz* (1980).[182] The crucifixion scene is very much a scene of mixed modes: in the background, as in *Petra von Kant*, a reproduction of Bosch's painting fills the wall; Franz Biberkopf is suspended on the cross against this backdrop; a tableau vivant of the Nativity forms the foreground;[183] a naked couple engaged in sex is evident in the middle distance; and a statue of a male body seen from the rear constitutes its left-hand frame. As in *Petra von Kant*, the figuration of the body across a wide spectrum of representational modes is centrally significant to this scene. Although this middle panel of Bosch's triptych is not clearly visible, one can discern its many naked human figures in strange conjunctions with animals, plants, and minerals, engaged in what appears, even at a distance, to be a celebration of corporeality. In Fassbinder's film, the naked couple engaged in sexual acts complements the male sculpture whose positioning, from a homosexual perspective, is sexually provocative. Franz's symbolic death, therefore, is staged within an erotic space created by painted bodies in the background, "living" bodies copulating in the middle distance, and a sculptural body in the foreground. In some sense other than the narrative, Franz's death seems to be the fulfillment of this space. Although Bazin's notion of the pleasure produced by the "ontological pornography" present in a graphic image of death is not the point here, nevertheless what Susan Sontag calls, in an analysis of Bataille, an "erotics of agony" is clearly at play.[184] After Franz has died, two angels of death clear away the dead bodies that litter what has become a corpse-strewn landscape, all the while reciting a paean to death.

Kaja Silverman, in her convincing reading of Fassbinder's films within the context of sadomasochism and what she calls the "ruination" of masculinity, rightly asserts that in Fassbinder "there is a kind of arrestation at the site of suffering" and that this site is highly eroticized.[185] In Silverman's reading of the crucifixion scene, however, the fact that Franz's dreamed death does not change him is evidence that Fassbinder rejects death as an avenue of escape from "the vicious circle of masculinity."[186] Silverman points out that pain is privileged rather than death, and that there is an "arrestation at the site of suffering" precisely because death would mean its termination. Deleuze's reading of masochism, however, claims that death may be seen as the "fantasy solution to masochistic desire."[187] A less literal reading of Franz's death might be in order. While death cannot be read as an escape from masculinity here, this scene with its tableau vivant and its overlay of painting and sculpture points to death's libidinal force within a masochistic aesthetic. This scene, then, finally comes down on the side of artifice rather than the real. Although Fassbinder's voice-over extolls the virtues of pain—associated with the real, with a corporeality insusceptible of representation[188]—Franz's death on the cross nevertheless incorporates him into the space of representation in which that cross is traditionally situated and to which it belongs in the form of sculpture or painted image.

In Fassbinder's work both aspects of the tension between body and image in tableau vivant are invested with significance. Associated with the painterly image, arrested movement, and the artifice of representation in general, death itself is eroticized as the fulfillment of masochistic sexuality. Its counterpart, the "maniacal obsession with the real," read by Baudrillard as an intensification of the corporeality of the body both as essentially pornographic *and* as a defense against death, is expressed—to

155

the extent to which it is capable—in moments of physicality and in the pain and pleasure they produce.[189] These two drives both intensify and undermine as they supplement one another.

INCORPORATION IN GREENAWAY

Beginning with its masterful credit sequence, *The Draughtsman's Contract* (1982) presents itself as a text that juxtaposes language and images. In this sequence, a series of controlled and hauntingly beautiful tableaux based on the lighting and compositional practices of Georges de La Tour are interspersed with the writing that constitutes the credits. Each of these tableaux presents a different arrangement of figures in the candlelit interior of a manor house, and each configuration in turn forms the backdrop for witty anecdotes in which figures of speech are foregrounded. The play of metaphor in these verbal exchanges evokes a set of exchanges and relations that will figure recurrently in *The Draughtsman's Contract*: women's bodies are multiply connected with property, fruit, and gardens to be arranged, consumed, and implanted. From the outset, therefore, the figural activity of this film takes place within the domain of language as well as that of image. Narrative activity, on the other hand, coded as plotting—as "symmetrical stratagem" or "interpretive plot"—is visually connected with the manner in which the viewfinder and the kind of drawing that it produces impose a grid or structure upon what is seen.

The support of both image and plot is the female body and its analogue, the natural landscape. In the scene that initiates the narrative proper—another tableau based upon Georges de La Tour—a transgressive contract is drawn up, arranging the exchange of drawings for sex.[190] This scene foregrounds the triangulated relation upon which the contract of the film is based: the draughtsman who draws up documents is the double of the one who produces drawings, and both have an interest in the body of Mrs. Herbert. Through her agency, *The Draughtsman's Contract* expresses the interaction of visual and verbal representation as the contract basic to film and suggests that it is an adulterous contract, much as Lessing suggests that the mixed mode of painterly poetry proceeds from the "adulterous fancy."[191]

Mr. Neville, the draughtsman Mrs. Herbert has commissioned to execute twelve drawings of her husband's estate at twelve different sites and times of day, is an artist who interprets his task as the mastery of a scene. His tyrannical arrangements concerning the disposition of each site stem from a fixation on strict mimesis. He has no wish, he says, to "distort or dissemble," and his concept of mimesis can accommodate change only with difficulty and cannot accommodate motion at all. Once Neville himself is shot through his viewfinder's frame, as though "penned into" his own rigid rules of representation. As Neville observes, although his art is mimetic, it is incapable of representing whistling and it does not admit color into its frames. It cannot, in other words, do what Geenaway's film can do. Nevertheless, at those moments when the cinematic frame is coterminous with the frame of the viewfinder, an alliance between these two modes of visual representation is expressed. Accordingly, the camera remains almost completely stationary in this film, refusing the mobile eye that distinguishes it from that of the painter. As if further to emphasize the connection between painting and film, Greenaway executed Neville's drawings himself. But drawing—or by extension, painting—is not the only art to which this film points. Indeed, the frame of his viewfinder having once composed each scene and imposed its central perspective upon it, Neville takes up his black pen and places it on the white paper in an act of authority that conjures up the act of writing.

Neville's authority over the landscape and his desire to arrange and control it in the act of representing it are paralleled by his relation to the body of Mrs. Herbert. His manipulation of the site of each drawing is mirrored in his manipulation of her body, mediated through the metaphor of the garden: the most telling instance of such conjoining involves an anecdote Neville relates concerning the branches and fruit of a pear tree while he is arranging Mrs. Herbert's arms and fondling her breasts. The site of each drawing, each arrangement of the scene, has an analogue in the position and sites of the sexual acts that take place between Neville and Mrs. Herbert. Tellingly, each act is connected with Neville's consumption of a different kind of fruit.

In *The Draughtsman's Contract*, representation (both visual and verbal) and sex are read as modes of appropriation: both the landscape and the women are inscribed by the pen of the draughtsman. But in his obsession with mimesis Neville is not content to inscribe. Not wishing simply to duplicate reality, he seeks a more intimate relation to it. Unable to appropriate the landscape by introducing it literally into the space of representation, Neville displaces this drive. As a "realist," Neville most intensely desires that objects will materialize within his drawings, but he is aware that the real is able to "enter" this space only obliquely. Neville accomplishes this oblique entry through the metaphoric agency of fruit and woman: his desire for the real within representation is displaced onto the consumption of fruit and woman that fetishistically accompany his drawing. Since he cannot represent the real, Neville confines himself to experiencing it and, insofar as this is possible, to incorporating it into his own body. This solution is pursued at various other junctures in Greenaway's films.

At least two situations in *The Draughtsman's Contract* support the view that Neville's interest in the real is shared by Greenaway. One such situation speaks to the drive to incorporate the real within language, while the other makes the same suggestion concerning visual representation. In a scene that is gratuitous to the film's diegesis, but overdetermined in a number of other ways, a governess teaches the current young heir to the Herbert estate the alphabet while strolling in the garden. Reciting the letters, she "illustrates" each letter with the name for a different fruit, conjuring it up in the process and thus coming as close as possible to suggesting a natural language, an alphabet of fruits.[192] The other example is embodied in the "natural man," a belching and urinating creature whose unexplained presence in a variety of scenes disturbs the symmetrical arrangements that structure the garden as well as the social decorum. Insofar as this figure is genuinely natural, he evades both the draughtsman's and society's attempts at mastery. His naked body, covered with a thin veneer of paint—aestheticized—is arranged in a variety of poses in various different garden locales, where he functions as the statuary that graced landscape gardens during the time in which this film is set (1694), slightly anticipating the eighteenth century, which admired the incorporation of the real within artifice. Not surprisingly, this naked figure can only be imperfectly appropriated by art: he takes great delight in performing bodily functions meant to remind the spectator that he is a *living* statue.[193] What the natural man as statue represents, of course, is precisely the desire to bring the real in the form of the body into representation. Resembling in this the figures of tableau vivant, he raises similar questions about the ontology of a mixed mode of representation.

Life, the living body, is precisely what the draughtsman cannot capture, no matter how mimetic his art. With his large black glove covering the graph paper as he draws, the draughtsman kills off life—as indeed he must—when he consigns it to representation. In the ominous thirteenth drawing, the drawing that definitively seals his doom, he draws the statue of a horse, but omits from his frame the "natural man" who has posed as its rider. Neville's riderless horse speaks to the absence of Mr. Herbert from his estate: when the mystery around which the film's plot is constructed is to that extent resolved, Mr. Herbert is discovered to be a corpse. Later, the ritualized act of murder in which the draughtsman is killed culminates in the dumping of the draughtsman's corpse in the place where Mr. Herbert's had been. This act of substitution, one of the many upon which this film is structured, is the punishment for Neville's struggle for visual as well as sexual mastery: before he is killed, his eyes are put out in a symbolic act of castration. Since the visual artist is represented indirectly as an agent of death, the draughtsman has met a fitting end.

In *The Draughtsman's Contract* Greenaway analyzes cinema with respect to the drive for visual mimesis and visual mastery over space that the central perspective of the draughtsman's art implies. While the film acknowledges the capability of cinema to render life more fully than drawing, complete with movement and sound, both visually and on the level of its narrative, it rejects the idea of mastery of *any* kind by disrupting the symmetries on which it only appears to thrive. When Mrs. Herbert's daughter suggests to Neville that narratives incriminating him may be devised to explain his drawings—when, that is, she alerts him to the fact that paintings may be narrativized and read, and by this means definitively ensnares him in her own "interpretive plot"—she provides a paradigm both for this film's conjunction of word and image and for its resistance to univocal interpretation.

One of the techniques by means of which Greenaway seeks to infuse language with a sense of the real—as in the example of the governess with her alphabet fruit—involves taking metaphors literally, causing them to be enacted and embodied in his narratives and visualized by the camera—as, for example, in the variations on "eating the apple" that accompany Neville's sexual encounters with Mrs. Herbert. Indeed, the central conceit of *In the Belly of an Architect* (1987) is based on precisely this kind of literalization. An architect, Stourley Kracklight, figuratively gestates for nine months and "gives birth to" an exhibition in Rome while his wife is pregnant with his child. In the meantime, Kracklight's own belly grows large with a tumor of whose status—real or imagined—the spectator is at first uncertain.

One of Kracklight's central obsessions in this film is the belly of a sculpture of Augustus of which he has a photograph. Kracklight enlarges a detail from this photo and photocopies it repeatedly—subjects it, that is, to a process of multiple reproduction that both sustains and, as it is technological, undermines the metaphor of pregnancy. Kracklight places this image upon his own belly, and then examines himself in a mirror, setting up an astonishingly complex series of relations between the real and the copy. One of the purposes of this sequence is to establish a fractured relationship between Kracklight's belly and the image (copy) of an image (photo) of an image (sculpture) of a belly (that of the long-dead Augustus). By pressing the image to his own body, Kracklight both comments upon the inauthenticity of this image and seeks to recuperate its corporeality. Later, Kracklight suggests an intimate connection between the detail of the sculpted abdomen and his own body when he draws intestines upon it as a doctor might draw the location of a tumor on an X ray. These gestures reflect, in a contemporary idiom, upon the issue posed by the figure of the natural man in *The Draughtsman's Contract* who, as a living sculpture, stands for the collapse of reality into representation. In examining the conjunction of the many copied images surrounding his body in a mirror, Kracklight is able to effect an ironic synthesis of sorts by turning both into something like a cinematic image and thus merging them within the space of representation, effecting, therefore, a postmodern solution to the breakdown between real and copy.

As Kracklight's preoccupation with the image of a sculpture's belly may already suggest, Greenaway's film is much concerned with the cultural tradition. Kracklight is not staging an exhibition of his own architectural drawings, but of the work of the French visionary architect Etiènne-Louis Boullée (1728–1799) in whom, as in Augustus, Kracklight sees an alter ego. Rome is, of course, a locale in connection with which the anxiety of influence is a cliché. Hawthorne's *Marble Faun* is only one of the various literary texts that struggles to come to terms with the pressure exerted by Rome's works of art, and Greenaway's awareness of this struggle in the visual arts is discernible in his allusion to Fuseli's "Artist Contemplates the Grandeur of Rome," which represents an artist sinking his head in despair as he places his hand upon a huge sculptural fragment of a foot. The fact that this foot is three-dimensional suggests that Fuseli's anxiety (how to convey the materiality of the body on canvas or paper) is also figured through Kracklight, since the two-dimensional image of Augustus's abdomen suggests a diminishment of corporeality even vis-à-vis its sculptural "original."

In a film that is replete with larger-than-life representations of the human body in sculpture, the issue of corporeality introduced by the reference to Fuseli signals a preoccupation with the ability of the photographic and the cinematic image to "capture" the human body. The high-tech studio of the photographer, Flavia Speckler, for instance, is revealing in the manner in which it juxtaposes a variety of representational systems: it displays fragments of sculptures—heads, primarily—and its walls are covered with black-and-white snapshots arranged in collage-like fashion that could easily, in fact, be stills from the film itself.[194] Unified by the camera's long traveling shot, their status as photographs is undermined; rather, they evoke the montage quality of film, suggesting a continuity between the projects of film and photography. The three-dimensionality of the sculptural body parts comments on the two-dimensional images, which record, among other things, sex between Kracklight's wife and Flavia's brother and the pregnant belly of Kracklight's wife. It is not the act of voyeurism implied by the photographs that is suggestive, but rather the question as to what extent they are "pornographic," as Kracklight says of those that display the naked body of his pregnant wife. Are these images pornographic, do they present an excess of reality, or are they in actuality, as his wife suggests, art, a preoccupation with organic form? Perhaps these images represent neither and both of these alternatives. Especially in light of the sculptural heads, perhaps they also point simply to the camera's effort to bring the three-dimensional body into a mode of representation that is two-dimensional by virtue of its connection to the photographic image, but that gestures towards three-dimensionality in the ways that we have noted.

After Flavia has developed a roll of film featuring shots of the bellies of sculptures, she hangs it around Kracklight's neck as though it were a rope, suggesting his entrapment by his obsession and echoing his own act of applying the photocopied image to his abdomen. Pulling Kracklight behind a translucent white shade that suggests nothing so much as a movie screen and thus an entry into the representational space of film, Flavia begins to make love to him. This shot is followed by a very abrupt cut to a camera on a tripod that both blocks and metaphorically produces our view of this couple embracing on a couch. As is repeatedly the case in Greenaway's films, signifying practices are closely linked to sexual practices as part of the effort to make film corporeal.

Given the materialist dimension of Greenaway's project, it is predictable that Boullée's influence upon Kracklight will find physical expression. Boullée is said to have died, as Kracklight thinks he himself will, of pancreatic carcinoma. Kracklight feels linked to Boullée via his expanding belly, just as he does to Augustus, who died of eating poisoned figs. As we noted with regard to *The Draughtsman's Contract*, eating has erotic significance in Greenaway and functions more generally as an act of appropriation. It is also linked with death: when Neville finally eats the pomegranate—Pluto's fruit—freely offered to him by Mrs. Herbert, he metaphorically consumes his own death, much as Augustus did when he ate the famous figs. It comes as no surprise, then, that Greenaway, with his penchant for tableaux, makes perhaps his most notable allusion to painting in *Belly of an Architect* by quoting of da Vinci's *Last Supper*. Not only does the moment represented in this painting record Christ's last meal before the crucifixion, but it is the scene in which he instructs his disciples concerning communion, the act of commemorative participation in Christ's body. The tantalizing chain of signification suggested by Christ as the "Word made Flesh" and, on the other hand, by bread as the symbolic body of Christ is experienced by Greenaway much as it is by Kleist. Rohmer's *The Marquise of O. . . .* , which Greenaway cites as one of the two films that influenced *The Draughtsman's Contract*, was not only a model for its authentic period style and for its address of the literary and visual arts, but also for how it addresses the theme of "body language," of bringing the body into signification.[195]

Naturally, the Greenaway film in which food and eating move to center stage is *The Cook, The Thief, His Wife, and Her Lover* (1990). This film develops the theme of ingestion as appropriation that is already present in *The Draughtsman's Contract*, but allows it to emerge more obviously as a means of incorporating the real, an idea that is overtly and ironically addressed by the cook when he wonders whether Georgina wishes him to cook her dead lover so that she can eat him and absorb him into herself.[196] Georgina's husband Spica has a desire for mastery, signaled by his oral relationship to the world, which is even more fanatical than Neville's: Spica's drive is similar to that of Freud's infant in the oral stage, who wants to abolish "the separate existence of the erotic object through incorporation."[197] In its concluding scene, this film literalizes that wish, as we shall see, in the act of cannibalism.

Like several of Hitchcock's films, *The Cook, The Thief . . .* represents itself as theater, its first frames beginning with the opening of theater curtains and its last frames ending as they close, thus encasing the entire film within a set of representational brackets. After the opening frames, the theater is revealed to be a movie set with steel rafters, thus introducing another level of representation, another set of brackets; further, two trucks whose back doors open to reveal still lifes of meat and fish, shot frontally, are rendered as though they were particularly successful trompe l'oeil canvases. In *The Cook, The Thief . . .* , bodies are repeatedly suggested to be continuous with representation. To this effect, the actors' costumes are color-coded to match each space: when, for instance,

Georgina leaves the predominantly red dining room for the white ladies' room, her dress changes from red to white. In this way, her body is trapped within the mise-en-scène, subsumed within the palette much in the manner in which the bodies of Gustav Klimt's female figures are trapped behind the excessively decorative quality of their clothing. Spica himself is attired in seventeenth-century Dutch costume, and tableau vivant moments of Spica's carousing men at table are visual echoes of seventeenth-century Dutch painting. This kind of painting sets the tone as well for the still lifes of fish and dead fowl that decorate kitchen and dining room. Displays of rotting sides of meat and eviscerated fish also recall Diderot's defense of Chardin's "Gutted Skate," as well as the more general interest in connecting death with representation among theoreticians of the picturesque.[198] Of course, the most horrifying example of *nature morte* and of the body's containment within the space of representation involves the presentation of the dead, cooked lover in aspic, complete with a *garni* of parsley and mushrooms. By virtue of this *pièce de résistance*, the French chef of the restaurant "Le Hollandais" has become a Dutchman in his ability to bring the real into representation, a movement that governs all of the preceding examples.

Suggesting most obviously the continuity of the body with representation from the other direction—figured as the represented entering the real—is an enlarged reproduction of Frans Hals's "Banquet of St. Joris' Shooting Guild," whose figures seem to reside within the same space as the actors, again in part because of the manner in which the colors of the painting harmonize with those of the room. Moreover, in turning its painted figures at table—who look straight out of the painting—into spectators of its beholders, Hals's painting positions both viewer and viewed within a shared space. Representation also enters the space of the real when Spica and his men murder Georgina's lover by stuffing pages torn from his books down his throat: the lover ingests signification, literally eating the word that is metaphorically eaten in the act of communion.[199] Her lover's manner of dying makes Georgina's demand at gunpoint that her husband eat her lover's cooked penis—the corporeal version of the phallic signifier—all the more just, as this pays Spica back in reverse while literalizing his threat that he will kill her lover and eat him.[200]

The unusual death experienced by Georgina's lover makes a point about the nature of representation that alludes to the painting competition between Zeuxis and Parrhasios, a competition during which both

Fig. 12. Greenaway suggests a continuity between the space of the Frans Hals painting and the dining room of "Le Hollandais."

birds and human beholders confuse representation with the real. It is the naive beholder capable of such confusion who is satirized by Goethe in an anecdote concerning a pet ape whose owner, a natural scientist, finds him in the library one day, sitting on the floor with a large, unbound volume of a scientific work scattered about him. Surprised by the sight of his ape engrossed in study, the scientist discovers to his chagrin that, after all, the ape is not reading the text but eating its illustrations of bugs.[201] For Goethe, those who demand realism of art—who, like the ape, take it literally—demonstrate their incapacity to understand the nature of arbitrary signs. Greenaway, in a move that is very much in opposition to Goethe's, wants to suggest a continuity between the real and representation established by the reciprocal movement from one to the other that we find, for example, in Diderot's attitude towards genre painting: in the imagined entry into the painting, on the one hand, and in the imagined "removal" of one of its life-like images, on the other.

Death is what is finally at issue in this movement. As the cook says to Georgina, black foods are the most expensive because "People like to remind themselves of death. Eating black food is like consuming death. Like saying 'Ha, death, I am eating you.'" The act of bringing death into the self in the form of representation—as though Diderot were actually to "'pick up [Chardin's painted] biscuits and eat them'"—renders death innocuous, subject to mastery by the body.[202] On the other hand, to use an example from Greenaway's A Zed and Two Noughts (1985), when the surgeon Van Meegeren who has amputated a woman's legs, expresses a burning desire to "be a Dutch painter" and paints this same woman in a costume straight out of a Vermeer, he is making a gesture through which representation makes the wounded body whole.[203] Frequently referred to as the filmmaker's painter for his use of light, the presence of Vermeer in A Zed and Two Noughts mediates the representation of the filmmaker in his rejected roles of surgeon and painter—both of whom, it might be added, in this instance ironically arrest movement.[204]

Greenaway guest-curated an exhibit at the Louvre called "Le bruit des nuages," which closed in February of 1993. In devising this exhibition, not surprisingly, Greenaway displayed his far-ranging knowledge of theories of the visible. Among the works displayed were drawings animated into a primitive "film" by means of a lighting device; visitors entering the exhibition were incorporated into what became a representational space as they moved among watercolor clouds in a blue sky.[205] A reviewer of Greenaway's exhibition wrote that during a film screening that accompanied this exhibit, the audience "gasped at the image of a live butterfly and snail framed as a Dutch 17th century still life."[206] This image, perhaps an allusion to the drawings of Jacques de Gheyn, may also point to Mothlight (1963), an experimental film by Stan Brakhage that does not use photography, but literally incorporates the real into film: its original was made of actual flowers, leaves, and moth wings pressed between transparent strips of editing tape. Greenaway's image of the live butterfly and snail encapsulates better than any other single image the problematic of the image and the real, recalling the "blind drive" of Goethe's collector to render representation increasingly real until it is life, and presenting the spectator with a "drawing" that reverses Herder's contention that painting pins the (dead) body onto the canvas. By including these framed living

165

things within the cinematic frame that is able to render their movement, Greenaway's astonishing collage claims that only film can contain their living bodies over time, painlessly, within the image.

PAINFUL IMAGES

The pornographic film, the slasher film, and the snuff movie focus on the "opened body" in its quest for "the fleshy secrets of normally hidden things."[207] But violence to the body is represented in less marginal, if related, films as well: in Rohmer, Hitchcock, Fassbinder, and Greenaway, it circles around the topics of castration, rape, dismemberment, and evisceration, sometimes displaying the assaulted body to the view. In presenting such a body, films play upon what Michael Fried, with reference to the painting of Thomas Eakins and of Caravaggio, has called "a wounding of seeing." By this wounding Fried is led "to imagine that the definitive realist painting would be one that the viewer literally could not bear to look at."[208] The paintings of Caravaggio, Fried suggests, are both difficult to look at and difficult to look away from because their images of violence to the body confer upon their beholder the sense of bodily reality that he or she craves. Such is the nature of the fascinated hold that images of pain have upon us.

It is not surprising, then, given the subject matter of Caravaggio's paintings, that Derek Jarman's film *Caravaggio* (1986) is organized around images of the suffering painter on his deathbed and that, after illustrating each of the memories narrated by a voice-over, the camera returns to Caravaggio's dying body in order to anchor it there.[209] Jarman seeks repeatedly to create a corporeal link between Caravaggio's painting and his body: on several occasions, human blood and paint are presented as interchangeable, and painting, at least Caravaggio's kind, is represented as visceral, a mode of expression for which tableau vivant is innately suitable. Jarman's film strains at the boundaries of tableau vivant when Caravaggio is shown using the body of his dead lover among a group of living models for "Death of the Virgin," thus ironically literalizing tableau vivant's—and painting's—connection with death. Introducing the body into representation involves the urge to rescue it (metaphorically) from temporality; embalmed within the "death" of representation, the body is secure from actual wounding or decay. In the scene immediately following upon the tableau vivant, Caravaggio is shown engaged in a necrophilic act with the corpse, thus literalizing the erotic pull of tableau vivant as well.

Like Fassbinder's epilogue to *Berlin Alexanderplatz*, *Caravaggio* ends with an allusion to the crucifixion—with another tableau vivant, that is, in which the body of the painter assumes the role of Christ in his painting, "The Burial of Christ." As the quintessential image of suffering, crucifixion promises the transformation of matter into spirit. In Jarman's film, however, in keeping with the corporeality with which it (rightly) invests Caravaggio's painting, matter remains precisely that: Caravaggio chose, after all, to paint the burial of the body, not its transfiguration. We might look to Andres Serrano's photograph "Piss Christ" as a gloss on this scene: Serrano's much-debated photograph representing a plastic image of Christ under urine literally introduces the real in the form of body substances (Serrano has also used blood and sperm as "paint") into the site of representation. This is body language par excellence. Serrano's photograph records the troping of realism, imposing the stuff of the body upon the inauthentic, plastic image; at least a part of the photograph's shock value derives from this effect alone.

The representation of the body in pain and the introduction of the real into the space of representation, acts of assertion that are materialist in nature, attempt, like Hitchcock's camera in *Vertigo*, to provoke affective responses in the spectator, to promote feelings of disgust and nausea. The deliberate production of affective responses is at bottom an eclipse of Kantian aesthetics, a return to a pre-Kantian, eighteenth-century aesthetics closely tied to the body that was never abandoned by some artists and is enjoying a resurgence in a postmodern era troubled by problems of reference. As a representational system, film perceives itself as having a special relation to materiality.[210] The spectator's nausea and vertigo, symptoms of the cinema's reality effect, serve to bridge the subject/object gap that necessarily inheres in cinema, a gap that some films take pains to overcome.

Afterword

UT PICTURA POESIS

In a recent essay aimed against the interest in pictorialism and the visual image that informs current critical debates, Claudia Brodsky Lacour represents film studies as having "spearheaded" the tendency of theories of the visual media to promote the image by adopting "the metalanguage of language."[1] Locating the current crisis of aesthetic theory in "the structural exchange of vision and words," Brodsky Lacour's essay inveighs simultaneously against postmodern theories of the image and the institutionalization of the cultural studies that they make possible.[2] Quite predictably, the villains of this piece are Foucault and Barthes, together with those who, like W.J.T. Mitchell and David Wellbery, have read Lessing's *Laocoön* against the grain. The writings of the Frankfurt school—in particular Benjamin's work on images and objects—are seen as their unwitting accomplices. Holding the fort against this imputed lack of rigor are Lessing and his proper readers, those who uphold the self-identity of the arts, an identity determined by the empirical limitations of each—the precise means, as Brodsky Lacour sees it, through which each gains its "critical edge."[3]

Cogent as such an argument may be, it suffers from the same difficulties that beset Lessing's. Indeed, Brodsky Lacour's essay seems to share the *Laocoön*'s somewhat beleagured historical position, its origin in what occasionally appears to be Lessing's Rousseauistic disapproval of the visual arts per se as well as of the generic boundary crossings he describes. (I share with Mitchell the view that Lessing's female gendering of painting has a role to play here.)[4] Pre- and proscriptive, this essay, like the *Laocoön,* seeks to create an ideal system that struggles against unaccommodating acts of artistic—and critical/theoretical—praxis. The doctrine of *ut pictura poesis*—"as is painting, so is poetry"—in the eighteenth century draws upon a long history, firmly in place before Lessing. When, for example, Lessing speaks of the poet as one who leads us through a whole gallery of paintings, his no doubt inadvertent borrowing from the vocabulary of the sister arts alludes to the Renaissance genre of the *galeria*, a collection of ecphrastic poems or poems on pictures. Surely this represents a lapse in rigor on Lessing's part rather than "a conceptual play on

words" or an ambiguous response to an ambiguous term.[5] Unaccommodating acts of artistic praxis persist, some no doubt inspired by Lessing
himself. In the context of Lessing's remark that Milton's poetry does not
produce such a gallery, for instance, it is ironic that towards the end of his
century, a "Milton gallery"—a series of paintings based upon *Paradise
Lost*, perhaps the result of Lessing's interdiction—was undertaken by the
painter Fuseli.

Today, the reorientation of praxis in contemporary art has elicited a
fresh look at the constraints modernism places upon the arts to uphold
the integrity of their respective mediums. One theoretical response to this
reorientation in the domain of the postmodern is Rosalind Krauss's "expanded field theory," a theory that seeks to account for work that exists
between media in a radically different way.[6] Concerning sculpture in the
1960s, Krauss notes that it had become "a kind of ontological absence,
the combination of exclusions."[7] (Alluding to a famous debate concerning the representation of beauty, Brodsky Lacour fears that a painting of
Helen in which Helen was not visible, but behind clouds, "would be like
a display of nonfigural painting in which the paintings were not visible,"
a situation that could easily be elaborated as Concept Art.) The terms
within which such sculpture is created remain identifiable and of interest,
however, leading Krauss to develop her notion of the expanded field as a
result of problematizing the oppositions within which this work is situated. As Krauss sees it, "within the situation of postmodernism, practice
is not defined in relation to a given medium—sculpture—but rather in relation to the logical operations on a set of terms, for which any medium—
photography, books, lines on walls, mirrors, or sculpture itself—might be
used."[8] In postmodern artistic practice, in which film is used as a vehicle
of expression by painters, sculptors, and photographers as well as by
filmmakers, we might well ask within what predominant cultural oppositions it is located. One of these is certainly the configuration image-stasis-
space versus that of narrative-movement-time whose separation Lessing
is at pains to maintain, despite painting's acknowledgment of temporality
dating back at least to the Renaissance. The synthesis of these oppositions—mediated by Bergson—is effected most notably for film theory in
Deleuze's movement-image, expressing time through movement, and his
time-image, through which modern cinema is said to effect an expression
of time directly.[9]

As an intrinsically heterogeneous medium that borrows from both the
literary and the painterly, film has always been determined by the modal-

169

ities of both time and space. Erwin Panofsky's famous assertion that film's unique possibilities lie in its "dynamization of space" and "spatialization of time" is not the first such claim.[10] Given film's heterogeneity, it is hardly surprising that attempts at defining the particularity of the cinematic medium have from the beginning led its theorists to stray into the territories of neighboring arts. Treating film as metalanguage is not just a recent vogue. Among the earliest attempts to come to terms with film's composite nature is Vachel Lindsay's *Art of the Moving Picture* (1915), best known for its discussion of "hieroglyphics": this is the first attempt at an analysis of the cinematic sign and the first important discussion—though by no means the last—to situate cinema within the doctrine of ut pictura poesis. By focusing on the semantic quality of film's images—already confirming Brodsky Lacour's suspicion of film theory's appropriation of the "metalanguage of language"—Lindsay points to the composite nature of the hieroglyphics of which cinematic writing—"the new universal alphabet"—is constituted.[11]

For Lindsay, the definition of cinematic genres entails boundary crossings as well; *Art of the Moving Picture* compares "photoplays of action," "intimate photoplays," and "splendor films" to sculpture-, painting-, and architecture-in-motion. In relating types of films to specific visual arts, Lindsay bases his distinctions somewhat impressionistically on what he takes as each genre's appeal to the plastic sense, on the degree of three-dimensional relief that each genre suggests, breaking down his categories further to reflect the nature of the temporal and spatial relations within them. In its preoccupation with the spatiality of the visual arts, Lindsay's system does not neglect the literary, somewhat predictably suggesting connections between the photoplay of action and drama, the intimate photoplay and lyric, and the splendor film and epic. An intimate photoplay as defined by Lindsay, for example, would be characterized by the tableau-space of painting, by the motion of planes as in a kaleidoscope, and likened to the Imagist poetry of Ezra Pound or Amy Lowell. For Lindsay, both the (silent) intimate photoplay and Imagist poem are defined by "space measured without sound plus time measured without sound."[12]

In his writings on film of the 1920s through the 1940s, Eisenstein, too, must be judged guilty, from Brodsky Lacour's standpoint, of the easy movement back and forth among literature, painting, and film that characterizes the sister arts principle. Like Lindsay, Eisenstein is interested in the notion of cinema as a pictorial language, comparing the hierogplyph to the Japanese ideogram whose function is at once denotative and depictive.[13] In his cinematic genealogy Eisenstein traces what he calls a "genetic line of descent" from the Griffith film back to the Dickensian novel; *Paradise Lost* likewise comes in for praise as a model for montage practices and for the study of audio-visual relationships.[14] Among painters, Van Eyck, Picasso, and especially El Greco are singled out as forefathers of filmic montage, while Kandinsky, Gauguin, and Van Gogh are praised for their "psychological" use of color in an essay that also includes, significantly, an analysis of Rimbaud's "Voyelles."[15] Indeed, Eisenstein's study of audio-visual relations examines the synaesthetic elements in texts whose *correspondances* produce a synchronization of the senses—if only for the sake of the dissonances and ruptures produced by montage. Eisenstein, then, is concerned both with the common affects that the materials of each sister art induce in the spectator and with the structural affinities among literature, painting, and film that allow for the organization of these affects.

For Arnheim, the position of film remains irrevocably "in-between" from several points of view. One of these focuses on the issue of reality versus illusion, another of the central cultural oppositions within which film itself and debates about its nature have been repeatedly situated. Governed by his interest in perception, Arnheim's writings on film are at pains to distinguish between film and reality on the basis of differences between the camera's eye and embodied human vision. For Arnheim, too, film's "in-between" situation derives from its composite nature, but in "A New Laocoön" (1938)—following Lessing—Arnheim stresses the diversity of the perceptual media, believing their separateness retained even when the media are combined. At once planar and solid, between the two- and three-dimensional, between photograph and theater, film "is always at one and the same time a flat picture post card and the scene of a living action."[16] Although Arnheim's aesthetic is based upon conceptions of unity and the whole, he does not participate in the metaphor of the family romance that explains the origins of cinema for Eisenstein. For Arnheim, the combination of the media "resembles a successful marriage, where similarity and adaptation make for unity but where the personality of the two partners remains intact."[17] It does not resemble the child of such a marriage, in whom both personalities are inseparably combined: for Arnheim film is by definition unstable. Thus if he shares Brodsky Lacour's emphasis on the self-identity of the arts, he is obliged nevertheless to maintain that the self-identity of film is precisely its composite status.

171

More recently, of course, Derridean influences on film criticism have intensified the interest in cinematic writing and developed the semiotics of cinema as theorized by Christian Metz, stressing film's heterogeneity and the inherent instability of the cinematic text. Predictably, they have also renewed interest in the hieroglyph, which for Derrida implies not the marriage but the "organized cohabitation" of figurative, symbolic, and phonetic elements: the work of Marie-Claire Ropars-Wuilleumier, for example, proceeds from the conjunction of Derridean assumptions concerning the hieroglyph with Eisensteinian concepts of montage.[18] At the same time, variously inspired by Barthes (*Camera Lucida* looms large), by Lacan's work on the gaze, and by Derrida's *Truth in Painting*, the French in particular have shown a burgeoning interest in the relation of film to painting—witness the work of Pascal Bonitzer and Jacques Aumont.[19] Bonitzer's interest in point of view, in the framing of the image, and in trompe l'oeil owe a great deal to Lacan, while his meditation on film's relation to the *grain de réel* of photography finds its origin in the writings of Barthes. Like Aumont, Bonitzer addresses—directly and indirectly—aspects of the oppositions (reality /illusion, movement /stasis) that together govern film within the double perspective supplied by photography and painting. Fittingly, Lessing resurfaces in Aumont's book in the chapter on "Formes des Temps" where, also following Barthes, Aumont reads Lessing's pregnant moment in painting as artificial and abstract, contrasting it with the decisive photographic instant and the "any-instant-whatever" that characterizes film.[20]

In a recent review of Jacques Rivette's *La Belle Noiseuse*, Elsaesser interprets the current interest in painting and cinema evinced by French filmmakers and critics as an attempt to ally film with the "authentic" art of painting in a cultural battle against the digital image; Aumont shares this belief, as does Patrice Rollet.[21] But perhaps it is precisely by way of *La Belle Noiseuse*, a story of painters and their models adapted from *The Hidden Masterpiece* by Balzac, that we can move back to the issue of film's relation to writing. Like *Sarrasine*, Balzac's novella is concerned with his own realist project, a project whose impossible realization would lie in the Pygmalion-like ability to bring the body it represents to life. In his painting, Balzac's Frenhofer claims to have mastered the art of lifelike rendering that lies in "the secret of relief": "the body turns, the limbs stand out, we feel the air circulating around them."[22] When this painting of the *belle noiseuse* is finally revealed, however, to two other painters, one of them Poussin, what its beholders see is not a beautiful woman, but "a mass of confused color, crossed by a multitude of eccentric lines, making a sort of painted wall."[23] The beholders' dismay at the missing figure is a variant on Lessing's reaction to the suggestion that the beautiful Helen be represented veiled.

Clearly, Frenhofer's maddened imagination leads him to believe that his canvas is covered with the figure of a beautiful woman rather than a mere palimpsest of colors. Interestingly, it is Frenhofer's vivid verbal description of the female figure—of a figure so lifelike as to be breathing—that paints an animated picture in the imagination of the two other painters. As Poussin notes, "He is a poet even more than he is a painter."[24] Balzac, himself a writer, proves himself a disciple of Lessing in believing that poetry gives freer rein to the imagination than painting, though, unlike Lessing, he has no qualms about describing and thus anatomizing the human body. In *The Hidden Masterpiece*, painting fails in its mission to render the body and requires the assistance of language—poetic description, verbal images—in order to do so. Insofar as Frenhofer's painting is nonrepresentational, it provokes the imagination as well; in fact, however, the painting, "crossed by a multitude of eccentric lines," is a hieroglyph of sorts, at once the product of painting and writing. Yet in one corner of the canvas a naked foot emerging from the colors, tones, and formless shadows—"an enchanting foot, a living foot"[25]—seems so real as to cause the painters to suspect that there may in fact be a living woman beneath the layers of paint. Itself a fetish, a fragment of a body, the foot is synechdochic for the heterogeneity of the protocinematic, composite work produced by the conjunction of Frenhofer's poetic description and the hieroglyph that he has painted upon the canvas.

"There," says one of the painters on beholding Frenhofer's masterpiece, "is the ultimate end of our art on earth."[26] The title of Elsaesser's review, "Rivette and the End of Cinema," plays on this line from Balzac's novella, just as his description of Rivette's customary technique of "layering one text with another" finds its model there. It appears that what is at stake in the issue of the *nouvelles images*, the electronic and digital images that are sending the French back to painting, is a "crisis of the real": the body that should function as their support isn't merely hidden, it simply isn't there.

Notes

INTRODUCTION

1. Vivian Sobchak, *The Address of the Eye: A Phenomenology of Film Experience* (Princeton: Princeton University Press, 1992), 9.

2. See Teresa de Lauretis, "Imaging," *Alice Doesn't: Feminism, Semiotics, Cinema* (Bloomington: Indiana University Press, 1984), 45.

3. Christian Metz, "On the Impression of Reality in the Cinema," *Film Language: A Semiotics of the Cinema*, trans. Michael Taylor (New York: Oxford University Press, 1974), 8–9.

4. Jean-Louis Comolli, "Machines of the Visible," *The Cinematic Apparatus*, ed. Teresa de Lauretis and Stephen Heath (London: Macmillan, 1989), 141.

5. W.J.T. Mitchell, "Space and Time: Lessing's *Laocoön* and the Politics of Genre," *Iconology: Image, Text, Ideology*, (Chicago: University of Chicago Press, 1986), 112.

6. Denis Diderot, "The Salons," *Selected Writings*, ed. Lester Crocker (New York: Macmillan, 1966), 172.

7. Roland Barthes, "Diderot, Brecht, Eisenstein," *Image, Music, Text*, trans. Stephen Heath (New York: Hill and Wang, 1977), 69–78.

8. Indeed, there have been many such adaptations. See Klaus Kanzog, ed., *Erzählstrukturen, Film-Strukturen: Erzählungen Heinrich von Kleists und ihre filmische Realisation* (Berlin: Schmidt, 1981).

9. This is displaced into the figure of Marianina, one of Zambinella's doubles, of whom the narrator explicitly claims that she is "the embodiment of that secret poetry, the common bond among all the arts, which always alludes those who search for it." Honoré de Balzac, "Sarrasine," in Roland Barthes, *S/Z: An Essay*, trans. Richard Miller, (New York: Hill and Wang, 1974), 223.

10. Balzac, "Sarrasine," 228.

11. Ibid., 230.

12. Ibid., 208.

13. Raymond Bellour, "The Film Stilled," *Camera Obscura* 24 (1990): 123.

14. Anne Hollander argues for a tradition of "proto-cinematic paintings" that "attempted and prefigured what cinema actually did, and that form a background and foundation for movies." Hollander, *Moving Pictures* (Cambridge, Mass.: Harvard University Press, 1991), 4. Although there are obviously paintings whose point of view seems to be "aligned with camera vision" (p. 13) and painting has often made use of devices by means of which it appears to represent motion, this aspect of painting is not the focus of attention here. In my reading, film's perception of painting is under discussion, and film, in contradistinction to itself, tends to read painting as essentially static.

15. Undoubtedly the argument can be made that culturally specific pressures incline the texts of German cinema in particular to conform to the norms of high culture, but that concern cannot, regrettably, be within the purview of this study. See Anton Kaes, "The Debate about Cinema: Charting a Controversy (1909–1929)," *New German Critique* 40 (1987): 7–33.

16. Max Horkheimer and Theodor Adorno, *Dialectic of Enlightenment* (New York: Seabury Press, 1972), 124. On Adorno and Horkheimer, see Miriam Hansen, *Babel and Babylon: Spectatorship in American Silent Cinema* (Cambridge, Mass.: Harvard University Press, 1991), 190. Elucidating Adorno and Horkheimer, Hansen comments: "Sound films are just as much 'written,' but industrialized film practice amalgamates dialogue, image, and music into a fictive homogeneity which suppresses the antithetical and discursive quality of the filmic materials." (343n.5).

17. Hansen, *Babel and Babylon*, 343.

18. De Lauretis, "Imaging," 45.

CHAPTER ONE

1. Stephen Heath, "Body, Voice," *Questions of Cinema* (Bloomington: Indiana University Press, 1981), 183.

2. "Das Wesen des Kinos ist die Bewegung" (trans. mine), Georg Lukács, "Gedanken zu einer Asthetik des Kinos," *Kino-Debatte: Texte zum Verhältnis von Literatur und Film 1909–1929*, ed. Anton Kaes (Tübingen: Niemeyer, 1978), 113.

3. Quoted by Stephen Heath, "The Cinematic Apparatus: Technology as Historical and Cultural Form," *The Cinematic Apparatus*, ed. Teresa de Lauretis and Stephen Heath (London: Macmillan, 1980), 1.

4. Yvan Goll, "Das Kinodram," in Kaes, *Kino-Debatte*, 137.

5. Carl Hauptmann, "Film und Theater," in ibid., 124.

6. See Lukács, "Gedanken," in ibid., 113. In the same volume, see also Paul Ernst, "Möglichkeiten einer Kinokunst," 118–23, and Carl Hauptman, "Film und Theater," 123–30.

7. In an argument grounded in idealism, Lukács asserts that "das Phantastische ist aber kein Gegensatz des lebendigen Lebens, es ist nur ein neuer Aspekt von ihm: ein Leben ohne Gegenwärtigkeit, ohne Schicksal, ohne Gründe, ohne Motive; ein Leben, mit dem das Innerste unserer Seele nie identisch werden will, noch kann." ("The fantastic is not in opposition to living Life ["das lebendige Leben"], it is a new aspect of it: a life without presence, fate, reason, motives, a life with which the innermost recess of our soul will never—nor can ever be—identical"—trans. mine.) ("Gedanken," 113).

8. Ernst, "Möglichkeiten," 119.

9. Hauptmann calls this an "Urbereich" and refers to an "Urmitteilung der Gebärde." Hauptmann, "Film und Theater," 125–26. See also Egon Friedell's

"Prolog vor dem Film," which also insists that verbal language not be given hege-mony—that glances, gestures, and the way the body is held signify more than verbal utterance in the modern age (in Kaes, *Kino-Debatte*, 43).

10. Walter Benjamin, "Rückblick auf Chaplin" (1929), in Kaes, *Kino-Debatte*, 173: "die Maske des Unbeteiligtseins macht ihn zur Marionette in einer Jahrmarktsbude."

11. Miriam Hansen, "Benjamin, Cinema, and Experience: 'The Blue Flower in the Land of Technology,'" *New German Critique* 40 (1987): 203.

12. Quoted by Lotte Eisner in *The Haunted Screen: Expressionism in the German Cinema and the Influence of Max Reinhardt*, rev. ed. (Berkeley and Los Angeles: University of California Press, 1977), 33.

13. Gilles Deleuze, *Cinema 1: The Movement-Image*, trans. Hugh Tomlinson and Barbara Habberjam (Minneapolis: University of Minnesota Press, 1986), 23. It should be noted that Deleuze takes the writings of Henri Bergson as his point of departure, thus making the similarity of concern between Deleuze and Wegener less surprising.

14. Eisner, *Haunted Screen*, 40.

15. In a fascinating article on Muybridge and Méliès, Linda Williams traces the beginnings of the cinematic mise-en-scène to the props and situations that Muybridge gives his human figures in order to better illustrate certain movements, and argues that the presence of women in the frame engenders "a fetish response on the part of the male image-producer to restore the unity which this body appears to lack." Linda Williams, "Film Body: An Implantation of Perversions," in *Narrative, Apparatus, Ideology: A Film Theory Reader*, ed. Philip Rosen (New York: Columbia University Press, 1986), 522.

16. Deleuze, *Cinema 1*, 25.

17. Eisner, *Haunted Screen*, 33.

18. "The spatial and fixed shot tended to produce a pure movement image." Deleuze, *Cinema 1*, 25.

19. Eisner, *Haunted Screen*, 33.

20. See Eisner, *Haunted Screen*, 40. The director of this film was technically Stellan Rye, a Dane, who worked with Ewers, with the cameraman Guido Seeber, and with Wegener, a Max Reinhardt actor. Many, though not all, film historians consider this film to be Wegener's. It is just such a blurring of the question of authorship that reminds us vividly of the collaborative nature of filmmaking. For further background, see Heide Schlüpmann, "The First German Art Film: Rye's *The Student of Prague*," *German Film and Literature: Adaptations and Transformations*, ed. Eric Rentschler (New York: Metheuen, 1986), 9–24.

21. Siegfried Kracauer, *Theory of Film: The Redemption of Physical Reality* (London: Oxford University Press, 1960, rpt.1978), 28–40. See also Gerald Mast, "Kracauer's Two Tendencies and the Early History of Film Narrative," *The Language of Images*, ed. W.J.T. Mitchell (Chicago: University of Chicago Press, 1980), 129–50.

22. Eisner, *Haunted Screen*, 35–36.

23. Paul Coates, *The Story of the Lost Reflection: The Alienation of the Image in Western and Polish Cinema* (London: Verso, 1985), 12.

24. Thomas Elsaesser, in his provocative essay "Social Mobility and the Fantastic: German Silent Cinema" (*Wide Angle 5* [1982]: 14–25), to which I will refer frequently, has made the claim that *The Student of Prague* sets up generic expectations that link it with two of the most popular commerical genres of the German cinema of this period, the comedy and the musical, both of which the film then works to disavow (17). Although these genres are certainly alluded to, the conflicting generic bracket in which the narrative is enclosed—with the reference to Musset, at least, pointing to "high culture"—makes one question to what extent a spectator could ever think he or she was watching an "entertainment" film.

25. Ibid., 20.

26. Thomas Elsaesser, "Film History and Visual Pleasure: Weimar Cinema," *Cinema Histories/Cinema Practices*, ed. Patricia Mellencamp and Philip Rosen, The American Film Institute Monograph Series, vol. 4 (Frederick, Md.: University Publications of America, 1984), 66.

27. Leon Hunt remarks that in this film "the division of the frame and distinction between foreground and background of an image composed in depth becomes the basis of a textual system of repeated and alternated spatial articulations" and claims that *Student of Prague* is a film " 'about' movements from the background (far space) to the foreground (near space) and back." Hunt, "*The Student of Prague*," *Early Cinema: Space, Frame, Narrative*, ed. Thomas Elsaesser with Adam Barker (London: BFI, 1990), 390.

28. Miriam Hansen was helpful in pointing out that this doubling of diegetic configurations can be found in French art films as well as in American films competing with this tradition, such as *Intolerance*.

29. Deleuze, *Cinema 1*, 23.

30. André Bazin, "Painting and Cinema," *What Is Cinema?*, vol. 1, ed. and trans. Hugh Gray (Berkeley and Los Angeles: University of California Press, 1967), 164–69.

31. Taking up Elsaesser's point that this film, like the other films of the fantastic in German silent cinema, both represents social conflicts and disguises them, I would like to suggest that the presence of the servant in the scene I described obviously serves to underscore the problem of a rigid social hierarchy that Elsaesser discusses. In fact, the servant's presence reminds us that the mural represents essentially feudal social relations directly, and also points to tapestry making itself as a collective art form that is also dependent upon such relations. (The drawings for tapestries were usually done by established artists or masters, while they were executed by groups of skilled workers.) Recalling Erwin Panofsky's comparison between cathedral building and filmmaking ("Style and Me-

dium in the Motion Pictures." [1934], a comparison also made by Walter Benjamin ("The Work of Art in the Age of Mechanical Reproduction" [1935–1936]), we may well wonder whether any parallel is intended here between tapestry making and film.

32. Peter Gay points out that Kleist's popularity in Germany increased during the early years of the century, and that later, during the Weimar period, Kleist actually became a cult figure. *Weimar Culture: The Outsider as Insider* (New York: Harper and Row, 1970), 61.

33. "Er sähe wohl Geister." Heinrich von Kleist, "Über das Marionettentheater," *Sämtliche Werke und Briefe*, vol. 2, ed. Helmut Sembdner (Munich: Hanser, 1961), 343.

34. Cynthia Chase, "Mechanical Doll, Exploding Machine: Kleist's Models of Narrative," *Decomposing Figures: Rhetorical Readings in the Romantic Tradition* (Baltimore: Johns Hopkins University Press, 1986), 146.

35. A noteworthy, if somewhat surprising, exception is Paul de Man's "Aesthetic Formalization: Kleist's *Uber das Marionettentheater*," *The Rhetoric of Romanticism* (New York: Columbia University Press, 1984), 263–90.

36. As de Man puts it: "The splinter-extracting ephebe thus becomes a miniature *Laokoön*, a version of the neo-classical triumph of imitation over suffering, blood, and ugliness," ibid., 280.

37. Simon Richter has analyzed the treatment—or lack thereof—of pain in commentaries on the *Laocoön*. See Richter, *Laocoön's Body and the Aesthetics of Pain: Winckelmann, Lessing, Herder, Moritz, Goethe* (Detroit: Wayne State University Press, 1992).

38. The complete remark reads: "Ein junger Mann von meiner Bekanntsschaft hätte, durch eine blosse Bemerkung, gleichsam vor meinen Augen, seine Unschuld verloren." Kleist, "Marionettentheater," 343.

39. See de Man, "Aesthetic Formalization," 277; Chase, "Mechanical Doll," 143.

40. "Immer ein Reiz nach dem anderen verliess ihn." Kleist, "Marionettentheater," 344.

41. Coates, *Story of the Lost Reflection*, 12.

42. Walter Benjamin, "The Work of Art in the Age of Mechanical Reproduction," *Film Theory and Criticism*, ed. Gerald Mast and Marshall Cohen, 2nd ed. (New York: Oxford University Press, 1979), 860. This version of Benjamin's essay does not include all material relevant to this topic. For an account of this essay's publication history, see Joel Snyder, "Benjamin on Reproducibility and Aura: A Reading of 'The Work of Art in the Age of Its Technical Reproducibility,'" *Benjamin: Philosophy, History, Aesthetics*, ed. Gary Smith (Chicago: University of Chicago Press, 1983), 172 n.1. See also Susan Buck-Morss, *The Origin of Negative Dialectics* (New York: Free Press, 1977), 286n.98.

43. Elsaesser, "Social Mobility and the Fantastic," 19.

44. Elsaesser makes the point that:

One way of recovering the historical dimension of the uncanny motif, therefore, is to point not so much to the emergence of the machine but to the changing relations of production during the Romantic period, especially as they affect the artists and intellectuals increasingly thrown upon the market with their products and finding there that they no longer control the modes of reproduction and distribution of their works. For many of Hoffmann's tales, notably the *Sandman* or *Mlle. de Scudéri* and the goldsmith Cardillac, apply what Marx wrote as early as 1830 about consumerist fetishism, namely, that in the capitalist production process, the product confronts the producer as something alien, and his own person comes to seem to him uncanny (p. 20).

One might also remark that in *The Student of Prague* the moving cinematic image—the mirror image—is sold, as though in an allegory of the consumer-dependent nature of this new art form.

45. It is a well-known fact that the psychoanalyst Otto Rank was inspired by *The Student of Prague* to pursue his study of the Double, and that he formulates his ideas using the work of Romantic writers such as Hoffmann, Lenau, Heine, and Dostoyevsky. See Otto Rank, *The Double: A Psychoanalytic Study*, trans. and ed. Harry Tucker, Jr. (Chapel Hill: University of North Carolina Press, 1971).

46. Sigmund Freud, "The 'Uncanny,'" *On Creativity and the Unconscious: Papers on the Psychology of Art, Literature, Love, Religion*, ed. Benjamin Nelson (New York: Harper and Row, 1958), 132.

47. Ibid., 132.

48. Ibid., 151.

49. Eisner, *Haunted Screen*, 33.

50. See de Man, "Aesthetic Formalization," 272.

51. "Trägheit der Materie." Kleist, "Marionettentheater," 342.

52. Quoted by Heath, "Body, Voice," 184. Heath's source is Lillian Gish, *The Movies, Mr. Griffith, and Me* (London: W. H. Allen, 1969), 59–60.

53. Ernst, "Möglichkeiten," *Kino-Debatte*, 122.

54. Ibid., 120.

55. See Chase, "Mechanical Doll," 146 : "The puppet theater is a model of the text as a system for the production of figures. That system would need to be understood, were we to follow the implication of the dancer's appended explanation, as a mechanism entailing mutilation; the puppet-theater text would be a mutilating machine."

56. Barthes, "Diderot, Brecht, Eisenstein," 71–72.

57. See Williams, "Film Body," 523–32.

58. Ibid., 525.

59. Elsaesser, in "Social Mobility and the Fantastic," notes: "It has often been pointed out that *The Cabinet of Dr. Caligari* is in fact an allegory of the film-

maker" (p. 20). See also Tom Gunning, "The Cinema of Attractions: Early Film, Its Spectator and the Avant-Garde," in Elsaesser, *Early Cinema: Space, Frame, Narrative*, 59. Gunning's significant article on the "direct address of the audience" by a "cinema showman" is important for *Caligari*, where we find a self-conscious evocation of this earlier "cinema of attractions."

60. Elsaesser reads this scene as "the very epitome of the 'dirty old man' exposing himself" and Cesare as a "phallus-fetish" ("Social Mobility and the Fantastic," 23), while Patrice Petro argues that Cesare is "in many ways the double for Jane," basing her reading upon Linda Williams's suggestion of the close affinity between monster and woman in early horror films. See Patrice Petro, *Joyless Streets: Women and Melodramatic Representation in Weimar Germany* (Princeton: Princeton University Press, 1989), 148.

61. Janet Bergstrom has made this point concerning Weimar cinema as a whole. She writes:

> The German film industry took pride in characterizing itself as superior to other national cinemas artistically, and developed a commercial appeal for its films based on a "high art" self-identification. There are constant references to film as art in the trade and popular journals of the twenties in Germany. This became a selling point both in competing for domestic audiences, primarily with American films, and in building up a healthy and widely-reviewed export business. (Bergstrom, "Sexuality at a Loss: The Films of F. W. Murnau," *Poetics Today* 6 [1985]: 192).

62. Mike Budd makes the following claim: "The genuine aesthetic surprise we might feel before these men's work, the ways it productively combines with the work of others in a conventional accessible narrative to expand our sense of the possibilities of movies, must always be tempered with a countervailing sense of how the parts of *Caligari* congeal into separate entities and reveal the traces of the commodity form that constricts human fulfillment." Budd, "The Moments of *Caligari*," *The Cabinet of Dr. Caligari: Texts, Contexts, Histories*, ed. Mike Budd (New Brunswick, N.J.: Rutgers University Press, 1990), 27.

63. Noël Burch's brilliant reading of pictorial space in *Caligari* takes a somewhat different approach to the issue. Burch also reads *Caligari* as an avant-garde film whose "primitivism" is simulated, designed to call into question the "homogenization of pictorial space" typical of what Burch calls the Institutional Mode (mainstream narrative cinema).

> The imagery in *Caligari* continually plays upon a carefully contrived ambiguity. The film's famous graphic style presents each shot as a stylized, flat rendition of deep space, with dramatic obliques so avowedly plastic, so artificially 'depth-producing' that they immediately conjure up the tactile surface of the engraver's page somewhat in the manner of Méliès. Yet at the same time, the movement of the actors within these frames is systematically perpendicular to the picture plane, in a way reminiscent of Primitive deep-field

blocking. The same images thus seem simultaneously to produce two historical types of pictorial space, superimposed one upon the other. (Burch, "Primitivism and the Avant-Gardes," in Rosen, *Narrative, Apparatus, Ideology*, 497).

64. Michael Fried, *Absorption and Theatricality: Painting and Beholder in the Age of Diderot* (Berkeley and Los Angeles: University of California Press, 1980), 77.

65. Typically in early German cinema, reading and writing are problematized. In one of the earliest tableaux in the narrative proper of *Caligari*, for instance, the student Alan is shown walking about his room with an agitation that can only, as far as the film ever tells us, have been motivated by the book that he is reading; no other explanation is ever given. Later on in the film, we discover that Caligari had become interested in the subject of somnambulism by reading an old manuscript, and that he keeps detailed notes on Cesare's condition; his tyrannical obsession has its origin in a written text.

66. Elsaesser, "Social Mobility and the Fantastic," 20.

67. Ibid., 21; Burch, "Primitivism and the Avant-Gardes," 496.

68. Jean-Francois Lyotard, "Acinéma," in Rosen, *Narrative, Apparatus, Ideology*, 349–59.

69. It is commonly accepted that early cinema derives its tableau form from the staged melodrama, but it is not a question of actual influence that I am concerned with when reading *Caligari*'s tableaux in the context of Diderot. Rather, I find in the Diderotian tableau an evocative theoretical context for a discussion of bodies in staged, painted, or cinematic scenes.

70. Fried, *Absorption and Theatricality*, 78.

71. Ibid.

72. Peter Szondi argues that Diderot's tableaux depict "Versöhnung"—the family reconciled and made whole. See Szondi, "Denis Diderot: Theorie und dramatische Praxis," *Die Theorie des bürgerlichen Trauerspiels* (Frankfurt: Suhrkamp, 1974), 105–6. See also Szondi, "*Tableau* and *Coup de Théatre*: On the Social Psychology of Diderot's Bourgeois Tragedy," *NLH* 11 (1980): 323–43. Karlheinz Stierle claims that "For Diderot the *tableau* as the culmination of the *drame* designates the moment when, under the conditions of pathos, the acting persons lose their individualities to become representations of the unchanging order of human nature." Stierle, "Baudelaire and the Tradition of the *Tableau de Paris*," *MLN* 11 (1980): 347. See also Jay Caplan, *Framed Narratives: Diderot's Genealogy of the Beholder* (Minneapolis: University of Minnesota Press, 1985).

73. Bergstrom, "Sexuality at a Loss," 188.

74. Herbert Dieckmann, *Cinq leçons sur Diderot* (Geneva, 1959), 118. Cited and trans. Fried, *Absorption and Theatricality*, 86.

75. Siegfried Kracauer, *From Caligari to Hitler: A Psychological History of the German Film* (Princeton: Princeton University Press, 1947), 68.

76. Barthes, "Diderot, Brecht, Eisenstein," 73.

77. Gilles Deleuze, *Masochism: An Interpretation of Coldness and Cruelty*, trans. Jean McNeil (New York: George Braziller, 1971), 62.

78. Comolli, "Machines of the Visible," 136.

79. Elsaesser, "Social Mobility," 23.

80. Petro, *Joyless Streets*, 148.

81. As Petro reads this moment, "Cesare recognizes in Jane his own difference from the other male figures in the film, [but] there nevertheless exists an important difference between Cesare and Jane," *Joyless Streets*, 148–49.

82. I am not concerned here with the distortion that the framing narrative imposes upon the political and ideological significance of the "inner" narrative and its representation of Caligari and Francis. See Kracauer, *From Caligari to Hitler*, 61–87, for an account of the film's genesis.

83. Kracauer, *From Caligari to Hitler*, 71.

84. See Samuel Weber, "The Sideshow, or: Remarks on a Canny Moment," *MLN* 88 (1973): 1102–33. Weber convincingly demonstrates the manner in which Freud misreads the final scene of Hoffmann's tale.

85. Friedell, "Prolog vor dem Film," 44.

86. Weber, "The Sideshow," 1132–33.

87. Freud, "The 'Uncanny,'" 151.

88. Lou Andreas-Salomé is quoted by Jean-Louis Baudry in "The Apparatus: Metapsychological Approaches to the Impression of Reality in Cinema," in Rosen, *Narrative, Apparatus, Ideology*, 301.

89. Ibid.

90. Lukács, "Gedanken zu einer Ästhetik," *Kino-Debatte*, 114.

91. Janet Bergstrom, "Alternation, Segmentation, Hypnosis: Interview with Raymond Bellour," *Camera Obscura* 3–4 (1979): 102.

92. Russell Merritt makes the following comment concerning psychoanalysis and American cinema in the pre-Hollywood period: "As post-Freudians we might expect these films [films containing dream sequences] to represent an early interest in human psychology and to evolve into increasingly sophisticated studies of the human subconscious. But in America, this is precisely what did not happen." Merritt, "Dream Visions in the Pre-Hollywood Film," *Before Hollywood: Turn-of-the-Century Film from American Archives*, ed. Charles Musser (New York: The American Federation of Arts, 1986), 70.

93. Gay, *Weimar Culture*, 34–37. For instance, Gay quotes Rudolph Loewenstein concerning a lecture he had heard Freud deliver: "It was one of the greatest esthetic, scientific-esthetic experiences I've ever had in my life."

94. Alan Trachtenberg, "Photography/Cinematography," in Musser, *Before Hollywood*, 75.

95. Comolli, "Machines of the Visible," 130.

96. Williams, "Film Body," 523.

97. Stephen Jenkins, in his convincing essay concerning the "troubling presence of the woman" in Lang's films, connects the loss of Rotwang's hand with the

threat of castration emblematized by the female robot that he creates. Jenkins, "Lang: Fear and Desire," *Fritz Lang: The Image and the Look*, ed. Stephen Neale (London: British Film Institute, 1981), 84. See also Andreas Huyssen, "The Vamp and the Machine: Fritz Lang's *Metropolis*," *After the Great Divide: Modernism, Mass Culture, Postmodernism* (Bloomington: Indiana University Press, 1986), 65–81. Huyssen sees Rotwang as creating the "android as an artifact, as an initially lifeless thing which he can then control and dominate" and as an example of "the ultimate technological fantasy: creation without mother" (71). See also Elsaesser's discussion of Burch in "Film History and Visual Pleasure":

> Burch is suggestive, especially in his remarks about those inventors of the cinema whose *idée fixe* was the recreation of life in its entirety by means of a mechanical apparatus. . . . Behind the Edisonian project of the kinetograph, he detects, rightly I think, the ambition of Frankenstein: to reproduce life artificially and mechanically, *à rebours*, so to speak, and in defiance of nature (77).

98. Quoted by Lucy Fisher, "Dr. Mabuse and Mr. Lang," *Wide Angle* 3 (1979): 26.

99. Jenkins, "Fear and Desire," 66.

100. For example, see Fisher, "Dr. Mabuse and Mr. Lang," 22.

101. Mary Ann Doane, "The Voice in the Cinema: The Articulation of Body and Space," *Yale French Studies* 60 (1980): 34–35.

102. See Tom Conley, *Film Hieroglyphs: Ruptures in Classical Cinema* (Minneapolis: University of Minnesota Press, 1991). As Conley sees it, "Writing appears to generate the elemental fissure; it leads to and draws away from image and voice" (xv). Conley's book includes a chapter on Lang's *Scarlet Street*.

103. Vachel Lindsay, "Hieroglyphics," *The Art of the Moving Picture* (New York: Liveright, 1970), 199–216. Walter Benjamin mentions Gance's notion of the hieroglyph in "The Work of Art in the Age of Mechanical Reproduction," 857. See also Miriam Hansen's discussion of the hieroglyph in "The Hieroglyph and the Whore: D. W. Griffith's *Intolerance*," *South Atlantic Quarterly* 88 (1989): 361–92. Here Hansen notes that "the space of *Intolerance* is a reading space, a training ground of hieroglyphic signification and interpretation," a "reading space [that] exceeds and unmakes the confines of the book" (369). In *Babel and Babylon*, Hansen points out that it is the "irreducibly composite character" of the hieroglyphic sign that is of interest to film, as well as the connection that Freud and Derrida make between "hieroglyphic writing and the figurative script of dreams"; Hansen reads the hieroglyph as a "master trope designed to marshall the film's diverging textual elements" (191; 197). Also on the use of hieroglyph in Derridian film theory, see Marie-Claire Ropars-Wuillemier, "The Graphic in Film Writing: *À bout de souffle*, or the Erratic Alphabet," *Enclitic* 5 (1981–1982): 147–61; Peter Brunette and David Wills, *Screen/Play: Derrida and Film Theory* (Princeton: Princeton University Press, 1989); Conley, *Film Hieroglyphs*.

104. See Fisher, "Dr. Mabuse and Mr. Lang":

The lab technician's process of deciphering the name of Mabuse seems like nothing so much as a procedure for printing an image from film. The glass pane is like a negative that must be "developed" with certain chemicals in order to strike a "print." Similarly the process by which the lab technician shows Lohmann the word scratched into the pane bears a striking relation to what we must do to read a word etched into the emulsion of a film frame as it comes off the reel; we must flip it laterally and turn it upside down. As if the parallels were not clear enough, there is a camera visible within the laboratory and Lohmann's image is pictured on the glass frame (26).

105. An interesting example of this Expressionist writing occurs on the windshield of a car in *Dr. Mabuse the Gambler,* where the word "melior" is spelled out; like *Caligari, Dr. Mabuse the Gambler* is a film about the creation of illusion, one which would like to "do it better" than the earlier film.

106. Although it was fashionable at this time to feature multiple narratives in one film—Griffith's *Intolerance* (1916) and Paul Leni's *Waxworks* (1924), for example—Lang uses this technique not only to offer the spectator greater variety, but in order to make a point regarding the structure of narrative. As Stephen Jenkins suggests, *Destiny* is about the process of narrativity itself. See Jenkins, "Fear and Desire," 65.

107. Julia Kristeva, "The Father, Love and Banishment," *Desire in Language: A Semiotic Approach to Literature and Art* (New York: Columbia University Press, 1980), 150–51.

108. This scroll may be a reference to *Diagonal Symphony,* one of several experimental films made by Hans Richter and Viking Eggeling at the time that *Destiny* was being shot. Richter and Eggeling were experimenting with drawings on scrolls resembling Chinese scrolls; the dynamism of the images created by the unrolling of the scrolls so intrigued them that they decided to pursue the idea on film. Robert Motherwell, *The Dada Painters and Poets: An Anthology* (New York: Wittenborn and Schultz, 1951), xxxii.

109. Timothy Corrigan, "Cinematic Snuff: German Friends and Narrative Murders," *Cinema Journal* 24 (1985): 12.

110. Raymond Bellour, "On Fritz Lang," *Fritz Lang: The Image and the Look,* ed. Stephen Neale (London: BFI, 1981), 35.

111. Ibid.

112. Eisner, *Haunted Screen,* 106.

113. H. Börsch-Supan, *Die Bildgestaltung bei Caspar David Friedrich* (diss. University of Munich, 1960), 50. Joseph Leo Koerner, *Caspar David Friedrich and the Subject of Landscape* (New Haven: Yale University Press, 1990), 114. See also Bryan Wolf, "The Aesthetics of Parody," *Romantic Re-Vision: Culture and Consciousness in Nineteenth-Century American Painting and Literature* (Chicago: University of Chicago Press, 1982), 18–23, whose brief reading of Friedrich is highly suggestive.

114. This becomes more pronounced in some of Friedrich's later paintings, such as "Landscape with Graves," 1835–1837, one of many graveyard paintings that feature a vulture sitting upon a spade handle, looking down into an open grave. Here the diffused moonlight in the background contributes strongly to the uncanniness of the scene, enveloping the other grave markers in the near distance. By means of this minimal composition and the ominous quality of the moonlight that fills the sky, Friedrich is able to suggest that the imagination itself—figured by the moonlight—is a negative and oppressive force in its orientation towards death.

115. Paul M. Jensen, *The Cinema of Fritz Lang* (New York: Barnes and Co., 1969), 23, 33.

116. Koerner, *Caspar David Friedrich*, 114.

117. The many caves in Lang films, overtly marked as female spaces, have their analogue in the human anatomy as well. The film in which this is perhaps most obvious is *The Woman in the Moon* (1929). With regard to gaps or holes in the Lang text, see Frieda Grafe, "Für Fritz Lang: Einen Platz, kein Denkmal," *Fritz Lang* (Munich: Hanser, 1976), 74. Grafe puts the problem somewhat differently, claiming: "Die Löcher sind bedrohlich, weil sie Passagen fürs Chaos sind, aber das Chaos wiederum ist die Erettung vor der Erstarrung durch Geplantes, durch System." ("The holes are threatening because they are passageways for chaos, but chaos, on the other hand, is salvation from the immobilization brought about by planning, by systems"—trans. mine.)

118. Benjamin, "Work of Art," 859. Henceforth cited parenthetically.

119. As Miriam Hansen has pointed out in her thought-provoking article, there is a sense of belatedness about Benjamin's essay—it "belongs to the avant-garde of the Twenties." Hansen, "Benjamin, Cinema and Experience," 182.

120. This is also the apparatus of the alchemist and the medieval "philosopher," familiar to us from Faust's study. It is noteworthy that it is the apothecary who gives the young woman the potion that provokes her "dream," the three narratives contained within the frame story that constitute the body of the film.

121. See Miriam Hansen, "Benjamin, Cinema and Experience," 214. Although this particular insight is not developed, Hansen suggests that Benjamin's "theory of experience hovers over and around the body of the mother. . . . The image of the mother's body, as disturbing to Benjamin as to patriarchal discourse in general, shortcircuits desire and mortality—of which castration is perhaps the most powerful metaphor."

122. Lee Atwell, "The Silent Period: Toward an Individual Style," *G. W. Pabst* (Boston: Twayne, 1977), 41. In another amusing instance of the confusion concerning the boundaries of film and reality during this period, Pawlow is said to have played his role so well that a group of American analysts asked him to lecture—perhaps simply mistaking him for Pavlov the behaviorist. (34).

123. Benjamin puts it differently, however: "The camera introduces us to an unconscious optics as does psychoanalysis to unconscious impulses" (865).

124. Donald Spoto, *The Dark Side of Genius: The Life of Alfred Hitchcock* (New York: Ballantine Books, 1983), 563–64.

125. Vittorio Giacci put it as follows:

The relationship between sex and death . . . finds its most powerful imagery of transgressed desire in the crime with sexual undertones, and in the consequent choice of its representation in terms of the "thriller." The symbolic rapport between crime and sexuality is the *knife* (and its derivatives, scissors and razor) which assumes the connotations of the mortal weapon as in rape (murder, like the sex act occurs through "penetration"), in impotence and in the terror of castration. (Giacci, "Alfred Hitchcock: Allegory of Ambiguous Sexuality," *Wide Angle* 4 (1980): 8.)

126. Raymond Durgnat, *The Strange Case of Alfred Hitchcock*, (Cambridge, Mass.: M.I.T. Press, 1974), 161.

127. Spoto points out that "Hitchcock absorbed the Teutonic spirit" during the direction of two films in Munich at the Emelka Studios in 1925. During this period he met Lubitsch, Murnau, and Lang, the latter of whom had a decisive influence on his work. (Spoto, *The Dark Side of Genius*, 74.) As Robin Wood notes (and, indeed, it is a critical commonplace), Hitchcock was influenced by the style of German Expressionism; Fritz Lang's *Destiny* was one of Hitchcock's most important cinematic experiences. Robin Wood, "Retrospective," *A Hitchcock Reader*, ed. Marshall Deutelbaum and Leland Poague (Ames, Ia.: Iowa State University Press, 1986), 27.

128. See Patrice Petro, "Rematerializing the Vanishing 'Lady': Feminism, Hitchcock, and Interpretation," in Deutelbaum and Poague, *A Hitchcock Reader*, 129.

129. Ibid., 126.

130. Tania Modleski, *The Women Who Knew Too Much: Hitchcock and Feminist Theory* (New York: Routledge, 1989), 79. See also Robin Wood, *Hitchcock's Films* (South Brunswick, N.J.: A. S. Barnes and Co., 1977), 71. Wood reads the film as an enactment of a "therapeutic experience" that releases Jeffries from the compulsion to commit murder himself.

131. See especially Robert Stam and Roberta Pearson, "Hitchcock's *Rear Window*: Reflexivity and the Critique of Voyeurism," in Deutelbaum and Poague, *A Hitchcock Reader*, 193–206.

132. Raymond Bellour, "Hitchcock, The Enunciator," *Camera Obscura* 2 (1977): 66–91; also, "Psychosis, Neurosis, Perversion," in Deutelbaum and Poague, *A Hitchcock Reader*, 311–31.

133. This is suggested in Stam and Pearson, "Hitchcock's *Rear Window*," 196.

134. Some work has been done on the significance of painting in Hitchcock. In her essay, "'Never to Be Thirty-Six Years Old': *Rebecca* as Female Oedipal Drama," Tania Modleski makes the argument that woman poses the greatest threat to man as portrait, that her gaze renders that of the male impotent (*Wide*

Angle 5 (1982): 34–41). She later revises and elaborates upon her argument in *The Women Who Knew Too Much*. This, however, is only one aspect of this problem in Hitchcock; see my discussions of Hitchcock in chapters 2 and 3.

135. See Stephen Heath, "Narrative Space," in *Questions of Cinema*, 19–20, for another moment in which a detective looks at a painting, in this case an abstract painting, in a Hitchcock film. Heath reads this moment in *Suspicion* as pointing to an alternative space outside the confines of Quattrocento perspective and outside the space of the film.

136. Modleski, *Women Who Knew Too Much*, 80.

137. The subject of painting is already articulated in *The Lodger* (1927), which includes a painting depicting a scene of rape.

138. Deborah Linderman, "The Screen in Hitchcock's *Blackmail*," *Wide Angle* 4 (1980): 27.

139. In his reading of *Psycho*, William Rothman makes the following observation: Norman's hobby, "stuffing things" is "analogous to Hitchcock's hobby, fixing the human subject with a camera." Rothman, *Hitchcock—The Murderous Gaze* (Cambridge, Mass.: Harvard University Press, 1982), 279.

140. Bellour, "Psychosis, Neurosis, Perversion," 311–31.

141. Barbara Klinger, "*Psycho*: The Institutionalization of Female Sexuality," in Deutelbaum and Poague, *A Hitchcock Reader*, 336.

142. See André Bazin's reading of the "mummy complex," art's "defense against time." Bazin, "The Ontology of the Photographic Image," *What Is Cinema?*, 1: 9–11.

143. Bellour, "Psychosis, Neurosis, Perversion," 328.

144. Donald Spoto, *The Art of Alfred Hitchcock: Fifty Years of His Motion Pictures* (New York: Hopkinson and Blake, 1976), 155–56.

145. Stanley Cavell, "*North by Northwest*," in Deutelbaum and Poague, *A Hitchcock Reader*, 263.

146. Deutelbaum and Poague, "Hitchcock in Britain," *A Hitchcock Reader*, 64.

CHAPTER TWO

1. Horace, "Art of Poetry," *Criticism: The Major Texts*, ed. Walter Jackson Bate (New York: Harcourt, Brace, Jovanovich, 1970), 51.

2. This territory is a disputed one: for a reading of early film history that credits Griffith with these achievements, see David A. Cook, *A History of Narrative Film* (New York: W. W. Norton, 1981), 63–75; John L. Fell, *Film and the Narrative Tradition* (Norman, Okla.: University of Oklahoma Press, 1974), on the other hand, is interested in establishing links between protocinematic forms and early cinema; A. Nicholas Vardac, *Stage to Screen: Theatrical Method from Garrick to Griffith* (Cambridge, Mass.: Harvard University Press, 1949) also traces cinematic syntax to various earlier forms. For more contemporary readings of

Griffith, see Hansen, *Babel and Babylon*, and Tom Gunning, *D.W. Griffith and the Origins of American Narrative Film: The Early Years at Biograph* (Chicago: University of Illinois Press, 1991).

3. Sergei Eisenstein, "Dickens, Griffith, and the Film Today," *Film Form: Essays in Film Theory*, trans. and ed. Jay Leyda (New York: Harcourt Brace Jovanovich, 1949), 232. For another consideration of Dickens with regard to cinema, see Garrett Stewart, "Leaving History: Dickens, Gance, Blanchot," *Yale Journal of Criticism* 2 (1989): 145–82.

4. Eisenstein, "Dickens, Griffith, and the Film Today," 195.

5. For this and other relevant details surrounding the film's production, see Vance Kepley, Jr., "Griffith's *Broken Blossoms* and the Problem of Historical Specificity," *Quarterly Review of Film Studies* 3 (1978): 37–48.

6. As Dudley Andrew notes: "Indeed it might be suggested that it was Griffith's megalomania, inflated by the fame he had achieved in 1916, that allowed this more acceptable notion of art to be admitted in America, where the sort of subculture of the French impressionists could never exist and where every alteration in the institution of cinema had to be ratified by the single dominating culture, Hollywood." Dudley Andrew, "*Broken Blossoms*: The Vulnerable Text and the Marketing of Masochism," *Film in the Aura of Art* (Princeton: Princeton University Press, 1984), 17.

7. Kepley, "Griffith's *Broken Blossoms*," 42.

8. Ibid., 43.

9. Ibid., 44.

10. Siegfried Kracauer, "Cult of Distraction: On Berlin's Picture Palaces," *New German Critique* 40 (1987): 92.

11. See Miriam Hansen's discussion of title cards in Griffith's *Intolerance*, whose Babylonian narrative has title cards with a background of stone-engraved hieroglyphics and whose Judaean narrative uses title cards with a background of Hebrew tablets. Hansen, *Babel and Babylon*, 190.

12. See Chapter 3, below.

13. Comolli, "Machines of the Visible," 122.

14. Neil Harris, "A Subversive Form," in Musser, *Before Hollywood*, 47.

15. Andrew makes a noteworthy distinction along these lines: "The oriental's oblique liquid movements come to rest in gently curved poses which concentrate and contain the dramatic energy within the frame, while the burly boxer thrashes about abruptly and gracelessly, thrusting our attention out of the frame and to the object of his aggression." Andrew, "The Vulnerable Text," 21.

On the topic of the one-upmanship that I read in this moment, Alan Trachtenberg's insight that film is interested in "wresting authority" from photography is suggestive and pertinent; the long-lens, close-up "portraits" of Lillian Gish in *Broken Blossoms* are a case in point. See Alan Trachtenberg, "Photography/Cinematography," in Musser, *Before Hollywood*, 78.

16. Andrew, "The Vulnerable Text," 19.

17. Deleuze, *Cinema 1*, 31.

18. Mitchell, "Space and Time," 112.

19. Deleuze, *Cinema 1*, 31. For an important discussion of parallel editing in Griffith, see Tom Gunning, "Weaving a Narrative: Style and Economic Background in Griffith's Biograph Films," *QRFS* 6 (1981): 11–25.

20. Barthes, "Diderot, Brecht, Eisenstein," 74.

21. On the topic of the female portrait in Hitchcock, see Modleski, " 'Never to Be Thirty-Six Years Old,' " 34–41. See also Teresa de Lauretis, "Desire in Narrative," in *Alice Doesn't*, 154.

22. Spoto, *The Dark Side of Genius*, 38ff.

23. Bellour, "Psychosis, Neurosis, Perversion," 329. An obvious instance of Hitchcock's substitution of his own body for a female body occurs in the trailer for *Frenzy*, where he allows his effigy (a model of his head attached to a dummy) to float down the Thames just as the film's first female corpse had done. See Spoto, *The Dark Side of Genius*, 548.

24. François Truffaut with Helen G. Scott, *Hitchcock*, rev. ed. (New York: Simon and Schuster, 1983), 319.

25. A feminist reading of this moment would stress the utopian aspect of this self-representation, for the heroine is not yet prepared to act.

26. When Rebecca wears the costume, she is masquerading as an innocent (as the sexual woman, her mode is black velvet) and probably provokes a reaction in her husband much like the reaction Midge calls forth in Scottie (*Vertigo*) when she represents herself as Carlotta. It is for this reason that Maxim is shocked when the second Mrs. de Winter also dresses as Lady Caroline, for the sight of the costume awakens in him the fear that she, too, may simply be masquerading, and that in reality she shares Rebecca's phallic—castrating—power.

27. See Modleski, " 'Never to Be Thirty-Six Years Old,' " 34–41. Mary Ann Doane makes the following point: "The films construct an opposition between different processes of imaging along the lines of sexual difference: female desire is linked to the fixation and stability of spectacle refusing the temporal dimension, while male desire is more fully implicated with the defining characteristic of the cinematic image: movement." *The Desire to Desire: The Woman's Film of the 1940s* (Bloomington: Indiana University Press, 1987), 171.

28. When portraits of men are featured in Hitchcock films, as in the portrait of General MacLaidlaw in *Suspicion*, or the portrait of the dead father in *The Birds*, they function quite obviously as reminders of the law of the father and of the Oedipal power that he exerts.

29. Stephen Heath begins his brilliant essay, "Narrative Space," with a reference to a disconcertingly different kind of space suggested by a Picasso-like rendering of the human body, a painting that captures the attention of a detective in *Suspicion*. Heath suggest that this painting problematizes point of view, framing, and the law for this film, that it is "somewhere else again, another scene, another story, another space." Heath, "Narrative Space," 19–20. Actually, the fear of

abstract paintings of the human figure in Hitchcock (the second Mrs. de Winter's brother-in-law, for instance, does not like modern art because bodies are not recognizable in it) has a good deal to do with the fear of fragmentation discussed in chapter 1. It is another theme that Hitchcock may have picked up from Lang, where the fear of Cubism is mocked (*Dr. Mabuse the Gambler*).

30. Cavell, "*North by Northwest,*" 256.

31. It also strongly resembles the outfit that Marlon Brando wears for similar effect as a bounty hunter in *Missouri Breaks*.

32. Rothman, *Hitchcock—The Murderous Gaze*, 60.

33. Once again there is a connection between Fane and Norman Bates, whose phallic power resides in his knife and bird beak.

34. See chapter 1 above.

35. Rothman, *Hitchcock—The Murderous Gaze*, 90. Rothman's detailed discussion of this intricate scene is well worth reading.

36. Ibid.

37. This moment of spectacle featuring Fane should not be understood exclusively as interrupting the progress of the narrative; it, too, develops the narrative and is subject to its pressures, and hence can be legitimately called diegetic.

38. See Linda Williams, *Hard Core: Power, Pleasure, and the "Frenzy of the Visible"* (Berkeley and Los Angeles: University of California Press, 1989), 201.

39. Lotte Eisner, *Murnau* (Berkeley and Los Angeles: University of California Press, 1973), 84. Eisner quotes from notes of Murnau's.

40. Here I am in disagreement with André Bazin, who says of Murnau that "the composition of his image is in no sense pictorial." Bazin, "The Evolution of the Language of Cinema," in *What Is Cinema?*, 1:27.

41. Eric Rohmer, *L'organisation de l'espace dans le "Faust" de Murnau*, (Paris: Union Générale d'Editions, 1977), 18.

42. For a reading of the relation of these two texts, see Judith Mayne, "Dracula in the Twilight: Murnau's *Nosferatu* (1922)," *German Film and Literature: Adaptations and Transformations*, ed. Eric Rentschler (New York: Methuen, 1986), 25–39.

43. For an interesting discussion of mediation in Friedrich, see Bryan Wolf, *Romantic Re-Vision: Culture and Consciousness in Nineteenth-Century American Painting and Literature* (Chicago: University of Chicago Press, 1982), 18–23.

44. Rohmer, *L'organisation de l'espace dans le "Faust" de Murnau*, 15–18.

45. Alexandre Astruc, "Fire and Ice," *Cahiers du Cinéma in English* 1 (1966): 69–73.

46. Mitchell, "Space and Time," 101–4.

47. This reading was first suggested by Robin Wood, " F. W. Murnau," *Film Comment* 12 (1976): 7.

48. De Lauretis, "Desire in Narrative," 139.

49. Ibid., 144.

50. Ibid., 132. Nosferatu's ship is called the "Demeter."

51. Eisner, *Murnau*, 116.

52. Bazin, "Painting and Cinema," 164–69.

53. Janet Bergstrom, "Sexuality at a Loss: The Films of F. W. Murnau," *Poetics Today* 6 (1985): 201.

54. Bergstrom is careful, however, not to reduce her argument to biographical terms.

55. See Linda Williams, "When the Woman Looks," *Re-Vision: Essays in Feminist Film Criticism*, ed. Mary Ann Doane, Patricia Mellencamp, and Linda Williams (Frederick, Md.: University Publications of America, 1984), 87.

56. Herlth and Röhrig, set designers of *Caligari* and *Destiny*, also designed *The Last Laugh*. See Cook, *A History of Narrative Film*, 121–25.

57. It is well known that Karl Freund, the cameraman, rode down a glass-sided elevator with the camera, that he shot film while riding a bicycle and on roller skates, transported the camera along cables, and hoisted the camera up the ladder of a fire truck, thus creating the genuinely cinematic space that structures the film's scenes. See ibid., 120–21. As Elsaesser claims, the so-called unchained camera is "an attempt to 'narrativize' and anthropomorphize the possibilities inherent in the camera's inhuman vision." Elsaesser, "Film History and Visual Pleasure," 79.

58. Interestingly, as soon as the doorman and the night watchman are constituted as an alternative couple in this film, the camera becomes more objective, as though the camera's relation to its subject (primarily Jannings as the night watchman) had been displaced into this relation. This occurs in the epilogue of the film, which does have a different style. The epilogue actually sets up a traditional "romantic" restaurant scenario, complete with flowers, gifts, oysters, and champagne; the couple leaves this scene in a wedding coach, while the film proper had featured motorized vehicles prominently. If Murnau was forced to make this happy ending, as some contend, how happy he must have been to be able to represent a disguised homosexual narrative within it.

59. Elsaesser, "Film History and Visual Pleasure," 79.

60. There has been a good deal of controversy concerning the extent to which Freund, Murnau's cinematographer, and Carl Mayer, the screenwriter, shaped this film. At the risk of sounding auteurist in reading cinematic texts, I share the view held by those film historians who consider Murnau's control over his films absolute.

61. Arnold Höllriegel, quoted by Eisner, *Murnau*, 85.

62. See chapter 1 for a discussion of this issue.

63. Hayden White, "The Noble Savage Theme as Fetish," *Tropics of Discourse: Essays in Cultural Criticism* (Baltimore: Johns Hopkins University Press, 1978), 190.

64. Wood, "F. W. Murnau," 11.

65. Molly Haskell, "Sunrise," *Film Comment* (1971): 18.

66. See Mary Ann Doane, "The Moving Image," *Wide Angle* 7 (1985), 44, 48.

Doane quotes Wolfgang Schivelbusch (*The Railway Journey: Trains and Travel in the Nineteenth Century*), who compares the manner in which railroad travel provokes a reorganization of space and time with that necessitated by cinematic montage, both reflecting "the new reality of annihilated in-between spaces."

67. Astruc said of Murnau films that "every frame of Murnau's is the story of a murder." Astruc, "Fire and Ice," 69.

68. Dudley Andrew, "The Turn and Return of *Sunrise*," *Film in the Aura of Art*, 28–58: 34.

69. See Deleuze on the "gothic geometry" of Expressionism. Deleuze, *Cinema 1*, 51–52.

70. Anton Kaes, "The Debate about Cinema: Charting a Controversy (1901–1929)," *New German Critique* 40 (Winter 1987): 10–15. Similarly, in *The Last Laugh* it is apparent that the camera belongs to the world of cars, trams, lights, and trains—the modern world of technology in which the natural processes of living (the porter's aging) cannot be accommodated humanely.

71. Andrew, "Turn and Return," 51.

72. Bazin, "The Ontology of the Photographic Image," 14.

73. Andrew, "Turn and Return," 48.

74. It is interesting that the narrative of *The Last Laugh* also subjects the porter, its emasculated main character, to the hostile and mocking stares of a group of harpy-like women; this is so much on the surface of the film that critics have mentioned Murnau's "misogyny" in writing of these scenes. Eisner, *The Haunted Screen*, 219.

75. According to Eisner, four films intervened between these two: two of these were rediscovered, and two remain lost. Eisner, *Murnau*, 27–57.

76. George O'Brien, the actor who played the husband, wore shoes with twenty-pound weights in them in order to produce that effect. Wood, "F. W. Murnau," 12.

77. Andrew, "Turn and Return," 53.

78. The story of Murnau's discontent with Hollywood, his Gauguin-like flight to Tahiti on a sailboat, and his plan to make a film there with Robert Flaherty can be pieced together only imperfectly. See the chapter entitled "The Culmination: Tabu," in Eisner's *Murnau*, 202–20, as well as Robert Plumpe Murnau's account of his own visit to Tahiti after his brother's death, also in *Murnau*, 24–26. See also Robin Wood, "Tabu," *Film Comment* 12 (1976): 23–27; Richard Griffith, "Flaherty and Tabu," *Film Culture* 20 (1959): 12–13; and David Flaherty, "A Few Reminiscences," *Film Culture* 20 (1959): 14–16. Although Murnau and Flaherty initially planned to make a film together, Flaherty (noted, of course, for his documentaries) apparently abandoned the project because Murnau, who was personally financing the film, was "romanticizing" the story on which they had worked together. See F. W. Murnau and Robert J. Flaherty, "Tabu (Taboo), A Story of the South Seas," *Film Culture* 20 (1959), 27–38.

79. Eisner, *Murnau*, 208.

80. Ibid.

81. Ibid., 211–12.

82. Ibid., 211.

83. Ibid., 219.

84. Richard Griffith, in "Flaherty and Tabu," mentions an essay by Maurice Scherer, "La Revanche de l'Occident" (*Cahiers du Cinéma* 21 [1953]: 46–48), about which he says: "In this article the author says—with evident approval— that in *Tabu* Murnau has revenged [*sic*] Western art for the revolution against it which Gauguin began by imposing upon [Polynesia] a specific and traditional European imagery" (13). A footnote to this claim reads "Sous leur peau bronzée, c'est un sang blanc qu'il fait couler dans les veines de ces Polynésiens." (Under their bronzed skin, it is white blood that flows in the veins of these Polynesians"— trans. mine.) Eisner, referring to the Griffith article in *Murnau*, reveals that Maurice Scherer is a pseudonym for Eric Rohmer, and secondly implies that he has argued no such thing—despite the "white blood beneath their brown skins and . . . the Greek bas-relief of the Sleeping Hunter"(216). In fact, Scherer/Rohmer does argue this point, but in a generalizing manner.

85. His brother, Robert Plumpe Murnau, reported that Murnau built his house in Tahiti in the ancient Polynesian style, "showing the present generation what the art of its ancestors had been. He knew the history and culture of this people. He respected their traditions and their laws." In Eisner, *Murnau*, 25.

86. White, "The Noble Savage Theme as Fetish," 184, 187.

87. It is not my intention here to provide an exhaustive reading of this film; Wood, in "F. W. Murnau," points out the similarities in basic plot structure and style between *Nosferatu, Sunrise,* and *Tabu.*

88. Robert Plumpe Murnau reports this in Eisner's *Murnau*, 25.

89. Ibid.

90. Eisner, *Murnau*, 219.

91. Wood is also interested in the "dialectic between flux and stasis," and notes the connection between Hitu, stasis, and tribal law. Wood, "F. W. Murnau," 26.

92. Eisner, *Murnau*, 219.

93. Ibid., 218. This story suggests that Werner Herzog's shooting of *Fitzcarraldo* is a remake of Murnau's shooting of *Tabu.*

94. See Kenneth Anger, *Hollywood Babylon* (New York: Dell, 1975), 244–45. Anger writes: "Homosexuality, real or supposed, was a favorite topic. Few around the Fox lot had not heard that director F. W. Murnau favored gays when it came to casting. Murnau's death inspired a flood tide of speculation." Eisner offers two explanations for the car accident sharply differing from Anger's (*Murnau*, 222–23). Apparently, fortune-tellers and astrologers had predicted his death.

95. Reported by Robert Plumpe Murnau, in Eisner's *Murnau*, 26.

96. For a sampling of such responses, see Timothy Corrigan, ed., *The Films of Werner Herzog: Between Mirage and History* (New York: Methuen, 1986).

97. Corrigan, "Producing Herzog: From a Body of Images," in *The Films of Werner Herzog*, 11.

98. Thomas Elsaesser, "An Anthropologists's Eye: *Where the Green Ants Dream*," in Corrigan, *The Films of Werner Herzog*, 145; Gertrud Koch, "Blindness as Insight: Visions of the Unseen in *Land of Silence and Darkness*," in ibid., 81.

99. Kaja Silverman, "Kaspar Hauser's 'Terrible Fall' into Narrative," *New German Critique* 24–25 (1981–1982): 91.

100. Kraft Wetzel, quoted by Gertrud Koch, "Blindness as Insight," 76.

101. Corrigan, "Producing Herzog," 12.

102. Werner Herzog, *Vom Gehen im Eis* (Munich: Carl Hanser, 1978).

103. Elsaesser, "An Anthropologist's Eye," 155.

104. Herzog resists calling these characters "marginal," preferring to call them "pure": "They are just very *pure* figures that have somehow been able to survive in more or less pure form." Quoted by William Van Wert, "Last Words: Observations on a New Language," in Corrigan, *The Films of Werner Herzog*, 55. Van Wert makes the point that the "purest of the pure" are the entirely silent ones.

105. Silverman, "Kaspar Hauser's 'Terrible Fall,'" 77.

106. Brigitte Peucker, "Literature and Writing in the Films of Werner Herzog," in Corrigan, *The Films of Werner Herzog*, 105. As I point out, in making this claim Herzog denies the strong influence of literature in his films. I also argue this point in "Werner Herzog: In Quest of the Sublime," *New German Filmmakers: From Oberhausen Through the 1970s*, ed. Klaus Phillips (New York: Ungar, 1984), 168–94; and "The Invalidation of Arnim: Herzog's *Signs of Life*," *German Film and Literature: Adaptations and Transformations*, ed. Eric Rentschler (New York: Methuen, 1986), 217–30.

107. It is present, of course, in Herzog's adaptation of Büchner's *Woyzeck* (1978), which is quite faithful to the play.

108. Silverman, "Kaspar Hauser's 'Terrible Fall,'" 74.

109. Bergstrom, "Sexuality at a Loss," 199.

110. Herzog's films cannot, however, be said to displace erotic energy onto the male body as male body.

111. Paul Coates, *The Story of a Lost Reflection: The Alienation of the Image in Western and Polish Cinema* (London: Verso, 1985), 125.

112. Dana Benelli, "The Cosmos and Its Discontents," in Corrigan, *The Films of Werner Herzog*, 91.

113. Koerner, *Caspar David Friedrich*, 217.

114. Wolf, *Romantic Re-Vision*, 23.

115. Silverman, "Kaspar Hauser's 'Terrible Fall,'" 74.

116. Peucker, "In Quest of the Sublime," 170.

117. Although I believe this image to allude specifically to Lang's film, naturally the Romantic tradition connects the mountaintop experience with the sublime and with death. For a discussion of the translation of these images into film, see Siegfried Kracauer on the "mountain movies" made by Arnold Fanck and Leni Riefenstahl. Kracauer, *From Caligari to Hitler*, 110–12.

118. Thomas Elsaesser, *New German Cinema: A History* (New Brunswick, N.J.: Rutgers University Press, 1989), 20.

119. Peucker, "In Quest of the Sublime," 184.

120. Carl T. Dreyer, "New Ideas About the Film: Benjamin Christensen and His Ideas," *Dreyer in Double Reflection: Translation of Carl Th. Dreyer's Writings "About the Film" (Om Filmen)*, trans. and ed. Donald Skoller (New York: E. P. Dutton, 1973), 32.

121. Tom Milne, *The Cinema of Carl Dreyer* (New York: A. S. Barnes and Co., 1971), 20. As Milne notes: "This aspect of the film, it seems, had not occurred to Dreyer, who was advised by friends to flee the country before the Germans began to sit up and take notice."

122. Dreyer, "Imagination and Color (1955)," in Skoller, *Dreyer in Double Reflection*, 178–79.

123. "Call it witchcraft, vampirism, or simply the nature of love, Dreyer's heroines all live and die by this power," Milne, *The Cinema of Carl Dreyer*, 31.

124. Skoller, *Dreyer in Double Reflection*, 62.

125. Though this expression is used figuratively in the case of Dreyer, an experiment of this kind was actually carried out by Herzog, who hypnotized his actors for the shooting of *Heart of Glass*.

126. Milne, *The Cinema of Carl Dreyer*, 93.

127. Siegfried Kracauer, *Theory of Film: The Redemption of Physical Reality* (London: Oxford University Press, 1960), 81. See also David Bordwell, "Day of Wrath," *The Films of Carl-Theodor Dreyer* (Berkeley and Los Angeles: University of California Press, 1981), 127.

128. Mark Nash, *Dreyer* (London: BFI, 1977), 9. This film is based upon a novel by Herman Bang.

129. Ibid., 10.

130. In fact, this element of mother-son incest was played upon by the Italian title of the film, *The Lover of his Mother*. Ibid., 60.

131. Hélène Cixous and Catherine Clément, *The Newly Born Woman*, trans. Betsy Wing (Minneapolis: University of Minnesota Press, 1988), 12. In this essay, "The Guilty One," Clément draws heavily upon Jules Michelet's *La Sorcière (Satanism and Witchcraft)*. Joan of Arc was also tried for sorcery.

132. Raymond Durgnat, *Eros in the Cinema* (London: Calder and Boyars, 1966), 50.

133. In this film the camera moves around characters and creates a circular sense of space.

134. Bordwell notes: "By the time that the presence of the supernatural has been motivated by Anne's dead mother and Herlof's Marte, witchcraft becomes one side of the dialectic of natural/supernatural, the purpose of which is to displace perpetually the problem of woman's sexuality." Bordwell, "Day of Wrath," 126.

135. Robin Wood, "Murnau 1: *Nosferatu*," *Film Comment* 12 (1976): 5–9.

136. Nash, *Dreyer*, 32.

137. In *Joan of Arc*, a similar strategy is at work: Dreyer juxtaposes a written text, the transcript of the trial, with the text of images that is the film itself. Since Joan, who is virtually mute and expresses herself through her tears, forms such a striking contrast to the male world of language, spoken and written, several critics have discussed this juxtapositon in terms of Kristeva's notion of "signifiance," which combines the male symbolic order with the female semiotic process, of which tears are an example. See Nash, *Dreyer*, 16–19, and Deborah Linderman, "Uncoded Images in the Heterogeneous Text," in Rosen, *Narrative, Apparatus, Ideology*, 143–52.

138. Bordwell, "Day of Wrath," 137.

139. Svetlana Alpers, "Interpretation without Representation or, The Viewing of *Las Méninas*," *Representations* 1 (1983): 37.

140. Cixous and Clément, *The Newly Born Woman*, 54. Clement, summarizing Michelet's argument, qualifies this assertion: "At the time of medieval sorcery, incest has such a broad definition that it includes almost all the members of the same village," 30.

141. Bordwell is correct in saying that the text used here is not the traditional Latin *dies irae* text: he states that "English language prints have mistakenly translated the Latin poem and attached it to the illustrations." Bordwell, "Day of Wrath," 129. He is incorrect, however, in claiming that the film uses an "unorthodox" text; I am indebted to Thomas M. Greene for the information that this is a standard Danish translation of the Thomas of Celano poem on the same subject, dating from the Middle Ages.

142. Bordwell gives an excellent account of the function of sound and music in this film. In *Dreyer*, Nash argues that music in his films "heals the fragmented body of the text" (25), and that Dreyer had wanted *Joan of Arc* to be a sound film for this reason (31). I do not agree that music has this effect in *Day of Wrath*.

143. For a reading of the function of uncoded material in *Joan of Arc*, see Linderman, "Uncoded Images in the Heterogeneous Text," 143–52.

144. In this regard, see Antonin Artaud's essay, "Witchcraft and the Cinema," in which he makes the connection between the "secret movement" of the cinema, by means of which "objects obtain a life of their own. . . . Essentially, the cinema reveals a whole occult life with which it puts us directly into contact." Artaud, *Collected Works*, vol. 3, trans. Victor Corti (London: Calder and Boyars, 1974), 65–66.

145. Cixous and Clément, *The Newly Born Woman*, 39.

146. Nash, in particular, has made use of this term in *Dreyer*, 30–31.

147. Nash quotes Rasmussen in *Dreyer*, 30.

148. Mary Ann Doane, "The Voice of the Cinema: The Articulation of Body and Space," *Yale French Studies* 60 (1980): 35.

CHAPTER THREE

1. Diderot, "The Salons," 150.

2. Benjamin, "The Work of Art," 867.

3. Ian Hamilton Finlay, *Concrete Poetry: An International Anthology*, ed. Stephen Bann (London: London Magazine, 1967), 151.

4. Jacques Lacan's references to Zeuxis and Parrhasios in his seminar have undoubtedly sparked renewed interest in the story. Lacan, "Of the Gaze," *The Four Fundamental Concepts of Psychoanalysis* (New York: W. W. Norton, 1981), 67–119.

5. Norman Bryson makes the point that Zeuxis's painting was probably an example of skenography, painting for the theater. See Bryson, *Looking at the Overlooked: Four Essays on Still Life Painting* (Cambridge, Mass.: Harvard University Press, 1990), 30–31.

6. Norman Bryson, "The Natural Attitude," *Vision and Painting: The Logic of the Gaze*, (New Haven: Yale University Press, 1983), 3.

7. Svetlana Alpers, *The Art of Describing: Dutch Art in the Seventeenth Century* (Chicago: University of Chicago Press, 1983), 12.

8. Jonathan Crary notes that many accounts "single out as its most impressive feature its representation of movement." Crary, *Techniques of the Observer: On Vision and Modernity in the Nineteenth Century* (Cambridge, Mass.: M.I.T. Press, 1992), 34. Sabine Hake observes that the camera obscura's "small opening represents the primal scene of cinema." Hake, "Self-Referentiality in Early German Cinema," *Cinema Journal* 31 (1992): 39.

9. Christopher Hussey, *The Picturesque: Studies in a Point of View* (reprint, London: Frank Cass, 1967), 239.

10. Ibid., 241.

11. Joseph Addison, *The Works of Joseph Addison*, vol. 6, ed. George Washington Greene (Philadelphia: J. B. Lippincott, 1876), 338.

12. In the 1830s, this idea was still current. William Henry Fox Talbot wrote, for example, of the images produced by a camera lucida as "pictures of nature's painting." Talbot, "A Brief Historical Sketch of the Art," *Classic Essays on Photography*, ed. Alan Trachtenberg (New Haven: Leete's Island Books, 1980), 29.

13. Crary, *Techniques of the Observer*, 38–39.

14. Bryson, *Vision and Painting*, 119.

15. Bazin makes the following claim, which does not contradict mine: "Besides, just as the word indicates, the aesthetic of the *trompe l'oeil* in the eigh-

teenth century resided more in illusion than in realism, that is to say, in a lie rather than the truth. A statue painted on a wall should look as if it were on a pedestal in space." Bazin, "The Myth of Total Cinema," *What Is Cinema?*, 19.

16. Heinz Buddemeier, *Panorama, Diorama, Photographie: Entstehung und Wirkung neuer Medien im 19. Jahrhundert* (Munich: Wilhelm Fink, 1970), 19.

17. Alpers, *The Art of Describing*, 51.

18. Buddemeier, *Panorama, Diorama, Photographie*, 16.

19. Bryson, "The Glance and the Gaze," in *Vision and Painting*, 119.

20. Jean H. Hagstrum, *The Sister Arts* (Chicago: University of Chicago, 1958), 141.

21. C.C.L. Hirschfeld, *Theorie der Gartenkunst*, vol. 2 (Leipzig: Weidmann, 1785), 138–65. Hirschfeld frequently refers to his English models.

22. Although Hirschfeld does not see landscape gardens as mass entertainment exactly, he stresses their greater accessibility with respect to paintings. *Theorie der Gartenkunst*, 2:157.

23. Repton, quoted by Walter J. Hippel, *The Beautiful, the Sublime, and the Picturesque in Eighteenth-Century British Aesthetic Theory* (Carbondale, Ill.: The Southern Illinois University Press, 1957), 232. See also Hirschfeld, *Theorie der Gartenkunst*, 2:152. Hirschfeld takes this idea from Thomas Whately's "Observations on Modern Gardening" (1770). See Wolfgang Schepers, *Hirschfelds "Theorie der Gartenkunst, 1779–85,* (Worms: Werner, 1980), 67.

24. Buddemeier, *Panorama, Diorama, Photographie*, 16–17. These were often of prospects and, as such, were an attempt to control the distant space beyond the confines of the garden.

25. Michael Fried, *Absorption and Theatricality: Painting and Beholder in the Age of Diderot* (Chicago: University of Chicago Press, 1980), 118.

26. Diderot, "The Salons," 156.

27. Ibid., 150.

28. Ibid.

29. As Bryson points out, the Goncourts made a similar claim concerning the paintings of Chardin nearly one hundred years later; Bryson himself stresses their "sensuous materiality." Bryson, "The Gaze and the Glance," 130.

30. Eric Cameron, "Food Related Thick Paintings," *Descant* 71/72, 21 (1991): 207–14.

31. Johann Gottfried Herder, "Plastik," *Herders Sämmtliche Werke*, vol. 8, ed. Bernhard Suphan (Berlin: Weidmann, 1892), 12–13.

32. Kirsten Gram Holmström, *Monodrama, Attitudes, Tableaux Vivants: Studies in Some Trends of Theatrical Fashion, 1770–1815* (Stockholm: Almquist and Wiksell, 1967), 117, 203.

33. Ibid., 110ff.

34. Ibid., 111.

35. Ibid., 116, 120.

36. Ibid., 204.

37. Goethe himself speculates that the source for the tableau vivant lies in the tradition of the Neapolitan "cribs," which represented pivotal events in the Christmas story from the Annunciation to the birth of Christ. Goethe is probably wrong in making this assumption. Cribs tended to use real actors along with sculptural figures, and they further juxtaposed images with reality by incorporating distant prospects into the representation. Realistic in all details, "a perfect harmony in proportions and perspective," cribs were arranged to be viewed in sequence by a moving spectator, resembling the landscape garden in this respect also. See Holmström, *Monodrama, Attitudes, Tableaux Vivants*, 209–14.

38. J. W. von Goethe, *Elective Affinities*, trans. R.J. Hollingdale (London: Penguin, 1971), 191.

39. J. W. von Goethe, "The Collector and His Circle," *Goethe on Art*, trans. and ed. John Gage (Berkeley and Los Angeles: University of California Press, 1980), 33.

40. Here Goethe refers pointedly to the architectural meaning of the trompe l'oeil as false door or window.

41. Goethe, "The Collector and His Circle," 37.

42. Martin Price, "The Picturesque Moment," *From Sensibility to Romanticism: Essays Presented to Frederick A. Pottle*, ed. Frederick W. Hilles and Harold Bloom (London: Oxford University Press, 1965), 210.

43. Quoted by Price, "The Picturesque Moment," 286.

44. Uvedale Price, "Dialogue on the Distinct Characters of the Picturesque and the Beautiful," quoted in Hussey, *The Picturesque*, 74.

45. Ibid., 119.

46. Jean Baudrillard, *Seduction*, trans. Brian Singer (New York: St. Martin's Press, 1990), 46.

47. Charles Baudelaire, "The Painter of Modern Life," *"The Painter of Modern Life" and Other Essays* (New York: Garland, 1978), 9.

48. Ibid.

49. Ibid., 9, 12.

50. Ibid., 9. In *The World Viewed*, Stanley Cavell reads Baudelaire's essay as "an anticipation of film." "Baudelaire and the Myths of Film," *The World Viewed* (Cambridge, Mass.: Harvard University Press, 1979), 43.

51. Walter Benjamin, *Charles Baudelaire: Ein Lyriker im Zeitalter des Hochkapitalismus*, ed. Rolf Tiedemann (Frankfurt am Main: Suhrkamp, 1990), 48. By this time, of course, the connection of the cityscape with cinema had been made many times over. In noting this image in Dickens, however, Benjamin anticipates Eisenstein's interest in the cinematic quality of Dickens's writing by a number of years. Eisenstein wrote "Dickens, Griffith, and the Film Today" in 1944; Benjamin worked on *Charles Baudelaire*, a text that was never completed, from 1937 to 1939.

52. Benjamin, "Work of Art," 867.

53. Ibid., 866.

54. Ibid.

55. Bryson, "The Glance and the Gaze," 119.

56. Theodor W. Adorno, "Der wunderliche Realist," *Noten zur Literatur III* (Frankfurt: Suhrkamp, 1965), 96. Translation mine.

57. Thomas Elsaesser, "Cinema—The Irresponsible Signifier or 'The Gamble with History': Film Theory or Cinema Theory," *New German Critique* 40 (1987): 79. Kracauer's "Cult of Distraction" is in the same issue, 91–96; "The Mass Ornament" is available in *New German Critique* 5 (1975): 66–76.

58. Kracauer, "Cult of Distraction," 92.

59. Siegfried Kracauer, *Theory of Film: The Redemption of Physical Reality* (Oxford: Oxford University Press, 1960), ix.

60. Ibid., 196.

61. Ibid.

62. Ibid.

63. Bazin, "The Ontology of the Photographic Image," 11.

64. Ibid., 15.

65. Bazin, "The Evolution of the Language of Cinema," *What Is Cinema?*, 1:35. It is not my intention to analyze the significance of "deep space" for Bazin here. See Comolli, "Machines of the Visible," 134–36, for one reading.

66. Metz, "On the Impression of Reality in the Cinema," 8–9.

67. For Comolli, what Bazin calls the "psychological ambition" of the plastic arts is read as an ideological aim. Comolli, "Machines of the Visible," 133. Comolli takes up and revises a number of ideas put forward by Bazin in "The Myth of Total Cinema," 17–22. Bazin, for example, asks why, given the fact that nothing had stood in the way of the development of the phenakistoscope or zootrope since antiquity, they developed when they did. Comolli answers this question with the claim that the machine of the visible is "born immediately as a social machine" (122), a view taken by Jonathan Crary's *Techniques of the Observer*. Like Bazin, Comolli is interested in perspective in painting and cinema, stressing (unlike Bazin and like many contemporary art historians) its ideological function. See Heath, "Narrative Space," 19–75.

68. Jean-Louis Comolli, "Technique and Ideology: Camera, Perspective, Depth of Field," *Movies and Methods*, vol. 2, ed. Bill Nichols (Berkeley and Los Angeles: University of California Press, 1985), 51.

69. Mary Ann Doane, " 'When the direction of the force acting on the body is changed:' The Moving Image," *Femmes Fatales: Feminism, Film Theory, Psychoanalysis* (New York: Routledge, 1991), 193–94.

70. Ibid., 194.

71. Ibid., 196. It is important to distinguish, as Doane does, between Bazin's notion of realism as truth and his notion of trompe l'oeil as a lie, something meant to deceive. (291n.16).

72. Lacan, "What Is a Picture?" *Four Fundamental Concepts*, 112.

73. Richard Allen has argued recently that trompe l'oeil in the cinema would

imply mistaking the film for real life "in the manner of the proverbial spectators of Lumière's *Arrival of a Train at the Station*" but that the largeness of the image and "the context where it is seen (the cinema), simply rule out the possibility of trompe l'oeil illusion." Although cinema as a medium may not be able to accommodate trompe l'oeil in its pure form, films do make use of trompe l'oeil effects of various kinds by way of narratives and representational techniques that play upon the introduction of the real into cinematic representation. See Richard Allen, "Representation, Illusion, and the Cinema," *Cinema Journal*, 32 (1993): 41.

74. Noted by Doane, "The Moving Image," 191–92.

75. Comolli, "Machines of the Visible," 129. A recent and very interesting talk given by Antonia Lant, "Polishing Aladdin's Lamp: The Orientalization of Early Cinema," addressed the issue of three-dimensional and two-dimensional forms and tactile and visual responses in early cinema, relating tactility in the cinema to an interest in matters Egyptian (May 8, 1993; Yale University).

76. Kleist, *Sämtliche Werke und Briefe*, 2:650–51.

77. For a discussion of Kleist's relation to Rousseau, see Bernhard Böschenstein, "Kleist und Rousseau," *Kleist Jahrbuch* 81/82 (1983): 145–61.

78. Kleist, *Sämtliche Werke* 2:701.

79. See Alan Spiegel, "The Cinematic Text: Rohmer's *The Marquise of O . . .*," *Modern European Filmmakers and the Art of Adaptation*, ed. Andrew Horton and Joan Magretta (New York: Ungar, 1981), 316. For additional information, as well as a bibliography, see also *Erzählstrukturen—Filmstrukturen: Erzählungen Heinrich von Kleists und ihre filmische Realisation*, ed. Klaus Kanzog (Berlin: Erich Schmidt Verlag, 1981).

80. In German, the painting is known as "St. Michael mit der Lanze." See Peter Horvath, "Auf den Spuren Teniers, Vouets und Raphaels in Kleists *Michael Kohlhaas*," *Seminar* 5 (1969): 109. Other discussions of Kleist and the visual arts include Walter Silz, *Heinrich von Kleist: Studies in His Work and Literary Character*, (Philadelphia: University of Pennsylvania Press, 1961), 247–70; H. M. Brown, "Zwischen Himmel und Erde: Kleist and the Visual Arts, with Special Reference to Caspar David Friedrich," *German Life and Letters*, New Series 31 (1978), 157–66; Stuart Atkins, "Heinrich von Kleist and the Fine Arts—Kleist and Bury, or Kleist and Lethière?" *German Life and Letters*, New Series 31 (1978), 166–74; and Steven R. Huff, "Kleist and Expectant Virgins: The Meaning of the 'O' in *Die Marquise von O . . .*," *JEGP* 81 (1982): 367–75.

81. The German text reads "den Philosophen zu schaffen gibt." Kleist, *Sämtliche Werke* 2:329. Kleist, incidentally, refers indirectly in this letter to the concern of eighteenth-century aestheticians—Winckelmann and Herder among them—of whether and how the knowledge that Raphael's mistresses sat for his Madonnas ought to affect our reading of them.

82. Dorrit Cohn, "Kleist's *Marquise von O . . .* : The Problem of Knowledge," *Monatshefte* 67 (1975): 137.

83. Thomas Fries, "The Impossible Object: The Feminine, the Narrative (La-

clos' *Liaisons Dangereuses* and Kleist's *Marquise von O . . .*)," *MLN* 91 (1976): 1325–26.

84. Heinrich von Kleist, *The Marquise of O—and Other Stories*, trans. David Luke and Nigel Reeves (Middlesex, England: Penguin Books, 1978), 68.

85. Cohn, "The Problem of Knowledge," 131.

86. Kleist, *The Marquise of O . . .* , 83.

87. The body itself, simply because it is natural, is considered female; hence, men speak body language too.

88. See Ilse Graham, *Heinrich von Kleist: Word Into Flesh: A Poet's Quest for the Symbol*, (Berlin: de Gruyter, 1977), 242–43.

89. A literary precursor of this scene is undoubtedly an incident in letter 63 of Rousseau's *Nouvelle Héloise*, in which Julie, already "fallen," sits on her unknowing father's lap.

90. Kleist, *The Marquise of O. . . .* , 74.

91. Kleist, *Sämtliche Werke* 2: 123; Luke and Reeves formulate this somewhat differently, see Kleist, *The Marquise of O. . . .* , 74, 90.

92. Quoted by Spiegel, "The Cinematic Text," 316.

93. Ibid.

94. Rohmer's writings suggest that perhaps he is not aware of this interest, and he diverges quite sharply from other writers on this topic when, for instance, he makes the point that "the very nature of the screen . . . encourages a plasticity of gesture very different from what we are used to seeing on the stage." Eric Rohmer, *The Taste for Beauty*, trans. Carol Volk (Cambridge: Cambridge University Press, 1989), 21.

95. Kleist, *The Marquise of O. . . .* , 79.

96. Spiegel, "The Cinematic Text," 322.

97. Alpers, "Interpretation without Representation," 39. Further, as Pascal Bonitzer conflates tableau vivant with the tableau shot in cinema, one of his examples is Rohmer's quotation of the Fuseli painting. Pascal Bonitzer, *Décadrages: Peinture et cinema* (Paris: Cahiers du Cinema/Editions de l'Etoile, 1985), 31 ff. See also Lynne Kirby's excellent review of Bonitzer, "Painting and Cinema: The Frames of Discourse," *Camera Obscura* 18 (1988): 95–105.

98. Kleist, *The Marquise of O. . . .* , 112.

99. Spiegel, "The Cinematic Text," 322.

100. Rohmer, however, does extend the objectifying power of the gaze to the women themselves in the moment when the Marquise and her mother appraise the broad back of the groom Leopardo.

101. For a discussion of this issue, see Heath, "Narrative Space," 19–75.

102. See Fried, *Absorption and Theatricality*, 93–96.

103. This view of the relation of film to theater differs a good deal from that held by Stanley Cavell and his students. Basing his assertion on film's photographic nature, Cavell argues that the camera's photographic power privileges the flesh and blood actor and "reverses the relation between actor and character in

theater." Stanley Cavell, *Pursuits of Happiness: The Hollywood Comedy of Re-marriage* (Cambridge, Mass.: Harvard University Press, 1981), 157. Bazin, in "Theater and Cinema—Part Two," *What Is Cinema?*, 1:97, also says that it is false to claim that cinema cannot put us in the presence of an actor, but Bazin's notion of what constitutes presence and absence in cinema seems out of date: a mirror image does not, in my view, indicate presence. Cavell's view does not—on the one hand—seem to distinguish sufficiently between photography and film, overlooking the way our perception of the body is estranged when cinematic images are edited together—i.e., making one cinematic frame depend for its effect on its juxtaposition with other frames. (For another point of view see Richard Allen, "Representation, Illusion and the Cinema," *Cinema Journal* 32 [1993]: 21–48.) On the other hand, it does not take reactions of early spectators into account (i.e., the debate in the twenties concerning the difference between theatrical and cine-matic bodies, a debate that gives us historical insight into this relation. See chapter 1.) All of this is not to say that the identity of Hollywood stars does not affect the manner in which characters they play are perceived; I simply suggest that there are other mechanisms at work that relativize this effect.

104. Bazin makes the following observation: "If the plastic arts were put under psychoanalysis, the practice of embalming the dead might turn out to be a fundamental factor in their creation." Bazin, "The Ontology of the Photographic Image," 9.

105. Deutelbaum and Poague, "Hitchcock in Britain," 64.

106. Thomas M. Leitch, *Find the Director and Other Hitchcock Games*, (Athens, Ga.: University of Georgia Press, 1991), 1–2.

107. Ibid., 2.

108. Ibid.

109. "Hitchcock in Britain," 64.

110. Leitch, *Find the Director*, 3.

111. Edward Branigan argues that these shots cannot be justified within ordi-nary narrative logic. Edward Branigan, *Point of View in the Cinema* (Berlin: Mouton, 1984), 40–41.

112. Raymond Bellour, "Hitchcock, the Enunciator," *Camera Obscura* 2 (1977): 78.

113. *Vertigo* is perhaps Hitchcock's most complex film. My intention here is to throw one of its preoccupations into relief.

114. See my discussion of Midge in chapter 2.

115. As Robin Wood puts it, "Madeleine is presented in terms of the 'work of art,' which is precisely what she is. Her movement through the doorway suggests a portrait coming to life, or a gliding statue; when she pauses and turns her head into profile, the suggestion is of a cameo or silhouette, an image that will recur throughout the film." Wood, "Male Desire, Male Anxiety: The Essential Hitch-cock," in Deutelbaum and Poague, *Hitchcock Reader*, 228.

116. Gaston Bachelard, *L'eau et les rêves: Essai sur l'imagination de la matière* (Paris: José Corti, 1942), 111–13.

117. For a discussion of scopophilia see Laura Mulvey, "Visual Pleasure and Narrative Cinema," *Screen*, 16 (1975): 6–18; and Marian E. Keane, "A Closer Look at Scopophilia: Mulvey, Hitchcock, and *Vertigo*," in Deutelbaum and Poague, *Hitchcock Reader*, 231–48.

118. This problem will be pointed to in the Mount Rushmore sequence in *North by Northwest* one year later. See chapter 2 above.

119. Truffaut makes the comment that "*Vertigo* was undoubtedly a movie in which the leading lady was cast as a substitute for the one Hitchcock had in mind initially. The actress we see on screen is a substitute, and the change enhances the appeal of the movie, since this substitution is the main theme of the picture." Francois Truffaut, *Hitchcock*, rev. ed. (New York: Simon and Schuster, 1983), 325.

120. Interestingly, Eric Rohmer connects the visual theme of the spiral with the perception of the screen as three-dimensional. Rohmer, *Taste for Beauty*, 21.

121. Durgnat, *The Strange Case of Alfred Hitchcock*, 294.

122. Bazin, "The Myth of Total Cinema," 19.

123. Kracauer depicts Karl Freund, the cameraman who shot *Berlin: Symphony of a City* as a man "starved for reality." It was actually Walter Ruttmann, known for his work on abstract films, who, much to Kracauer's disgust, edited Freund's material and imposed a formal pattern upon it. Kracauer, *From Caligari to Hitler*, 183. David Caldwell and Paul W. Rea have commented on Wenders's evocation of the city symphony. "Handke's and Wenders's *Wings of Desire*: Transcending Postmodernism," *German Quarterly* 64 (1991): 46–53. See also Robert Phillip Kolker and Peter Beicken, *The Films of Wim Wenders: Cinema as Vision and Desire* (Cambridge: Cambridge University Press, 1993), 144.

124. Christian Metz, "On the Impression of Reality in the Cinema," 8–9.

125. See Kathe Geist, *The Cinema of Wim Wenders: From Paris, France to "Paris, Texas"* (Ann Arbor: University of Michigan Press, 1988).

126. Tony Rayns, "Forms of Address: Interviews with Three German Filmmakers," *Sight and Sound*, 44 (1974–1975): 6.

127. Ibid., 6. Bazin, "The Ontology of the Photographic Image," 14. Kracauer's essay on photography anticipates Bazin's thinking on a number of points. See Siegfried Kracauer, "Die Photographie," *Das Ornament der Masse*, (Frankfurt: Suhrkamp, 1977), 21–39.

128. Kracauer, *From Caligari to Hitler*, 182ff; Mary Ann Doane, "The Voice in the Cinema: The Articulation of Body and Space," in Rosen, *Narrative, Apparatus, Ideology*, 344.

129. In literary history, of course, we associate it with the modernism of James Joyce and of Döblin's *Berlin Alexanderplatz*, to which Wenders may be alluding. In my reading of Wenders's film I am indebted to Kevin Affonso, whose under-

graduate essay on Wenders (Yale University, May, 1991) informs some of my ideas.

130. Quoted by Doane, "Voice in the Cinema," 342.

131. Ibid., 340.

132. Ibid., 341.

133. Thomas Elsaesser, "Primary Identification and the Historical Subject: Fassbinder and Germany," in Rosen, *Narrative, Apparatus, Ideology*, 536.

134. Here Wenders plays upon the traditional conflation of circus trapeze acts with virtuoso displays of camera movement. See my discussion of Hitchcock's *Murder!* in chapter 2.

135. I am indebted to Katrin Schroeter of Brown University for this information.

136. Pascal Bonitzer reads this moment as an example of Lacanian *anamorphosis* in cinema. Bonitzer, *Décadrages*, 36.

137. Although I am intrigued by this film's theoretical project, I am also disturbed by its ideology: it is regressive, and does nothing to redeem the role of women in Wenders's films.

138. For a discussion of the way in which the Diderotian tableau is situated between the two arts, see Suzanne Guerlac, "The Tableau and Authority in Diderot's Aesthetics," *Studies on Voltaire and the Eighteenth Century* 219 (1983): 183–94. While Martin Meisel does not make this connection, he does note that Baron Grimm, through whom Diderot's *Salon* of 1765 was disseminated in Germany, added a note to Diderot's text in which he describes the tableau vivant. Martin Meisel, *Realizations: Narrative, Pictorial, and Theatrical Arts in Nineteenth-Century England* (Princeton: Princeton University Press, 1983), 47.

139. See Michael Moering, "Kleist und Frankreich," *Witz und Ironie in der Prosa Heinrich von Kleists* (Munich: Wilhelm Fink, 1972), 137–59.

140. Kleist, "The Foundling," *The Marquise of O—and Other Stories*, 278.

141. Peter Naumann suggests that some "postures" and certain tableaux vivant of this period were pornographic in nature. Peter Naumann, *Keyhole und Candle: John Clelands "Memoirs of a Woman of Pleasure" und die Entstehung des pornographischen Romans in England* (Heidelberg: Carl Winter, 1976), 318.

142. This scene also alludes to Catholic religious practices such as kneeling before an icon (art in its ritual function) and suggests the erotic overtones of such practices. Kleist's strong response to the sensuousness of the Catholic Mass—to its music as well as to its visual stimuli—makes these parallels predictable. Again we should keep in mind the Protestant Kleist's association, following Rousseau, of danger with an appeal to the senses.

143. Bernhard Böschenstein, "Kleist und Rousseau," *Kleist Jahrbuch* 1981/82 (1983), 145, 155.

144. Kleist, "The Foundling," 278.

145. In particular, we might recall the erotic encounter in which Diderot fancies himself participating with the young girl of Greuze's "Girl Weeping for her

Dead Bird" in the Salon of 1765. Diderot, "The Salons," 157. For a detailed account of the reception of Diderot's aesthetic writings in Germany, see Roland Mortier, *Diderot in Deutschland, 1750–1850*, (Stuttgart: Metzler, 1967), 261–91. For Kleist, empiricist (pre-Kantian) aesthetics, bound to the senses and to the body, are suspect as a source of erotic danger and perversion. It is at such moments that Rousseau and Kant appear to be in the ascendancy in the battle waged with empiricism in Kleist's mind.

146. Fried, *Absorption and Theatricality*, 118–32.

147. Here, too, we can detect an allusion to *Elective Affinities*, where the character Ottilie, always more text than body, is preserved in a glass coffin after her death, and so becomes an art object behind glass.

148. Jean-Francois Lyotard, "Acinéma," in Rosen, *Narrative, Apparatus, Ideology*, 356.

149. Lyotard goes on to say that "this institution is made to order for the phantasmatic of Klossowski, knowing as we do the importance he accords to the *tableau vivant* as the near perfect simulacrum of fantasy in all its pardoxical intensity." ("Acinéma," 356. These performances are related to Emma Hart's "attitudes." Freud's essay on Jensen's *Gradiva* ("Delusions and Dreams in Jensen's *Gradiva*," 1907, in vol. 9 of Strachey's *Standard Edition* [London: The Hogarth Press and the Institute of Psycho-Analysis, 1959]) is disappointing on the nature of the erotic fascination exerted by visual representations (usually of women) and explains the desire experienced by Jensen's archaeologist solely by virtue of his profession.

150. Jean Baudrillard, *Seduction*, trans. Brian Singer (New York: St. Martin's Press, 1990), 29.

151. Ibid., 46.

152. Bonitzer, *Décadrages*, 31.

153. Baudrillard, *Seduction*, 37.

154. Vladimir Nabokov, *Despair* (New York: G. P. Putnam's Sons, 1965), 26.

155. It is dedicated also to Unica Zürn, a German woman writer diagnosed as a schizophrenic who committed suicide in Paris in 1970.

156. Lynne Kirby, "Fassbinder's Debt to Poussin," *Camera Obscura* 13/14 (1985): 6–27. Interesting in this regard is a reading of Dreyer's film *Michael* by Mark Nash, who has similarly seen a triptych in Dreyer's film as a "barely masked representation of the problematic of bisexuality." Nash, *Dreyer*, 12.

157. See Peter Iden, "Making an Impact—Rainer Werner Fassbinder and the Theater," *Fassbinder*, ed. Tony Rayns (London: BFI, 1980), 17–23; Michael Töteberg, "Das Theater der Grausamkeit als Lehrstück. Zwishen Brecht und Artaud: Die experimentellen Theatertexte Fassbinders," *Text + Kritik* 103 (1989): 20–34.

158. See Brigitte Peucker, "High Passion and Low Art: Fassbinder's Narrative Strategies," *Ambiguities in Literature and Film*, ed. Hans P. Braendlin (Tallahassee, Fla.: Florida State University Press, 1988), 65–75.

159. See Thomas Elsaesser, "Tales of Sound and Fury: Observations on the Family Melodrama," *Movies and Methods*, vol. 2, ed. Bill Nichols (Berkeley and Los Angeles: University of California Press, 1985), 165–89.

160. In his thought-provoking chapter on this film, Timothy Corrigan writes that "the mannequins and Marlene are in fact nearly interchangeable." Corrigan, "Transformations in Fassbinder's *Bitter Tears of Petra von Kant*," in his *New German Film: The Displaced Image* (Austin: University of Texas Press, 1983), 58. Lynne Kirby reads the mannequins as insusceptible of being viewed psychoanalytically but rather as representing "nothingness." Kirby, "Fassbinder's Debt to Poussin," 22.

161. See chapter 1. For another discussion of theater in this film see Catherine Johnson, "The Imaginary and *The Bitter Tears of Petra von Kant*," *Wide Angle* 3 (1980): 20–25.

162. Bazin, "Painting and Cinema," 164–69.

163. Ibid., 166.

164. Corrigan, "Fassbinder's *Bitter Tears*," 56.

165. See Roland Barthes, "The Reality Effect," *The Rustle of Language*, trans. Richard Howard (Oxford: Basil Blackwell, 1986), 141–48.

166. Thomas Elsaesser, "Murder, Merger, Suicide: The Politics of *Despair*," in Rayns, *Fassbinder*, 51.

167. Robert Burgoyne, "Narrative and Sexual Excess," *October* 21 (1982): 59.

168. Christian Braad Thomsen, "Five Interviews with Fassbinder," in Rayns, *Fassbinder*, 96.

169. Renate Fischetti reads these moments in terms of the narrative. See Fischetti, "Querelle bei Fassbinder und Genet: Zur Frage von Repräsentation und Rezeption in Roman und Film," *Kontroversen, alte und neue: Akten des VII. Internationalen Germanisten-Kongresses*, vol. 10, *Medium Film—das Ende der Literatur?* (Tübingen: Niemeyer, 1986), 335. See also Thomas Elsaesser, "A Cinema of Vicious Circles (and Afterword)," in Rayns, *Fassbinder*, 24–53. In "Primary Identification and the Historical Subject: Fassbinder and Germany," Elsaesser reads the tableau shots as moments of "self-display" that have a great deal to say about the social imagery of Germany. In Rosen, *Narrative, Apparatus, Ideology*, 535–49.

170. Kaja Silverman, "Fassbinder and Lacan: A Reconsideration of Gaze, Look, and Image," *Camera Obscura* 19 (1989): 61.

171. On this point I am in complete agreement with Ed Sikov's review of *Querelle* in *Cinéaste* 13 (1983): 42.

172. Roland Barthes, *A Lover's Discourse: Fragments*, trans. Richard Howard (New York: Farrar, Strauss, and Giroux, 1978), 193.

173. See the discussion of *The Cabinet of Dr. Caligari* in chapter 1.

174. Kleist's text is protocinematic: Linda Williams points out that the keyhole shot was utilized in "primitive" pornographic films such as the German film

"Am Abend" (ca. 1910). Williams, *Hard Core*, 61. See also Sabine Hake's insightful discussion of the keyhole shot in "Self-Referentiality in Early German Cinema," 41ff. Further, as Bazin points out in "Theater and Cinema—Part One," *What Is Cinema?*, 1:92: "It was Cocteau who said that cinema is an event seen through a keyhole."

175. For another point of view, see Kaja Silverman's suggestive reading in "Fassbinder and Lacan," 70–71.

176. According to Michael Töteberg, Fassbinder originally knew Artaud at second-hand, through the Living Theater and Action Theater, then read him years later. Töteberg, "Das Theater der Grausamkeit als Lehrstück," 31.

177. Antonin Artaud, *Collected Works*, vol. 4, trans. Victor Corti (London: Calder and Boyars, 1974), 25–26.

178. Jacques Derrida, "The Theater of Cruelty and the Closure of Representation," *Writing and Difference*, trans. Alan Bass (Chicago: University of Chicago Press, 1978), 241.

179. It becomes obvious from these writings, in which Artaud also reads painting as "mute theater," that Artaud knew his Diderot. See the "Third Letter on Cruelty," *Collected Works*, 4: 120.

180. Ibid., 82.

181. Ibid., 120.

182. Bosch, Grünewald, Brueghel, and El Greco are the painters to whom Artaud refers in the "Letters on Cruelty."

183. It is interesting that Goethe erroneously thought the tableau vivant derived originally from the Neapolitan cribs (crèches). Hölmstrom, *Monodrama, Attitudes, Tableaux Vivants*, 211. In the film, this is not an ordinary Nativity, however. As Silverman points out, it has political implications. Silverman, "Masochistic Ecstasy and the Ruination of Masculinity in Fassbinder's Cinema," *Male Subjectivity at the Margins* (New York: Routledge, 1992), 279.

184. André Bazin, "Marginal Notes on *Eroticism in the Cinema*," in *What Is Cinema?*, 2: 173. Susan Sontag, "The Pornographic Imagination," *A Susan Sontag Reader* (New York: Vintage Books, 1983), 224.

185. Silverman, "Masochistic Ecstasy," 216–17.

186. Ibid., 283.

187. Gaylyn Studlar, "Masochism and the Perverse Pleasures of the Cinema," in Nichols, *Movies and Methods*, 2: 606.

188. As Elaine Scarry contends concerning pain, it is both "incontestably real" and it "resists language." Elaine Scarry, *The Body in Pain: The Making and Unmaking of the World* (New York: Oxford University Press, 1985), 27, 4. Richard Allen claims that "scenes of sex and violence are inarticulate" and "appeal directly to the senses." Allen, "Representation, Illusion, and the Cinema," 44–45.

189. Baudrillard, *Seduction*, 29ff, 37ff.

190. Greenaway claims that "the deliberate, thoughtful, visual quality of the film can be traced back to late 17th century painting—Caravaggio, de La Tour,

even late Raphael and so on and the famous interiors of the Dutch painters. Some of the compositions have been taken over and moved consciously into the film." Karen Jaehne, "*The Draughtsman's Contract*: An Interview with Peter Greenaway," *Cinéaste* 13 (1984): 13.

191. Mitchell, "Space and Time," 109.

192. Typically of Greenaway, this scene illustrates an opposite idea as well, suggesting the manner in which language (masculine) is imposed upon the natural world (feminine).

193. Greenaway's own explanation for this figure involves the suggestion that late seventeenth-century English landowners who were too poor or too stingy to buy statuary for their estates would ask as servant to pose as a statue. Jaehne, "*The Draughtsman's Contract*," 15.

194. Flavia, interestingly, given the self-representation of film as a hybrid, is said by Kracklight's wife to be a "hermaphrodite," and it is strongly suggested also that she conducts an incestuous relationship with her brother. The fragments of sculpture also point to the way in which the photographic image is capable of fragmenting the body.

195. The other film is Resnais's *Last Year at Marienbad*. Jaehne, "*The Draughtsman's Contract*," 13.

196. Once again a Kleist text comes to mind: in the drama *Penthesilea*, the heroine wishes to eat her lover Achilles.

197. Silverman, *Male Subjectivity at the Margins*, 234, based upon Freud's "Instincts and their Vicissitudes," *Standard Edition*, vol. 14 (London: The Hogarth Press and the Institute of Psycho-Analysis, 1957), 138.

198. In Uvedale Price's famous and amusing *Dialogue*, the carcass of an ox hanging in a butcher shop is redeemed as an object of aesthetic interest because it dislays " 'the blended variety of mellow tints' reminiscent of a similar image in Rembrandt." Quoted from Hussey, *The Picturesque*, 77. Much earlier, in 1763, Diderot's description of Chardin's "Gutted Skate" ends by exhorting painters to learn from Chardin to "redeem the distastefulness that is present in certain natural objects." Diderot, "The Salons," 150.

199. This is precisely what Kleist's Piachi in *The Foundling* refuses to do after he has killed Nicolo and is about to be executed. Piachi's belief in the principle of substitution—which leads him to adopt Nicolo in place of his natural son—has been so rudely undermined by Nicolo that he will not perform any further acts based upon this principle.

200. For an alternative reading of this film see Marlene Rogers, "Food and Defilement in Peter Greenaway's *The Cook, The Thief, His Wife and Her Lover*," *Descant* 71/72, 22 (1991): 215–24.

201. J. W. von Goethe, "On Truth and Probability in Works of Art: A Dialogue," *Goethe on Art*, trans. and ed. John Gage (Berkeley and Los Angeles: University of California Press, 1980), 29.

202. Diderot, "The Salons," 150.

203. Van Meegeren is the name of the man who most successfully faked Vermeer paintings; other references to Vermeer include a character named Caterina Bolnes (the name of Vermeer's wife), and allusions to Vermeer's method of composition. Greenaway's interest in Dutch painting undoubtedly extends beyond its claim that the seen and portrayed is the real; it is, as Alpers points out, "at ease with inscribed words" and no doubt also interests Greenaway because of its juxtapositions of image and text. See Alpers, *The Art of Describing*, 169.

204. See chapter 1.

205. From a review, "Light in Flight," in the *Guardian Weekly*, January 24, 1993, 25. I am indebted to Murray Biggs for this information.

206. Ibid., Another English artist, Damien Hirst, recently showed his "Mother and Child Divided" at the Venice Biennale. For Hirst's sculpture, "a cow and calf have been slaughtered, bisected lengthwise, and pickled in formaldehyde in clearglass cases." See Adam Gopnik, "Death in Venice," *The New Yorker*, August 2, 1993, 66.

207. Williams, *Hardcore*, 191. See also Claire Pajaczkowska, "Images and Pornography," *Explorations in Film Theory: Selected Essays from Ciné-Tracts*, ed. Ron Burnett (Bloomington: Indiana University Press, 1991), 72–85.

208. Michael Fried, *Realism, Writing, Disfiguration: On Thomas Eakins and Stephen Crane* (Chicago: Univeristy of Chicago Press, 1987), 65.

209. Paul Leduc's film *Frida* (1984), based on the life of Frida Kahlo, makes use of this same technique of alternating shots of the dying artist's intense physical pain with vignettes from her life based on personal memories and linked to the paintings. For a reading of Jarman's film that places it within what he calls an "aesthetics of homosexuality," see Timothy Murray, *Like a Film: Ideological Fantasy on Screen, Camera, and Canvas* (London: Routledge, 1993), 124–71.

210. Metz, "On the Impression of Reality in the Cinema," 8–9.

AFTERWORD

1. Claudia Brodsky Lacour, " 'Is that Helen?' Contemporary Pictorialism, Lessing and Kant," *Comparative Literature* 45 (1993): 232.

2. Ibid., 242.

3. Ibid., 240.

4. Mitchell does not, as Brodsky Lacour contends, claim that Lessing aligns women with *vision*, which, as she points out, has traditionally been associated with cognition, but rather with the spatial art of painting, which is tied to the body. See ibid., 238n.26.

5. Ibid., 242.

6. Rosalind E. Krauss, "Sculpture in the Expanded Field," *The Originality of the Avant-Garde and Other Modernist Myths* (Cambridge, Mass.: M.I.T. Press, 1985), 276–90. I am indebted to Andrew Anker for this reference.

7. Ibid., 282.

8. Ibid., 288.

9. Deleuze, *Cinema I; Cinema II: The Time-Image*, trans. Hugh Tomlinson and Robert Galeta (Minneapolis: University of Minnesota Press, 1989). Both Mitchell and Arnheim stress the interrelatedness of our perceptions of space and time. See W.J.T. Mitchell, "Spatial Form in Literature: Toward a General Theory," *The Language of Images*, ed. W.J.T. Mitchell (Chicago: University of Chicago Press, 1974), 274; Rudolf Arnheim, "Space as an Image of Time," *Images of Romanticism*, ed. Karl Kroeber and William Walling (New Haven: Yale University Press, 1978), 1–12.

10. Erwin Panofsky, "Style and Medium in the Motion Pictures," in Mast and Cohen, *Film Theory and Criticism*, 246.

11. Lindsay, *Art of the Moving Picture*, 203. See also Miriam Hansen's treatment of the hierogplyh in *Babel and Babylon*, 191ff.

12. Lindsay, *Art of the Moving Picture*, 267.

13. Sergei Eisenstein, "The Cinematographic Principle and the Ideogram," *Film Form: Essays in Film Theory*, ed. and trans. Jay Leyda (New York: Harcourt Brace Jovanovich, 1949), 28–44.

14. Sergei Eisenstein, "Dickens, Griffith, and the Film Today," in Leyda, *Film Form*, 195–255; "Word and Image," *The Film Sense*, ed. and trans. Jay Leyda (New York: Harcourt Brace Jovanovich, 1942), 58.

15. Eisenstein, "Synchronisation of the Senses," 101–2; "Color and Meaning," 113–18, both in Leyda, *The Film Sense*. For another essay concerning El Greco and the relation of film to the visual arts, including architecture, see writings collected under the title "Pathos" in *Nonindifferent Nature*, trans. Herbert Marshall (Cambridge: Cambridge University Press, 1987), 38–199.

16. Rudolf Arnheim, "Film and Reality," *Film as Art* (Berkeley and Los Angeles: University of California Press, 1966) 12, 26.

17. Arnheim, "A New Laocoön: Artistic Compsites and the Talking Film," *Film as Art*, 207–8.

18. Marie-Claire Ropars-Wuilleumier quotes Derrida to this effect in *Le Texte divisé* (Paris: Presses Universitaires de France, 1981), 61. Also see her essay "The Graphic in Film Writing," 147–61.

19. Bonitzer, *Décadrages*; Jacques Aumont, *L'Oeil interminable* (Paris: Librairies Seguier, 1989); see also *Cinéma et peinture: Approches*, ed. Raymond Bellour (Paris: Presses Universitaires, 1990). See an informative review of Bonitzer by Lynne Kirby, *Camera Obscura* 18 (1988): 95–105.

20. Barthes, "Diderot, Brecht, Eisenstein," 73.

21. Thomas Elsaesser, "Rivette and the End of Cinema," *Sight and Sound* 1 (1992): 20–23. (My thanks to an anonymous reviewer for this reference); Aumont, *L'Oeil interminable*, 254; Patrice Rollet, "Le mage et le chirurgien, Notes sur la relève de la peinture dans le cinéma selon Walter Benjamin," in Bellour, *Cinéma et peinture*, 31–45.

22. Honoré de Balzac, "The Hidden Masterpiece," *The Works of Balzac*, vol. 28, trans. Katharine Prescott Wormeley (Boston: Little, Brown, 1900) 346, 343.

23. Ibid., 360.

24. Ibid., 361.

25. Ibid.

26. Ibid.

Index

215

DATE DUE